Secret

Intelligence

Books by Ernest Volkman

LEGACY OF HATE (1982)
WARRIORS OF THE NIGHT (1985)

With John Cummings

THE HEIST (1987)

Secret

Intelligence

Ernest Volkman and Blaine Baggett

DOUBLEDAY
New York · London · Toronto · Sydney · Auckland

Published by DOUBLEDAY, a division of Bantam Doubleday Dell Publishing Group, Inc.
666 Fifth Avenue, New York, New York 10103

DOUBLEDAY and the portrayal of an anchor with a dolphin are trademarks of Doubleday,
a division of Bantam Doubleday Dell Publishing Group, Inc.

Library of Congress Cataloging-in-Publication Data

Volkman, Ernest.
Secret intelligence.

Includes index.
1. Intelligence service—United States—History—
20th century. I. Baggett, Blaine. II. Title.
UB251.U5V64   1989   327.1′2′0973   88-18963

To Miss Andrews

B.B.

For Eric and Michelle
Exegi monumentum aere perennius

E.V.

Preface

BILL KURTIS

IN WASHINGTON, there is no phrase more often quoted nor more frequently misunderstood than that of the two words "national security." Our government leaders are charged with this responsibility, but just how best to protect our land and its people is open to ferocious debate. The origins of the phrase officially date back to 1947 and the passage of the National Security Act, a legislative act signed into law by Harry Truman that created, among other things, America's first centralized intelligence agency, the Central Intelligence Agency.

Today, the CIA is but a portion of the vast espionage apparatus that is America's intelligence empire. This intelligence community exists to protect our nation, yet most Americans are uncomfortable with its inherent ability to also threaten individual liberties.

Fundamentally, *Secret Intelligence* is concerned with this problem, which has grown more critical as the secret empire continues to become more elaborate and enlarged. It is the theme that unites this history of American intelligence operations from their modern beginnings, in World War I, to the present day. This history sets American intelligence in the context of the unique nature of American democracy—and its constant conflict with secret intelligence operations.

The dilemma, as *Secret Intelligence* delineates, has never been resolved. Although it is generally agreed that America's place in a dangerous world requires an intelligence system of no small dimension, no one has yet been able to figure out how we can have such a system (and its secrecy) without endangering the Constitution and its individual guarantees of freedom. There seems no easy solution to having it both ways, and as this history records, the extremes of either too little intelligence or too much secrecy both bring with them disturbing consequences.

The only answer, it seems, is constant vigilance—vigilance that applies not only to potential enemies abroad, but also to those at home who secretly strive to protect the national security.

BILL KURTIS
Chicago
April 1988

Acknowledgments

THERE ARE A NUMBER of people to whom I owe a large debt of gratitude in the evolution of this book, but two of them merit special attention. The first dim spark of the central theme of this book was fostered by Jeri Winston and Jackie Lewis, publisher and editor respectively of the magazine *Espionage*. The magazine, for which I had the honor to serve briefly as executive editor, enjoyed an all-too-short life, but these two delightful women had often encouraged me in the idea of examining the role of secret intelligence in the American democratic system.

This small flame of an idea might have gone no further, except, by happy coincidence, it turned out that Blaine Baggett of KCET was already much further along in advancing the idea; *Secret Intelligence* is the result of a convergence between the two of us.

Like all such projects, this one required the aid of many people to bring it to life. A good number of them in the world of secret intelligence would prefer not to be named publicly. I have respected their wishes, but there are several people to whom I owe very large debts for their advice, encouragement, support, and willingness to devote much of their time in aiding this project:

John Cummings, valued friend and investigative reporter without peer; L. J. Davis of *Harper's*, whose instincts and ability to get to the heart of the matter are always unerring; Bob Roman, whose experience and knowledge of the secret world is unequaled; Tom Moon, formerly of the OSS and a shrewd, insightful observer of that extraordinary organization; and Knut Royce, infallible guide to the Washington core of the secret world.

And, above all, my agent, Victoria Pryor, of Arcadia, Ltd., for whom no challenge is too daunting and no project is impossible. Without her, this book would not exist.

ERNEST VOLKMAN
New York

THE GENESIS for this book—and the television series that bears the same name—began in the summer of 1983 with a visit to the Soviet embassy in Washington, D.C. The purpose of my visit —and subsequent ones—was research for a history of manned space travel for public television.

On September 1, 1983, a Korean civilian airliner was shot out of the skies by a Soviet interceptor jet after overflying Russian airspace. All 269 people aboard perished. The U.S. Government reaction was one of rage. Among Washington's punitive responses was the expulsion of the Soviet science attaché stationed in Washington, who was charged with being a spy. This alleged spy was also my principal resource for Soviet space research. Very shortly after the expulsion, I received a call from the FBI, inquiring as to the nature of my association with the Soviet Union. A forthright explanation seemed to satisfy the federal agent, and I never heard another word about my Soviet associations. A later Freedom of Information request showed no evidence of the inquiry ever having taken place.

My brief encounter with the FBI brought on two simultaneous but contradictory reactions. First, I was cognizant that my privacy had been violated, perhaps even illegally so. The second—

and diametric—reaction was one of comfort, knowing from first-hand experience that the U.S. Government seemed alert to contacts with the nation most Americans perceive as our greatest threat. It seemed a paradox worth exploring further.

I wish to thank the Public Broadcasting Service, the Corporation for Public Broadcasting, and public television stations throughout the country for their support; Phylis Geller and Bill Kobin of KCET/Los Angeles for their courage in embracing this project; KCET Senior Producer Arthur Barron for his wisdom and capable staff: Mitchell Koss, Greg Cooke, Lisa Samford, Susan Bellows, and Sandy Medof; Timothy Conroy, Glenn Schroeder, and agent Steven Axelrod for their advice, guidance, and general hand-holding; and Doubleday editors Nicholas Bakalar and Patrick Filley for their patience and counsel. Personal gratitude is also extended to researchers Joseph Angier, Ann Keisling, Kate Coe, and Wendy Lade, as well as Bonnie Winings, whose support went far beyond the call of duty. Special thanks, of course, go to my colleague and friend, Bill Kurtis.

A final word of appreciation goes to those intelligence officers who agreed to speak with us. I believe, like them, that American intelligence is, without question, a necessity. Unfortunately, most of what we know about this secret world has to do with their failures rather than successes. Those in the intelligence business learned long ago that this is an occupational hazard.

And because their work is done in secrecy, it must always be suspect. Besides, whether mythology or not, Americans have always held their government accountable to a higher standard of conduct than other nations. It is with this same high expectation that this writing is submitted.

BLAINE BAGGETT
Los Angeles, 1988

Contents

---

xiii

Introduction

"An Enemy to the Liberties"

"THE NECESSITY of procuring good Intelligence is apparent," George Washington wrote to a friend in 1777, "& need not be further urged—All that Remains for me to add is, that you keep the whole matter as secret as possible. For upon Secrecy, Success depends in Most Enterprizes of the kind, and for want of it, they are generally defeated, however well planned & promising a favourable issue."

However apparent, ten years later, the very same man who wrote that letter would say nothing about intelligence or secrecy when he presided over the great Constitutional Convention convened to forge the famous document. Indeed, there is no mention in the Constitution of intelligence, or spies, or intelligence agencies, or internal security—nothing of what some have called the "American national security state," the vast American espionage and internal security apparatus that form the most intriguing aspect of the greatest military and economic power the world has ever seen.

A curious paradox, and it is one created by that very document. The Constitution guarantees individual liberties, the right of the minority to dissent, and privacy. But it also gives the President of the United States broad powers in the conduct of foreign policy —and, implicitly, intelligence operations—thus creating a dilemma for American democracy. The problem centers on the questions of secrecy: the conduct of foreign policy and intelligence operations is largely secret, and secrecy is anathema to democracy.

Openness is deeply rooted in the American political tradition, and for that reason, most Americans are uncomfortable with intelligence operations. Although Americans have generally conceded the necessity of a national security apparatus in response to the two great threats to their democracy in this century—Nazism and communism—there remains a sense of uneasiness that the apparatus can represent just as great a danger to ourselves as the threats it is supposed to combat. No one yet has been able to figure out how America can have it both ways: wield the weapons of secrecy without damage to ourselves, and preserve secrecy without endangering the Constitution's guarantees of freedom.

One important reason for this uneasiness is the American historical record during the past century, filled with instances of presidents who decide that the Constitution is often an inconvenience in the pursuit of higher goals. These instances usually take place during times of crisis, when presidents seek blank checks to combat a perceived threat—even when the perception is not in accord with the general consensus. At such times, presidents tend to embrace secret intelligence operations as a means of accomplishing goals denied them by their own constitutional system. The result is often disaster and severe shock to the Constitution.

Perceived threats, both from without and within, can cause the gravest damage to the constitutional system. Consider, for example, the mind-set of otherwise reasonable men (chaired by the famous World War II hero James Doolittle) who were named to a presidential commission in 1954 at the height of the Cold War to consider how the United States could best undertake covert activities to counter the threat of Soviet communism.

"It is now clear," the group finally concluded, "that we are facing an implacable enemy whose avowed objective is world domination by whatever means and at whatever cost. There are no rules in such a game. Hitherto acceptable norms of human conduct do not apply. If the U.S. is to survive, long-standing American concepts of 'fair play' must be reconsidered . . . We must learn to subvert, sabotage and destroy our enemies by more clever, more sophisticated and more effective methods than those used against us . . . another important requirement is an aggressive covert psychological, political and paramilitary organization more effective, more unique and, if necessary, more ruthless than that employed by the enemy. No one should be permitted to stand in the way of the prompt, efficient and secure accomplishment of this mission."

It did not seem to have occurred to any member of this commission that in advocating methods "more ruthless" than the other side, and insisting that "no one should be permitted to stand in the way" of a reinvigorated effort against the Soviet enemy, the United States would be adopting the very methods used by the perceived enemy in the first place.

Perhaps in anticipation of such an eventuality, the Constitution's system of checks and balances wisely separates the powers of purse and sword, but these are precisely the two powers combined in intelligence agencies, which rarely are fully accountable for either their expenditures or deeds. This combination is what makes such agencies difficult to control, for since they also operate in secrecy, they represent extremely potent weapons in the hands of any president—as the country periodically has learned, to its cost. While the Constitution has made it difficult for us to declare war, it provides no easy answer to how this country can indulge in the expediency of ideological and foreign policy commitments (any number of which may be perfectly worthwhile)— and at the same time have a continuing commitment to an open society.

Even George Washington might have been hard-pressed to arrive at an answer on how such a delicate balance can be achieved.

Washington was the father of American intelligence, as well as the father of his country. Appalled at the low state of intelligence during the French and Indian War, when he served as a militia officer with the British—and watched their troops get hacked to pieces by enemies they had failed to spot in time—Washington was determined that no men under his command would ever again die because of intelligence failure. During the American Revolution, he created large networks of agents that kept his meager forces out of the clutches of numerically superior British formations, including the only spy hero American popular culture ever produced, Nathan Hale. Still, Washington was aware that his countrymen associated intelligence operations with sinister maneuvering and secrecy, among the very aspects of European culture they most despised.

It is sometimes argued that the American intelligence apparatus is of recent vintage, the response to unprecedented dangers not experienced or foreseen by the Founding Fathers. But in fact, America's first intelligence agency was formed in 1775. Called the Committee of Secret Correspondence, it was the intelligence arm of the Continental Congress, a fledging organization whose perception of grave threats facing the independence-minded colonists compelled it to resort to secrecy.

And yet, twelve years later, when the Constitutional Convention convened, the necessity for Secret Committees was rejected. Americans had learned a great deal in those intervening years, chiefly that a strong central government, equipped with extraordinary powers and wrapped in secrecy, would be a far greater "enemy to the liberties" than any external threat. Certainly the threats facing the new nation in 1787 were just as real as those in 1776: Spanish and French empires to the south and west, British empire to the north, no navy of consequence, virtually no army, and an economic system that was a shambles. Nevertheless, the delegates created a document whose emphasis was on personal liberties, an open society, and a governmental system restrained by checks and balances. The only crime specified in that document is treason, defined as "levying war against them, or, in adhering to their enemies, giving them aid and comfort."

As men who had been forged in the fire of struggle and war, the authors of the Constitution were perfectly aware that the United States could not live in an isolated Eden of its own creation. Sooner or later, the Constitution would be subjected to the strain of an external threat, one that would cause an American government to carry out secret operations without the knowledge and consent of Congress or the people (or conduct an undeclared war)—in other words, to forget "first principles," as Thomas Jefferson's elegant phrase had it.

That strain came quickly enough, in 1798, when the Federalists, confronting a quasi-war with France and a sudden surge of Irish and French immigrants, reacted by enacting the infamous Alien and Sedition Acts. The most dangerous portion of those acts was the one covering sedition, which banned all speech against the government that, in the words of the act, would bring it ". . . into contempt or disrepute." In other words, a virtual ban on free speech. One Federalist newspaper, the Boston *Columbian Sentinel,* summarized the motive that lay behind enactment of the statute: "It is patriotism to write in favor of our government—it is sedition to write against it."

The government imprisoned twenty-five of its most outspoken critics under the terms of the Alien and Sedition Acts, but in 1800, when Thomas Jefferson and the anti-Federalists came to power, the acts were repealed or allowed to lapse. The entire episode was instructive, however, for it demonstrated that the Constitution could be shunted aside whenever the government decided that there existed a grave threat to the established order. The argument made by the Federalists—that the sheer weight of the threat was so vast that constitutional niceties had to be temporarily put aside—would be repeated, in different contexts, on a number of occasions later in American history. Indeed, there is a remarkable similarity between the Federalists' argument in 1798 and the arguments for Abraham Lincoln's suspension of certain civil liberties of suspected Confederate sympathizers during the Civil War, the Wilson administration's "Red Scare" of 1919, the imprisonment of Japanese-Americans in World War II, the anti-Communist crusade during the Truman administration, and attempts during the Reagan administration to enact new restrictive legislation to "protect American secrets."

These and other clashes with the Constitution stemmed, in part, from American forays into the world of secret intelligence. They range from the first recorded instance of an American covert intelligence operation—the attempt by Benjamin Franklin and others in 1776 to acquire Quebec as the fourteenth colony of the United States—to recent U.S. intelligence operations in Central America aimed at overthrowing the ruling regime in Nicaragua. Inherently, all of them have carried the virus of serious trouble, for organized and operated in a mantle of secrecy, they have sometimes existed free from the constraints of constitutional democracy; without oversight and driven by the often-narrow view of the policymakers who devised them, they assume a life of their own.

The experiences of other democracies with almost no constitutional constraints on secret intelligence operations demonstrate the dimension of the problem. In Israel, for example, that country's intelligence service in 1972 was assigned the task of murdering a long list of Palestinian political activists the Israeli Government decided were dangerous to the state. An appalling decision, and it could take place only in a condition of the deepest secrecy —and with no restraints, parliamentary or otherwise, on intelligence agencies. It apparently did not occur to anyone involved in that decision to ask a simple question: if the government has the power to secretly order the execution of men it considers dangerous, what is to stop a future government from murdering its *domestic* opponents?

Similarly, the French intelligence service, free of any parliamentary control or oversight, has for years been involved in kidnappings and murders of people the government did not like, including what it later called "disposal" of several thousand Algerians. A more recent example of French lawlessness occurred on July 10, 1985, when the ship *Rainbow Warrior* was sabotaged by French intelligence agents while at harbor in Auckland, New Zealand. The bombing, meant to deter protests against French nuclear weapons testing, killed one photographer on board and caused an international furor. And in Great Britain, even more recent disclosures show an intelligence apparatus involved in "dirty tricks" against political dissidents, at one point the Labor Prime Minister Harold Wilson himself.

For nearly the first century and a half of its existence, the United States had limited involvement in the secret world. Among the few operations was the Lewis and Clark Expedition (in fact partly a cover for mapping fortifications), the Pike Expedition (also a reconnoitering of Spanish territory), the abortive mission led by Jed Poinsett to secretly purchase Texas for $5 million (Poinsett was later immortalized by the holiday flower he discovered), and the covert missions in aid of the rebels in Cuba (ultimately resulting in the Spanish-American War).

But in 1917 came a singular event which was to become the most significant political development of the twentieth century, with reverberations in the United States which are felt to this day. How America dealt with that event was to determine much of its history over the next seventy years.

PART ONE

The One-Eyed Giant
1917–1945

ONE

On the Road
to Shevogarsk

JUST AFTER DAWN, the Russian attack began. The Americans, alerted by artillery fire, saw the Soviet soldiers moving in a skirmish line toward the U.S. positions, struggling through three-feet-deep snow. The steam from their breaths could be clearly seen, as though the Russians were wearing white plumes; it was forty-five degrees below zero.

The forty-seven men of Company A of the U.S. Army's 339th Infantry Regiment saw they were vastly outnumbered. Judging by the accuracy of the artillery fire, the Soviet spies had been busy again, pinpointing every American bunker and machine gun post. More ominously, the American allies, the anti-Communists, did not appear very willing to join the fight. The Russian spies had been busy there, too, infiltrating their ranks, causing wholesale defections.

The Americans themselves were shaky. For months, they had been finding propaganda leaflets in their path, cleverly worded in perfect colloquial English, questioning why the Americans were fighting in this hopeless war, and why they were shedding their blood for the "capitalists." Some American soldiers agreed with the leaflets' sentiments, and there were rumors that a number of them had actually mutinied.

Under severe pressure from waves of attacking Russian soldiers, including white-clad troops with automatic weapons who seemed to appear out of nowhere, the Americans began to retreat. Hoping for covering fire from artillery manned by the anti-Communist allies, they heard nothing, for those allies had fled in panic at the sight of the hundreds of attacking Russian soldiers. The retreat now became a rout; the Americans, packing their wounded and supplies aboard sleds, fled at nightfall, and did not stop until they reached other American forces some miles away. It was a nasty setback for American arms, the first in a chain of disasters that resulted, finally, in a complete Soviet victory.

This sequence of events actually happened seventy years ago in Russia. On the morning of January 19, 1919, the Americans were routed out of their positions in the village of Nijni Gora, a speck in the vast sub-Arctic tundra of northern Russia. They retreated north, eventually, to a larger American position at Shevogarsk. From there, they retreated again, to their main base at the port of Archangel, where, facing total annihilation, they were packed aboard ships that summer, and sent back home in defeat.

Their defeat marked the climax of one of the most extraordinary adventures in American foreign policy, one that would have consequences for many years to come. On the Soviet side, they never forgave the Americans for invading their country, and as Nikita Khrushchev was to remark forty years after the event, "Never have any of our soldiers been on American soil, but your soldiers were on Russian soil." As for the United States, the consequences were in many ways more serious, for the entire American intervention in Russia was largely conducted ad hoc without the consent of Congress or the American people. And its failure touched off a long period of American isolation from the outside world.

The intervention remains a neglected episode in this country, an unfortunate oversight, since it was in many ways an eerie presage to future events that involved the United States.

To set the stage: in early 1917, the Czarist government of Russia was overthrown in a popular revolution, igniting a panic in Western Europe, which was then locked in a death struggle with Germany. There was grave fear, especially in London and Paris, that the war-weary Russians would sign a separate peace with the Germans, unleashing more than a million German troops for the Western front. Urged on by the British and French, the new head of the Russian government, Alexander Kerensky, vowed to keep Russia in the war. The Allies began shipping in huge amounts of supplies to the northern port city of Archangel to bolster the Russian armies.

The players: aside from Kerensky, the most important Russian was Vladimir Lenin, leader of the Bolsheviks, who was maneuvering to take power from Kerensky. Lenin had vowed to take Russia out of the war, and his party's slogan of "Peace, land and bread!" had broad appeal among the Russian masses. On the Allied side, there were three important figures whose attitudes toward events in Russia would shape history. One was British Prime Minister David Lloyd George, desperate to keep Russia in the war; the second was the American ambassador to Moscow, David Francis; and the third was the most important actor in the entire drama, President Woodrow Wilson.

Wilson was President of a nation that was sliding toward war with Germany—an event that would occur not long after in 1917 —and since only the United States had the resources to tip the balance of the war in the Allies favor, Wilson's views were obviously critical. But what exactly Wilson's views *were* proved somewhat difficult to fathom.

Wilson was a man seized with a messianic vision, a belief that since the old order was being destroyed in history's most terrible war, the opportunity now existed to seize history and redirect it. He intended nothing less than a complete restructuring of the Old World, replaced by his vision of liberal democracy everywhere. In Wilson's view, his particular concept of liberal democracy would serve as the middle road between reaction and revolution, the only way to maintain permanent peace and "make the world safe for democracy."

Among the Fourteen Points, Wilson's 1918 blueprint for the postwar world, was one that applied exclusively to Russia, whose fate had become a growing obsession to the American President. Russia, according to that document, would be allowed the opportunity "for the independent determination of her own political development and national policy," and the treatment accorded Russia by the rest of the world would be the "acid test" of the real intentions of nations in building the new postwar world.

Yet, only eight months after that ringing declaration, Wilson sent American troops into Russia, a mistake that undercut those words. How and why Wilson committed that folly are directly attributable to the event in October 1917, that fell like a thunderclap in the Western world: the Bolshevik revolution.

No other single event so unnerved the West. In the words of Winston Churchill, "We saw a state without a nation, an army without a country, a religion without a God." The fact that a Communist revolution had taken place was bad enough, but the new Bolshevik government's first foreign policy act, on November 8, 1917, was to issue a "peace decree" and seek immediate negotiations with the Germans. The nightmare had come to pass: the Bolsheviks would take Russia out of the war and the German troops would rush westward and defeat the battered British and French armies before the Americans arrived in strength. In the view of Lloyd George and the other Allied leaders, they were staring disaster in the face—unless they could do something about Russia.

To understand how Woodrow Wilson's own views about events in Russia evolved, it is first necessary to understand what he was being told about that country—especially what he was being told by American intelligence. That intelligence was in fact quite fragmented, with a number of curious characters.

The first American intelligence agent to attempt to understand events in Russia was a quasi-amateur, W. Somerset Maugham, a former British spy who preferred writing novels. Maugham's friend, William Wiseman, head of British intelligence in the United States, and close to Wilson's chief advisers, arranged for Maugham to go to Russia shortly after the Russian Revolution began to gauge Kerensky's strength and prospects of remaining in power. Maugham, under cover of writing a book, concluded that Kerensky could not stay in power; the Allies, he recommended, should begin covertly funding "self-determination movements" in the country as an alternative, but he underestimated the political chances of one of those movements, the Bolsheviks.

A similar intelligence error was made by a more high-level observer, diplomat Elihu Root, dispatched by Wilson to Russia in the spring of 1917 as head of a "special diplomatic commission" to report directly to him on the political power structure. Somehow, Root entirely missed the Bolsheviks—who already had won widespread support among workers and peasants—and did not even bother mentioning them in his report.

Meanwhile, the rest of the American intelligence presence in Russia was split among three main intelligence agencies, the standard American system for some years. First, there was the State Department, whose consuls and certain other employees carried out what might be termed legalized spying, the overt (and time-honored) collecting of information under diplomatic cover. They worked under the direction of the ambassador, David Francis, a multimillionaire businessman who hated the Bolsheviks (he occasionally referred to them as "vermin") and told his superiors in Washington that Kerensky would keep Russia in the war—if only the United States gave him sufficient support.

The State Department people in Russia also had hired a few agents for the more dangerous work of collecting secret information, mostly military. Among them was a Greek-American businessman with extensive commercial interests in Russia, Xenephon Kalamatiano, who in turn had employed a large network of over a hundred Russians on the American payroll.

The second American intelligence listening post, the U.S. Army's Military Intelligence Division (MID) operation in Russia, was run by the American military attaché at the U.S. embassy (he also functioned as chief of the U.S. Military Mission to Russia), Colonel James A. Ruggles, Jr. He had been assigned to his post shortly after the Bolshevik revolution, and like most officers of his time assigned to intelligence duties, he was insufficiently trained. On top of that, he was now thrust into an intelligence maelstrom. He faced the task of not only trying to make sense of the fast-moving events in Russia, he also had to contend with the vast intelligence apparatus run by the Germans. Moreover, he was trying to steer clear of the very active operations run by French and British intelligence.

In short, Russia at that time was a virtual spy novel, and Ruggles's job was complicated further by some disruptive amateurs who were working for him. Chief among them were the two leaders of the large American Red Cross mission in Russia, William Boyce Thompson, and his deputy, Raymond Robins. As information-gatherers, both men—wealthy philanthropists who had decided to devote their lives to social work—were ideally placed, for the scattered Red Cross operations around the country afforded the opportunity to travel to those outposts, giving them access to a wide range of information. Moreover, the Red Cross had many high-level contacts with government officials, and also tapped into several volunteer sources of information among the network of YMCA stations in the country. (The YMCA had been invited into Russia by Kerensky to perform relief work with Russian soldiers.)

Thompson and Robins were to prove more trouble than they were worth. Thompson became a rabid anti-Bolshevik, and with the tacit approval of the State Department, funneled $1 million of his own money to the Social Revolutionary political party, one of the chief opponents of Lenin. For his part, Robins suddenly became extremely pro-Bolshevik, and saw his mission as convincing the State Department and the White House that the Bolsheviks would fight Germany if given total support by the United States.

It was a serious misreading of the Bolshevik position, for both Lenin and his chief military aide, Leon Trotsky, had from the first moment made it clear that they intended to take Russia out of what they considered an "imperialist war" in which Russia had no stake. Robins had no grasp of that essential truth, nor did he even begin to comprehend what Trotsky meant when, storming out of the Russian-German armistice negotiations at Brest-Litovsk, announced that relations between Germany and Russia were now neither war, nor peace, a preview of what later would be called the Cold War.

The third arm of American intelligence was its oldest, the Office of Naval Intelligence, represented in the person of the naval attaché based in Petrograd, Vice Admiral Newton A. McCully.

The only American intelligence official then based in Russia who spoke the language, McCully warned his superiors that the Bolsheviks were there to stay, their White Russian opponents had no real support among the Russian masses, and that the Bolsheviks certainly would sign a separate armistice with Germany.

As McCully predicted—that report, like the others he wrote, appears to have been ignored—the Russians did finally sign a treaty taking them out of the war; less than a week later, in the spring of 1918, the great German offensive, buttressed with thirty-five divisions released from duty on the Eastern Front, fell upon the Western Front. Eventually, it would be checked, but at a cost of more than five hundred thousand casualties.

The treaty earned the Bolsheviks the enmity of the Allied powers, including the United States. Just to add more fuel to the fire, Edgar Sisson, the former editor of *Cosmopolitan* magazine, had been appointed by Wilson to the Committee on Public Information, America's wartime propaganda agency. A total amateur, Sisson paid a visit to Russia, where, he later claimed, he was handed a batch of documents allegedly stolen by anti-Bolsheviks from Lenin's headquarters. According to the documents, Lenin was a paid agent of Germany, and received all his orders directly from Berlin. Unfortunately for Sisson, who published the documents as authentic, they were crudely forged. Even the British, who despised Lenin, pronounced them inept forgeries, noting that although Sisson claimed the documents were from varied sources, close examination revealed that they had all been typed on the same typewriter.

The alleged secret documents caused a sensation in the United States, and how much of an influence they played in Wilson's fateful decision to intervene directly in Russia is impossible to say. Given the secrecy in which he made that decision, it is difficult, even today, to cite his exact motives.

Whatever the motives, Wilson further confused matters by offering shifting rationales for sending American troops. There were actually two interventions: one, a force of several thousand, was sent to Siberia via Vladivostok in August and September 1918, officially to guard the Trans-Siberian Railway and to help Czechoslovakian forces who had switched sides after the Russian Revolution and wanted to fight with the Allies on the Western Front. Its commander, Major General William S. Graves, was careful to keep his troops out of the real agenda in Siberia, which was an attempt by the Allies to create an entirely separate Siberian state to challenge the Bolsheviks. To that end, a motley collection of White Russian warlords was being propped up. Graves, who thought the whole thing idiotic, refused to have anything to do with conducting a war against the Bolsheviks.*

The second, and much more dangerous, intervention was at Archangel, ostensibly, according to Wilson, to prevent the large stores of military supplies there from falling into the hands of the Germans. Nearly five thousand American soldiers were sent to Archangel beginning in September of 1918, joining fifteen thousand French and British troops supposedly engaged on the same mission. But following the October Revolution, that mission began to assume dimensions probably intended from the start: destroy the Bolsheviks.

The Americans, mostly Polish-Americans from Michigan and Wisconsin who were originally trained to fight on the Western Front, found themselves in a bewildering situation that would presage the experiences of some of their descendants many years later in another foreign intervention. They were told that their presence in northern Russia was to help the war effort by denying that area and its supplies to the Germans. Then they were informed, following the October Revolution, that the Bolsheviks —people in the pay of the Germans—were also their enemies, and that the fight against the Bolsheviks was in fact a fight against Germany.

The argument took a new tack after the end of World War I: now, the Americans were helping the freedom-loving White Russians against the bestial enemy, the Bolsheviks. All around them, however, the American soldiers could see that there was something seriously wrong with that argument. Most of the Russians hated them as foreign occupiers, and the White Russians were led by corrupt generals who skimmed American aid money while their people were starving.

The Americans were subjected to a constant propaganda barrage by the Bolsheviks, who continually reminded them that they

* For some years afterward, Graves was the subject of FBI surveillance, the result of a suspicion by J. Edgar Hoover that Graves was some sort of Communist sympathizer for interpreting his orders in Siberia strictly and refusing to be drawn into the fighting between the Bolsheviks and White Russians.

were a long way from home, fighting against revolutionaries no different from their Founding Fathers. Militarily, the Bolsheviks reminded the Americans, the intervention was a disaster. While *The American Sentinel*, the official paper of the U.S. forces in Archangel, proclaimed the proverbial light at the end of the tunnel (sample headline: ADVANTAGE IS OURS IN PAST WEEK'S FIGHTS), the Americans could see the growing strength of Trotsky's Red Army. By February 1919, more than forty-two thousand Soviet troops were squeezing the Americans, British, and Canadians northward, away from the slivers of outpost lines they held.

Everything went wrong. Morale of the American troops plummeted—there were thirteen "official incidents," as the Army called mutinies by soldiers—and the Americans were appalled to see British troops moving Russians out of "suspected Bolshevik villages" and burning their houses down. Meanwhile, much further south in Moscow, the American intelligence operative Xenephon Kalamatiano foolishly became involved in a mad scheme by British and French intelligence to overthrow Lenin's government, a plot which included the idea of arresting the entire Bolshevik leadership and parading them through the streets of Moscow in their underwear. Like every other attempt to destroy the revolutionary government, it failed. Kalamatiano was arrested (he spent nearly two years in jail before being released in a prisoner exchange), and American diplomats fled the country—not to return until 1933, when U.S.–Soviet diplomatic relations were restored.

In this catalogue of disaster, Wilson found that his great vision of a postwar world had turned to ashes. It had been destroyed by his inability to build a consensus, and his blindness—caused by his fragmented intelligence agencies, which could not tell him the realities of the new Soviet state. He was a man trapped in a policy that had no exit, and in words that would be echoed a half-century later by another Democratic president caught in the coils of a failed intervention, he said in December 1918, "It is harder to get out than it was to go in."

It remained only to pick up the pieces and go home. Wilson finally gave up, and as Senator William Borah complained on the floor of the U.S. Senate, "We are not at war with Russia; Congress has not declared war against the Russian government or the Russian people," the Americans were withdrawn as the entire Allied intervention effort collapsed. It had cost the American Army 139 soldiers.

But there were further human costs. Admiral McCully, the Navy intelligence officer who had so accurately predicted the course of events, was head of the U.S. Navy forces at Archangel as the Americans evacuated. Behind them, begging to be taken along, were thousands of White Russian supporters, now being callously left to the mercies of the advancing Bolsheviks. McCully urgently requested that he be allowed to evacuate ninety-six thousand White Russians described as "seriously compromised." His request was refused.

And so these Russians stood at the dockside as the ships sailed away, weeping and begging to be taken to America—or anywhere; anyplace but Archangel, where the whispers had already started. *They* were coming, the grim men with documents and lists, leading execution squads for the Soviet state's revenge against "traitors of the revolution." There was no appeal from the judgments of these men, whose terrifying reputation would soon spread from Russia everywhere else, including America—the men of the Extraordinary Commission to Fight Counterrevolution and Sabotage. Its acronym already inspired great fear.

Cheka.

The Bolshevik revolution was only a day old when the Council of People's Commissars (Sovnarkom), the Bolsheviks' central command, created the first Soviet security organization, known as the Committee for Combating Pogroms. Less than two months later, determined to stamp out the considerable political opposition that ranged across the spectrum, it was replaced by a new entity: the Cheka, which was given wide powers that covered internal security, counterespionage, foreign intelligence, and ordinary police functions. Soon, Revolutionary Tribunals were formed to work with the Cheka, creating what amounted to a police-security-judicial network unparalleled in modern history. And this state security machine, in the hands of men like Lenin and Joseph Stalin, turned out to be a frightening weapon—even as it evolved from Cheka to GPU to OGPU to NKVD and, finally, the KGB.

Whatever the acronym, the apparatus owes its reputation to one man, the century's most extraordinary spymaster: Feliks

Dzerzhinsky. Son of a Polish nobleman, Dzerzhinsky was a committed revolutionary who had spent eleven years in the Czar's prisons. He was close to Lenin, and he was fanatically committed to the Revolution; totally without ambition, he sought only to be the "watchdog of the revolution." However intensely Dzerzhinsky sought this task, Lenin did not give him much in the way of resources to carry it out: at the time of its formation, the Cheka consisted of only two dozen men (some of them ex-officials of the Okhrana, the Czar's infamous secret police), and no vehicles.

But Dzerzhinsky had the heart and mind of a secret policeman. Wracked by a constant cough—heritage of his years of Siberian imprisonment—he worked nearly around the clock. He was that most dangerous of all revolutionary figures, the ruthless fanatic; invariably dressed in boots and gray cloak or military tunic, he dedicated his life to destroying the Revolution's enemies—the anti-Bolshevik "Whites," the foreigners, the Social Revolutionaries, the Mensheviks, anyone he and Lenin perceived to be a threat. Almost overnight, he created the vast machinery of repression and the Soviet mania for "state security," and made no effort to conceal its real purpose. "We represent in ourselves," he said in an interview in June 1918, "organized terror."

And terror it was: an estimated five hundred thousand Russians were executed by the Cheka during the first six years of its existence. Families of deserters were arrested, and in Kiev, the wives of Red Army officers who had defected to the anti-Bolsheviks (Whites) were executed. Groups of Cheka operatives, blandly called "special departments," roamed all over Russia during the Civil War that followed the Bolshevik revolution, rounding up and shooting whole groups of so-called "oppositionists."

The Russian people were not officially informed until 1922 that such an organization as Cheka even existed, but virtually all Russians were perfectly aware of that fact—especially the unfortunate people in Archangel who made the mistake of aiding the Allies. The ships carrying the Americans and the other Allies had hardly disappeared over the horizon when a terrible retribution arrived in the persons of Mikhail S. Kedrov and Aleksandr V. Eiduk, two Cheka operatives, with execution squads in tow. Sent to the city to "impose order," they set about to Bolshevize the city by the simple expedient of arresting and then summarily executing anyone known (or suspected) to be involved with the Whites and the Allies.

Eiduk had already prepared dossiers on many suspects, for he had been working as the Cheka's chief operative against the Americans since late 1918. Later, in 1921, he again worked against the Americans, serving under cover as Soviet government representative to the American Relief Administration (ARA) operations in Russia. The ARA, under Herbert Hoover, was distributing food to relieve a terrible famine; its large number of Russian employees were vetted, then closely watched by Eiduk's operatives, who also kept close tabs on all the Americans.†

Eiduk was among the first of what in a few years would become an army of counterespionage agents, a force whose sheer size and skill caught the Americans and their allies unaware. No one would have believed that Dzerzhinsky's organization could overcome the stark crises facing the new Bolshevik regime all at once: the outbreak of civil war, an invasion of foreign troops, vast areas of Russia occupied by the Germans, and an ongoing plot to overthrow the regime, including an attempted assassination of Lenin. In internal security terms, it was a nightmare.

Yet, within three years, the Cheka had infiltrated, then smashed the British-French plot to overthrow Lenin, neutralized the threat of the Whites, played a critical role in the removal of the foreign forces (as early as 1918, its cryptographers were reading coded American military messages in Russia), and secured the future of a regime that informed opinion gave no chance to survive. And, for good measure, the Cheka then mounted a brilliantly organized operation in 1921, creating a mythical center of opposition inside Russia, then luring White Russian exiles and Allied intelligence services into a trap. The operation, which lasted until 1927, wiped out the last remaining threats to the Soviet regime.

The success of these operations gave the Cheka a vaunted, if somewhat odious, reputation, but what really caused alarm in the West was Cheka's inevitable next step: expansion into foreign intelligence operations. Not an idle threat: Lenin had rung alarm

† Kedrov and Eiduk later perished in the Stalin purges, despite their bloody services to the infant Soviet state. Kedrov was one of the first purge victims to be publicly rehabilitated by Nikita Khrushchev during the de-Stalinization campaign of 1956.

bells everywhere in March 1919, with his famous declaration to the Third International: "Soon we shall see the victory of communism throughout the world; we shall see the foundation of the World Federative Republic of Soviets."

In other words, world revolution, the specter that haunted every capital outside of Moscow. Lenin's prediction seemed to be coming true: a Communist revolution in Hungary, Communist uprisings in Germany, and Communist-led unrest everywhere. In 1920, Dzerzhinsky formed the foreign branch of the Cheka for overseas intelligence operations, and now the specter had a new edge—Communist parties all over the world, aided and abetted by Chekhists who would organize the world revolution predicted by Lenin. Moreover, the Cheka would have ready-made armies of spies on hand, the members of the burgeoning Communist parties, prepared to do all for Moscow.

Ironically, this very real threat set off the greatest panic not among the Soviet Union's immediate neighbors, but in the United States. And what happened there was to rock the young republic to its foundations.

It was called "the Red Scare."

World War I, which marked America's first entry onto the world stage, demonstrated that, however wealthy and powerful, it was a country, oddly, that trembled at the first sign of a foreign "threat." The war ignited a wave of concern about internal subversion, which took the form of a belief that assorted dissidents in the United States were paving the way for a presumed horde of German spies and saboteurs. Actually, the German espionage effort in the United States—saboteurs or otherwise—never amounted to much, but President Wilson found himself steadily pressured into "doing something" about the alleged internal threat.

Theodore Roosevelt, Wilson's Progressive Party opponent in the 1912 election, proclaimed in 1917 that pacifists opposed to U.S. participation in the war "showed themselves traitors to America." By June of that year, Wilson, in a Flag Day speech, spoke of the Germans as "filling unsuspecting communities with vicious spies and conspirators" who "diligently spread sedition."

What resulted was a massive domestic surveillance effort to uncover this army of German agents, loosely defined as radicals, suspected radicals, academics critical of Wilson's views, "pro-revolutionary German conspirators"—in short, all domestic dissidents. New alien and sedition laws were passed, along with tough anti-espionage regulations; legislation authorized the government to confiscate property, wiretap, search and seize private possessions, censor writings, open mail, and restrict the right of assembly. Armies of private investigators, federal agents, and informers were created, operating under regulations that were vaguely drawn.

The very vagueness of the regulations, combined with the obsession over German spies supposedly lurking everywhere, was certain to cause trouble. In fact, the regulations created an American apparatus aimed not against German spies—who could neither be found nor identified‡—but against "agitators causing labor unrest," "radicals who undermine morale," and "Bolsheviks spreading subversive thought."

The victims were the most prominent dissenters. The Industrial Workers of the World union (the "Wobblies") headquarters was raided by Justice Department agents, who arrested IWW leaders, charging them with sedition, espionage, and "interference with the war effort." Based on highly questionable premises, the IWW leaders were found guilty and imprisoned (an experience that drove many of them into the American Communist Party).

What constituted dissent was interpreted rather broadly. The Wobblies were targeted, and so was the Harvard Liberal Club. All labor organizations were subjected to intense government spying efforts, as were Jews (regarded with special suspicion).

The panic over "subversives" supposedly aiding the German war effort began to be melded into another growing panic, the one concerned with "Reds." Since the U.S. Government had already produced an official report claiming that Lenin and the Bolsheviks were in the pay of the Germans (the forged Sisson documents), it was not unnatural to link both those entities as one, virtually indistinguishable, enemy. Ever more lurid news accounts of the excesses of the "Red terror" of the Cheka in Rus-

‡ The obsession over German spies carried over into all things German, leading to a wartime idiom that passed into the language: frankfurter was replaced by "hot dog" to make that popular dish less German-sounding. "Liberty cabbage" for sauerkraut did not survive the war, however.

sia helped create a climate in which the Bolshevik enemy began to assume even larger proportions than "Kaiser Bill" and the "Huns," especially after the Germans lost the war.

This internal security crisis burst into public view in February of 1919, when a U.S. Senate committee held hearings on the problem of "Bolshevik propaganda" and how it was threatening to subvert the United States. A parade of witnesses testified that Trotsky's Red Army was composed of depraved criminals and that the Russian Revolution was conducted largely by "East Side Jews," among other incredulities. David Francis, the former U.S. ambassador to Russia, was a star witness, testifying that Lenin was merely a "tool of the Germans," and that the Bolsheviks were killing any Russian who wore a white collar, was educated, or who was not a Bolshevik.

The depth of feeling was most marked in America's oldest intelligence agency, the Navy's Office of Naval Intelligence (ONI), created in 1882. Early in 1919, Captain Harry E. Yarnell, the chief war planner for the Chief of Naval Operations, asked that ONI purge the United States of "sinister Bolshevik influence," recommending as the best method a declaration of war against Soviet Russia, accompanied by treason trials for "American sympathizers." Small wonder, then, that the ONI in December of that year produced a report that claimed there was a massive nationwide plot to take over the entire country. According to the report, the plot was led by the noted anarchists Emma Goldman and Alexander Berkman, along with "German and Russian Jews," Mexican bandits, IWW "subversives," and a "Japanese master spy."* This incredible uprising, the ONI predicted, would take place sometime during January or February.

The fact that this plot did not come off as predicted caused not a ripple, for there were plenty of other alleged "plots" to keep military intelligence agents busy. Most of them spent their time during the war keeping tabs on people they regarded as potential subversives—labor union organizers, Jews, and Russian immigrants seemed to be favorite investigative targets. Now, the

* Goldman, known as "Queen of the Reds," had just two months earlier been set free after being imprisoned for violations of the conscription laws. In the same month that ONI named her as a lead conspirator in a secret national uprising, Hoover was busy having her and 248 other aliens deported under the Immigration Act.

agents were unleashed, without any legal restraint whatever, on a new subversive hunt; not surprisingly, they went after the same old targets.

The other major U.S. intelligence agency, the State Department, in 1919 created the Office of Chief Special Agent, assigned the task of investigating "organizations and individuals *suspected* of subversive activity." (Emphasis added.) The Office of Chief Special Agent had sole power to decide who was "suspected."

The lunacy also struck the U.S. Army's MID, first organized in 1917 to collect foreign intelligence, but almost immediately diverted into domestic operations, like ONI, busy searching for the "subversives" working to support Germany. Its first chief, Lieutenant Colonel Ralph H. Van Deman, was obsessed about the domestic subversion menace, and covertly supported networks of private vigilante groups all over the United States, who prepared reports on "labor agitators and anarchists." Van Deman also created files on hundreds of thousands of American dissidents—files which congressional investigators later discovered were still being updated and used by Army intelligence domestic spies as late as 1970.

Armed with vague directives that permitted them to spy on just about anybody, Army MID officers around the country also took it upon themselves to define who was a subversive. In Oregon, for example, one intelligence officer sent a letter to all county sheriffs seeking information on "all organizations and elements hostile or potentially hostile to the government of this country." He helpfully enclosed a list of such enemies, including the American Federation of Labor.

But the real focus of the government's panic was centered in a recently created arm of the Justice Department known as the Bureau of Investigation. One of its early chiefs was a political hack and ex-private detective named William J. Burns, whose achievements included surveillance of nude anarchist bathers in Puget Sound. The Bureau had a vague mandate to investigate "Communist subversives." It had a small intelligence division assigned the task of collecting dossiers on these "subversives." The division was headed by a devoted bureaucrat and up-and-comer named J. Edgar Hoover.

Hoover was just another low-level bureaucrat until the night of June 2, 1919, when a bomb went off outside Attorney General

Mitchell Palmer's home. The explosion killed the bomb-thrower, and a piece of paper found on his body with the words "Anarchist Fighters" offered no clue to the bombing: no such organization existed, and nobody had ever heard of the victim. Nevertheless, the incident electrified the country, and was seen as proof that the much-talked about threat of anarchist and Communist plots was real.

Palmer came up with an idea: "subversive aliens" who had not yet attained American citizenship would be rounded up and deported, thus sidestepping the inconvenience of formally charging them with criminal violations and being required to prove it at a trial. First, however, the aliens had to be identified—and that was where Hoover came in. No sooner had Palmer decided on deportations when Hoover produced names from the files he had been assiduously collecting, all of them, Hoover claimed, dealing with "subversives." The definition of who and who was not a "subversive," of course, was entirely Hoover's, and overnight made him the government's leading expert on Communists and similar subversives. He was to jealously guard this expertise the rest of his life.

Lists were drawn up, and on the morning of January 2, 1920, over four thousand people were rounded up and jailed, preparatory to being deported. They were denied legal counsel, and in most cases, there were no search or arrest warrants. A black day for individual rights in the United States, it led to the creation of the American Civil Liberties Union, which saw no "prairie fire of revolution" aflame in the country as Palmer did.

The real victim was civil liberties. As had happened before in American history, the government had reacted to a foreign crisis by turning on the enemy it most feared, dissidence. Palmer and Hoover did not, as they assumed, save America from the threat of Bolshevik revolution; in fact, what they injured was real freedom of expression for unpopular ideas. The line between dissent and treason became erased, replaced by teacher loyalty oaths, purging of textbooks of any mention of the dark sides of American history, and state sedition laws.

Yet, slowly a counterreaction was setting in. The level of hysteria during the "Red Scare" could not be maintained indefinitely; as the weeks and months passed without a mass revolution breaking out, Americans' attention began to turn elsewhere. The U.S.

Supreme Court, which had upheld sedition statutes, began to have second thoughts. The famous dissents of Oliver Wendell Holmes and Louis Brandeis, arguing that no one should be prosecuted simply for being an ideological nonconformist without a standard of "clear and present danger," began to sway the majority. Congress, which had willingly participated in the assault on civil liberties, roused itself and began asking awkward questions: just what were the intelligence agencies doing?

The Republican administrations during the years 1921 to 1932, concerned with "normalcy" and the American economic boom, had little interest in the preoccupations of the Wilson administration, and began dismantling the repressive machinery. The intelligence agencies that played such strong roles in the great domestic crackdowns were emasculated.

They had brought that destruction on themselves. Obsessed with the danger from within, they had wasted their resources on a whole series of operations that had nothing to do with the real issue, which was the larger world around them—where the real danger lay. Like it or not, America was part of that world.

But what kind of American eyes and ears were listening?

TWO

Papa's Crook Factory

COLONEL JOHN W. THOMASON, JR., shook his head. "No, not possible," he said to the man sitting opposite him. "There is absolutely no possibility that the Japanese Navy would be so foolish as to take on the United States Navy. That would be suicide, and the Japanese are not stupid people."

His listener strongly disagreed, but did not argue any further. He had already tried to make his point: based on what he had seen and heard in the Far East that spring of 1941, there was no doubt in his mind that Japan intended to attack the United States in the Pacific—and probably quite soon.

But Thomason, an impressive-looking Marine, could make a very persuasive argument that the facts, as he knew them, militated against such a possibility: the United States Navy was immensely superior to the navy of Japan, and was much better equipped. The Japanese knew that; therefore, they would not be so foolish as to attack the force certain to deliver them a terrible defeat.

His listener had remained silent during this learned exposition on the balance of forces in the Far East, a somewhat unusual occurrence, because Ernest Hemingway was not noted for deferential silence in anyone's presence. But Hemingway, a man usually combative and convinced that he knew more than anyone else on any given topic, could be quiescent if he thought someone had vastly superior knowledge and experience. And in Thomason, that certainly seemed to be the case. He was a highly decorated officer of twenty years' experience, the last ten spent in the Office of Naval Intelligence. Like many ONI officers, he had an intimate knowledge of Asia; when he said that the United States could easily handle any Japanese challenge, Hemingway listened with respect.

Seven months later, Hemingway—and the American people—learned that Thomason and the rest of American intelligence were wrong, tragically so. The "matchless Navy" Thomason had spoken of was smashed at Pearl Harbor, victim of an attack that none of them, somehow, had seen coming. The American military presence in the Philippines, another great bulwark that Thomason assured Hemingway would checkmate Japanese ambitions, had also been crushed in an attack that caught the defenders totally by surprise—even after commercial radio announced the news of the attack on Pearl Harbor.

Combined with the other drumrolls of disaster in the Pacific, it amounted to a perfect intelligence failure: seemingly, no one had seen it coming, no one made any preparations, and a nation the size of two American states had humbled the mightiest economic power on earth.

How was it possible for such an intelligence failure to occur? The reasons, it would turn out, were many and varied, but one of the more important ones was connected with a much narrower question: what was Ernest Hemingway doing in the Office of Naval Intelligence in the first place?

The arrangement between Hemingway and ONI was an informal one, largely the result of the writer's friendship with Thomason and another ONI officer, Marine Corps Colonel Charles Sweeny. For some years, Hemingway, who traveled extensively, had been providing the two men with assorted intelligence he encountered (accompanied, inevitably, with his own analyses).

He was among several dozen Americans, prominent and not so prominent, who served during the interwar years as the cutting edge of American intelligence. Very few were trained intelligence agents, but they were patriotic men and women who saw nothing wrong in those simpler times with combining professional duties with intelligence-gathering for American agencies. Almost all had been quietly recruited, a simple approach, usually from someone they knew in the intelligence trade, who asked if they would mind helping out their country. Almost no one refused.

Those years might be called the "time of the amateur American spy," which raises the question: why were the intelligence agencies so assiduously recruiting amateurs? Didn't they have their own agents? Not really, and that, for all intents and purposes, is the story of pre-World War II American intelligence.

The post–World War I era began in a burst of optimism. The United States had begun its great economic boom, and despite the unsettled nature of Europe, there was a prevailing conviction that World War I ("the war to end all wars") had made war as an instrument of national policy obsolete. The 1928 Kellogg-Briand Pact officially renounced war, and accompanied by naval arms limitation treaties and a series of bilateral arbitration treaties the United States negotiated, it seemed that, at last, the world would enter a prolonged period of peace.

The United States, for its part, was retreating from the world stage. President Hoover vowed withdrawal of U.S. troops from Haiti and Nicaragua, and pledged an open, honest government. Harding and Coolidge before him had already been busy dismantling the Wilsonian structure; the United States was withdrawing into itself to savor the fruits of prosperity.

And with it came the dismantling of the modest intelligence structure that Wilson and World War I built. The Army's Military Intelligence Division was cut from 1,441 men in 1918 to just 90 in 1922 (and a budget of only $225,000). The ONI was cut from nearly 1,000 men to 42. In 1927 the State Department's U-1 Bureau, its chief intelligence-gathering division, was eliminated altogether.

The result was a virtual halt in intelligence-collection activities at a time when they were most needed, for three great forces were at work in the outside world that threatened to involve, inevitably, the United States. One was the Bolshevik revolution and subsequent Soviet state, whose effects were reverberating everywhere; the second was the rise of fascism in Europe; and the third was the domination of the Japanese Government by military extremists whose program included expansion of Japan's borders by military conquest.

There was growing awareness of the dangers, but precious few resources to understand them. Even the resources available were woefully inadequate: because of minuscule budgets, Army intelligence ruled that officers assigned to military attaché duty overseas —the front line of intelligence collection—would be required to defray the expenses of life on the diplomatic circuit out of their own pockets. Thus, the officers assigned those jobs tended to have independent means of income, which solved the problem of paying the expenses, but it was not the kind of standard guaranteed to produce very good intelligence.

All of which meant that the intelligence agencies began to reach out for unpaid volunteers who might fill in the intelligence gaps. What they recruited turned out to be a very disparate collection, including people whose roles in secret intelligence work stood in sharp contrast with their public personalities.

On the afternoon of November 29, 1934, a tall, broad-shouldered American, speaking nearly flawless Japanese, walked into the reception area of the St. Luke's International Hospital in Tokyo. Bearing a bouquet of flowers, he asked the room number of Mrs. Cecil Burton Lyon, wife of the third secretary of the U.S. embassy, who was in the hospital giving birth to a baby girl. Assuming the American was a friend of the family, the Japanese nurses directed him to her room on the seventh floor.

The American got out of the elevator on the seventh floor, but immediately entered a fire exit door and walked up several flights of stairs to the roof of the hospital, at the time among the tallest buildings in Tokyo. Withdrawing a camera from under his kimono, the American spent the next hour photographing everything he could see, concentrating on industrial installations and several warships anchored in Tokyo Bay. When he had finished, he left the hospital, the camera and the flowers concealed under the kimono. As Japanese custom required, he smiled and gave a slight bow to the nurses on his way out.

The American's timing had been perfect. All Tokyo was preoccupied by events at the packed Omiya Grounds seventeen miles north of the city, where barnstorming American major league baseball all-stars were playing an exhibition game against some Japanese all-stars. The great Babe Ruth had awed the crowd with a gargantuan home run to deepest center field as the Americans romped, 23–5.

The American who visited the hospital was supposed to play in that game. His name was Moe Berg, catcher for the Washington Senators. He spent the next hour getting his film to the U.S. embassy.*

Later, Berg would claim to his American teammates that he had suddenly taken sick, and was unable to get to the ball park. No one pressed the issue, for Berg was considered a rather odd fish. Among the best catchers in the American League, he was a *magna cum laude* graduate of Princeton, a voracious reader of books, magazines, and newspapers in many languages, and a linguist who spoke at least twelve of those languages. What his fellow players did not know was that Berg was a volunteer spy. How he was recruited—and who recruited him—remains a mystery, but sometime during the early 1930s, he began carrying out intelligence-gathering missions during trips to Germany, where he vacationed, and Japan, where he had been sent in 1932 as part of a State Department-sponsored program to teach baseball to Japanese collegians.

Fellow major leaguers were somewhat awed by the man they sometimes called "professor," and who occasionally puzzled them with odd requests. Vernon (Lefty) Gomez, the New York Yankees star, thought it strange when, one day in 1936, Berg approached him while he was warming up for a game. Asked if he still had the snapshots he had taken during that 1934 tour of Japan, Gomez replied that he had. Berg asked to borrow them temporarily—he swore Gomez would get them back—claiming he was interested in some of the views of Japan. Gomez was thoroughly puzzled: he had visited Yokohama, not considered one of Japan's best tourist

* The pictures were used years later, in 1942, by U.S. air intelligence officers planning targets for the famous Doolittle bombing raid on Tokyo.

attractions. Nevertheless, something of a shutterbug, he had taken a pile of snapshots. What could Berg possibly want with pictures of the humdrum industrial city?

Berg did not tell him that Yokohama at the time contained Japan's largest and most important naval base. A few weeks after he turned over his pictures to Berg, Gomez got them back. They arrived in the mail in a package with no return address and a Washington, D.C., postmark.

Berg was later to join the OSS during World War II, and, still later, did some tasks for the CIA—none of which intelligence work he ever discussed publicly. A man shrouded in mystery, his prewar intelligence work is at least partially known. Much less is known about two other curious cases of interwar espionage, one of which involved a famous American.

Both cases were connected with one of the more knotty problems facing U.S. Navy intelligence: what exactly were the Japanese doing with the collection of Pacific islands awarded them by the Treaty of Versailles in 1919? The islands were scattered over an ocean area of four hundred thousand square miles and stood in the strategically important center of the Pacific. The fear was that the Japanese would fortify those islands, ideal bases from which they could then attack American installations.

Finding out what was happening on those Japanese possessions seemed impossible. The Japanese clamped tight security on the islands—considered a good indication that *something* was going on —and prohibited all visitors. ONI had no platoons of agents who could infiltrate the islands, but it did have an eager volunteer, Marine Corps Captain E. H. (Pete) Ellis.

A highly decorated World War I officer, Ellis also was an alcoholic, an affliction that did not prevent him from being among the most brilliant Marine staff officers. He was directly concerned with the question of the Pacific islands, for he was working on War Plan Orange, the basic strategic plan to be used in event of hostilities with Japan. But the plan had a major intelligence gap: were there extensive fortifications being constructed on the islands that would make them too costly to capture?

In 1922, according to the official records, Ellis applied for a ninety-day leave "to visit France, Belgium, and Germany." The application was approved in the uncommonly fast time of twenty-four hours. But Ellis never went to Europe; he next showed up in a hospital in Yokohama, Japan, and shortly afterward, disappeared. Six months later, the U.S. embassy was formally notified that an American citizen named E. H. Ellis, representative of the Hughes Trading Company of New York, had died in the Japanese-occupied Caroline Islands. He had died from illness, and his body was cremated.

Over the years, bits and pieces of the Ellis mystery have surfaced. Apparently, Ellis, under cover as a copra trader, cruised around the Japanese-occupied islands, trying to discover the extent of any fortifications work. There is no record that he found anything significant, or even got the opportunity: the Japanese, aware from the first moment that he was an American spy, kept him under close observation. Although attributed to acute alcoholism, Ellis' death, some native islanders later insisted, was actually the result of poisoning by the Japanese.

Concern over the islands was the backdrop to another, more sensational, interwar intelligence mystery that unfolded fourteen years after Ellis' abortive mission. This one concerned the famed aviatrix Amelia Earhart, who took off from Lae, New Guinea, on July 2, 1937, on a 2,556-mile flight to Howland Island in the central Pacific, part of a highly publicized attempt to fly around the world. But neither she nor her navigator, Fred Noonan, made it; somewhere in the vastness of the Pacific, she disappeared.

Her fate became one of the most intriguing mysteries of all time, and has spawned a small flood of articles and books positing various theories on what happened. One tantalizing part of the mystery concerns Earhart's possible intelligence connections, largely the result of stories told long after World War II by islanders who claim to have seen Earhart and Noonan captured by the Japanese after crash-landing near one of the mandated islands. According to these stories, the Japanese suspected that the Pacific portion of Earhart's flight, which overflew or skirted some of the mandated islands, was in fact cover for a spying mission.

It is difficult to determine how much credence to attach to these stories, but the entire episode has a number of tantalizing clues. For one thing, there was an extraordinary amount of U.S. Government help for what was supposed to be a strictly private effort: President Roosevelt personally ordered two U.S. Navy ships along Earhart's flight path to aid her, and a landing strip was built on Howland Island just for the flight, using Works Progress

Administration funds. Further, Noonan had once been employed at Pan American in the Pacific, in the days when the airline and the U.S. Navy had extremely close relations; Noonan and other Pan American employees were rumored to have provided, with encouragement from the company, freelance aid to ONI when requested. More intriguingly, U.S. Army intelligence agents after the war investigated the whole incident on the Japanese end—and discovered a curious lack of memory among Japanese officials thought to know something about the mystery. Nothing in the way of credible evidence has surfaced since, so the mystery remains.†

An even more famous aviation pioneer, Charles Lindbergh, did, in fact serve as an amateur agent. Many consider his one of the few really successful American intelligence operations before the war.

The idea of using Lindbergh was the brainchild of Major Truman Smith, the U.S. military attaché in Berlin. Concerned about reports in 1936 that Hitler was building the world's largest and most technically advanced air force, Smith realized he lacked the technical expertise to properly evaluate just how far the Luftwaffe had advanced. He noticed that the American hero Lindbergh was being invited to aircraft factories and air force installations all over Europe. Smith wangled an invitation for Lindbergh from the Germans, and then asked the "Lone Eagle" if he would perform a patriotic service: take a close look at everything the Luftwaffe has, and make a technical evaluation.

Lindbergh was the perfect spy; a shy and diffident man, he sometimes gave the impression of being a country bumpkin, but he did know airplanes. In private meetings with Smith and a stenographer, Lindbergh poured out an encyclopedia of details. In two state visits to Germany, he singlehandedly dictated the book on the U.S. Army intelligence picture of the Luftwaffe,

† If Earhart did in fact participate in a spying operation in the mandated islands, then she and Ellis both gave their lives in vain. It turned out that the strict Japanese security in the islands was designed to hide *weakness*, not strength; the Japanese did not want anyone to know the islands were virtually undefended. Fortification of the islands did not begin in earnest until nearly two years after Pearl Harbor. Using only locally available materials such as logs and coral, the Japanese nevertheless were able to create a formidable system of fortifications that required many American lives to overcome.

which he evaluated as superior to the French air force, but still inferior to the British Royal Air Force. (Lindbergh did make one serious error: accepting a medal from Hermann Goering, to President Roosevelt's fury. Lindbergh, head of the America First movement, was a leading political opponent of Roosevelt.)

Were it not for politics, Roosevelt would have savored Lindbergh's mission, for FDR himself was running a private network of amateur spies. Fascinated with spies (he devoured spy novels for relaxation), Roosevelt despaired of the constant infighting among his intelligence agencies, and generally found their work not very impressive. Shortly after taking office, he formed what amounted to his own informal intelligence service, a network of handpicked men he often dispatched on various missions. One of them was his close friend, New York financier Vincent Astor, along with another prominent New Yorker, William Donovan, a Republican but enthusiastic Rooseveltite. Called "The Room" by its members, the network included bankers, journalists, and others who brought FDR intelligence scraps and high-level gossip. Some of those "intelligence reports" could be terribly wrong, such as one Roosevelt received from one of his amateur spies, the journalist Edgar Ansel Mowrer. After completing a six-week tour of Asia in 1941, Mowrer confidently stated that "Japan would do nothing to provoke a major war." He delivered that assertion sixteen days before Pearl Harbor.

Roosevelt preferred such informal arrangements, but like other presidents who have "deniable assets" at hand, there was the temptation to use them to evade certain awkward constitutional or legal restrictions. Much of Roosevelt's attention was focused on the one single matter that dominated much of his thinking: clandestinely aiding Great Britain despite a groundswell of isolationism by the public at large. In one instance, he had the prominent journalist John Franklin Carter run a covert funding operation that used money taken from a special White House scholarship fund in order to evade congressional scrutiny.

Roosevelt's network provoked intense flak from the military intelligence agencies and the FBI, which complained that his band of amateurs were complicating the work of their own amateurs and agents. Given the agencies' poor record on intelligence in those years, however, it is difficult to understand how any of

Roosevelt's private intelligence agents could have made things much worse.

Consider the U.S. military attaché's office in Berlin, which insisted that the German invasion of Poland in 1939 would fail. The Polish defense plan, the office wrote in a report, was "being carried out as planned . . . and appears to be succeeding." At the very moment German panzers were cutting the Polish army to pieces, the report went on to say that the Poles were "making the Germans pay dearly for every kilometer gained and are exhausting the best German divisions." A week after that report was filed, Poland surrendered.‡

Of more serious consequence was ONI's belief that Japanese pilots were inferior to American pilots, and that Japanese military technology was far behind America's. ONI did not know until Pearl Harbor about the Japanese "Zero" fighter, which was faster, more maneuverable, and better armed than any American fighter; it took two years for the United States to come up with a fighter plane that finally overcame the product of the "inferior" Japanese.

Army intelligence held no such illusions about the Germans, but seemed to have no understanding about the revolution the German *blitzkrieg* theory had brought to ground warfare. At a time when the Germans were trying to develop new steel alloys for the treads of their tanks and increase their range, the U.S. Army's cavalry was debating whether tungsten-carbide horseshoes would allow the Army's cavalry horseshoes to last longer. (And as late as 1940, Major General John K. Herr, Chief of Army Cavalry, was telling congressional committees that the Poles lost to the Germans because of inferior cavalry—which would have been news to brave Polish cavalrymen slaughtered by German tanks.)

The full scope of the abysmal state of American intelligence in 1941 was immediately visible to the British Director of Naval Intelligence, Admiral J. H. Godfrey, when he made an official visit

‡ That office was part of the same U.S. Army intelligence organization that some years earlier, from its listening post in the Latvian capital of Riga, claimed that the United States faced a "serious menace" in the 1.2 million Eastern European Jews who had emigrated to the U.S., on the grounds that they were the "chief supporters of Bolshevism in Russia." The report went on to warn about "filthy Jewish quarters in American cities."

to Washington in June of that year as part of an effort to see what help British intelligence might be able to offer. Godfrey was appalled by what he saw: the U.S. agencies spent most of their time squabbling with each other, there was no joint evaluation, too many amateurs were running around playing spy, and American intelligence seemed obsessed over internal security, seemingly defined only in terms of domestic dissidents. The intelligence being collected, Godfrey discovered, was hopelessly wrong. Among other horrors, he was shown an ONI estimate on German U-boat strength that was 250 percent too high, and an Army intelligence report claiming that twenty German divisions were in Libya. (Godfrey was especially annoyed by that estimate, since the British had already told the Americans there were nowhere near that many Germans in North Africa because of inadequate port facilities and a severe shortage of shipping.)

Godfrey's visit was part of a revitalized cooperation between Great Britain and the United States to upgrade American intelligence, using the superior talent and organization of British intelligence. This influence would prove not all to the good, as we shall see, but for the moment, it was clear that American intelligence desperately needed help. Roosevelt sent one of his private spies, William Donovan, to Great Britain to study firsthand the structure and operations of British intelligence, from which emerged Roosevelt's first, cautious effort to centralize American intelligence (a key British recommendation): naming Donovan as Coordinator of Information, for which read intelligence.

The British had less to say on the more delicate matter of American intelligence's domestic operations, for these were jealously guarded by Roosevelt himself. Like all presidents, Roosevelt had a large appetite for domestic intelligence, particularly as it applied to his political opponents. One man who sensed that presidential need—and sought to become its exclusive provider—was J. Edgar Hoover. Named head of the Bureau of Investigation (later Federal Bureau of Investigation) in 1924 at the age of twenty-nine, Hoover cleaned up a corrupt organization and created the most famous law enforcement agency in the world. He had become a more bureaucratically cautious man since the "Red Scare," yet he was still eager for public support for his growing agency.

He shifted a significant part of his organization into a new role,

fighting notorious gangsters. This effort was a resounding success, and the resulting publicity made Hoover and the FBI extremely popular with the public. The success also redounded to
the Roosevelt administration, and FDR not only began to regard
Hoover as a guru of crime, but started to rely on him for domestic
intelligence as well.

Hoover, who fancied himself an intelligence expert, sought to
become eventually the czar of all American intelligence centralized in one office—the FBI. For his part, Roosevelt not only had a
long list of domestic enemies, he was also attempting to protect
his covert operations in support of Great Britain. One of his recurring nightmares was a linkup between his domestic enemies
and the extremists of left and right, all supported by Soviet and
Nazi money. As a possible threat it was not very credible, but
Hoover read Roosevelt's code immediately, and was soon sending
over frequent memos full of intelligence tidbits about Nazi sympathizers and domestic Communists, along with keyhole gossip
about assorted Roosevelt political enemies (sexual indiscretions
were a Hoover favorite).

Hoover was rewarded when Roosevelt asked for systematic intelligence on Communists, Nazis, and "all subversive activities,"
a rather broad term that Hoover understood to mean just about
anything Roosevelt didn't like. Now the cautious bureaucrat,
Hoover hesitated: none of these activities seemed to violate federal law, so on what basis could the FBI carry out such investigations? Roosevelt found the answer in a loophole in the law appro-
priating funds for the FBI. The law authorized the FBI to carry
out investigations of "subversive activities" if requested by the
State Department. Called in by Roosevelt, the Secretary of State
on the spot decided he wanted the FBI to investigate "certain
activities." On August 25, 1936, Hoover was handed a presidential
directive authorizing him to carry out investigations of internal
security threats—an authorization used by the FBI for the next
forty years to justify its domestic security investigations.

In June 1940, Hoover won his next great victory, the awarding
by Roosevelt of responsibility for all intelligence and counterintelligence operations in the Western Hemisphere. The President's authorization included the right to investigate individuals
engaged in activities *possibly* detrimental to the internal security
of the United States. This broad authority was unveiled at a con-

gressional appropriations hearing in November of that year, but none of the congressmen blinked an eye at what clearly was a blank check for domestic spying.

Hoover and Roosevelt in effect became mutual hostages, each aware of secrets neither of them wanted to see the light of day.* The model for the kind of relationship Hoover would have with five other presidents, its critical dynamic centered on the respective needs of each man (although both men distrusted one other): Roosevelt wanted the secrets Hoover could bring to him, and Hoover needed the close relationship with Roosevelt to make his FBI inviolable to outside political poaching, or inconvenient interference from Congress.

As a man primarily concerned with "domestic security," Hoover created a sprawling apparatus that collected intelligence on a lengthy list of "enemies," including Communist Party members, socialists, homosexuals, civil rights leaders, women's rights activists—in short, anybody Hoover considered "deviant" from his own rigid personal and political outlook. A rigid Presbyterian raised in a strict middle-class environment, Hoover never married (he was dogged all his life by rumors of homosexuality), and retained the attitudes of his upbringing in Washington, D.C., then a small Southern city. Hoover could not abide any deviation, however slight, from the established social norms. He established an FBI that was almost entirely in his own image, churning out agents in a quasi-uniform of business suits and wing-tip shoes, obedient organization men who were expected to share the director's views on life and politics.

With that sort of outlook, it was not surprising that the FBI domestic intelligence files were filled with reports on dissidents' personal habits. (A wholly separate and very secret "Hoover file" collected dirt on members of Congress, the White House, and high government officials; again, the emphasis was on personal habits.) The FBI's investigative targets often included people

---

* It is possible they both knew a deep secret about Herbert Hoover, Roosevelt's predecessor. Hoover, alarmed at hearing that the Democrats had a "very damaging file" on him, secretly arranged for ONI agents in 1930 to break into the offices of a Democratic party official in New York. The file was not found, and the President ultimately concluded that it probably never existed. The entire episode bears an eerie similarity to the Watergate break-in forty-two years later.

whose connection with "domestic security," even by the most stretched definition, seemed somewhat obscure. One especially obscure category was writers; a large-scale FBI effort, beginning in 1923 (and not ended until fifty years later) collected derogatory information on famous writers, all of whom were marked as security risks of varying degrees for their perceived connections with Communists or other extremists. The targets ranged from Edna St. Vincent Millay (because one of her poems was used on a greeting card by a suspected Communist) to Dashiell Hammett (because Hoover became convinced that a newspaper cartoon strip he had drawn might contain coded messages to Communists), eventually reaching a total of 134 writers who became the subjects of FBI investigations.

And among them was a man Hoover thought especially dangerous, Ernest Hemingway. In Hoover's view, Hemingway had committed three capital offenses: (1) he was a supporter of the Spanish Republican cause, regarded by Hoover as a purely Communist one; (2) he was a "sexual deviant," meaning he was a womanizer who was married four times; and (3) the most serious crime of all, he had intruded on the FBI's own turf—and insulted the Bureau in the process.

It all came down, really, to a piece of espionage tomfoolery known as "Papa's Crook Factory."

Hemingway had visions of himself as a super-spy, a role he first fancied during his visits to Spain in the 1930s. In the intrigue and spy-infested capital of Madrid, he became romantically attached to the world of secret intelligence and began to pass snippets of intelligence to various friends he knew to be involved in the intelligence business. It was fairly harmless stuff, although Hemingway later was to claim, inaccurately, that he had invented the Spanish Civil War's contribution to the espionage lexicon, the "fifth column." During this period he wrote a play, *The Fifth Column*, in which a thinly veiled main character modeled on Hemingway himself works as a counterspy in Spain, ferreting out "Fascist spy plots." The play is not a distinguished one, but many of its details suggest that Hemingway used incidents from his own experiences in the secret world.

As noted earlier, Hemingway also had an ongoing, if somewhat casual, relationship with American military intelligence.

Whether Hoover was aware of that relationship is not known, but it is probable that even if he had known, it would not have made much difference; the plain truth was that Hoover considered Hemingway a dangerous man. (Besides, Hoover was a bitter bureaucratic opponent of the military intelligence agencies, whose abilities he often denigrated as inferior to those of his own agents.)

Before World War II Hemingway lived in Cuba, part of Hoover's newly assigned intelligence empire. The island was of some concern to the Bureau, since it had strategic importance astride vital shipping lanes, and also had three hundred thousand Spanish refugees, of whom an estimated fifteen to thirty thousand were fascist sympathizers. That raised the possibility of an underground army available for use by the Germans.

The same thought occurred to Hemingway—called "Papa" by his friends and cronies—and he approached one friend, U.S. ambassador to Cuba Spruille Braden, with an offer. Papa would organize his own private spy ring that would keep tabs on all the Spanish fascists and any German agents entering Cuba. Since Hemingway seemed to know everybody, and had a large network of Spanish Republican exiles seemingly devoted to him, Braden told him to go ahead.

The FBI was horrified, for the thought of the brawling, heavy-drinking Hemingway stomping all over the island looking for spies struck them as the height of folly. To make matters worse, the FBI discovered, Braden had authorized Hemingway to dip into the embassy's fuel supply to use on his boat, the *Pilar*, which Hemingway intended to use for forays against German U-boats. How Hemingway planned to sink one of the submarines was not quite clear; apparently, the idea was to maneuver close to a surfaced submarine, cut down its crew with a machine gun, then heave a large explosive down the submarine's hatch—this latter task to be performed by two aging, former jai-alai players.

Hoover began to apply pressure to get this nonsense stopped, and did not find it funny when he discovered that Hemingway introduced the chief FBI agent on the island to friends as "Mr. Gestapo." Nor was he amused to learn that Hemingway had named his operation "Papa's Crook Factory" in honor of some of the assorted felons and Havana waterfront rats he had recruited. The quintessential bureaucrat, Hoover insisted that intelligence operations in Cuba were strictly the FBI's business, and Hemingway should stick to writing novels.

Hoover had his way, and Braden ordered Hemingway to close down his "crook factory." Its closing marked the end of the era of the amateur spy in American intelligence, for an event in Hawaii had caused shock waves everywhere. In one fell swoop, it had also changed the rules of the game, for revealed in a single moment were all the sins of American intelligence—and the penalty history exacts for unpreparedness.

Pearl Harbor, that perfect failure, is the standard by which all American intelligence is measured. The worst intelligence disaster in American history, the events even to this day are sifted and resifted: why did we miss it? How could we have done so badly? How was it possible for a Japanese Navy task force to sail, undetected, only several hundred miles from Pearl Harbor, launch planes, carry out an attack that lasted over an hour, and then casually sail away? How could we not have known, considering the tension between the two nations for months beforehand? Why was Pearl Harbor so unprepared for an attack many knew was certain to come?

The answer, summarily, is that Pearl Harbor—or something like it—was an inevitability. Given the problems of American intelligence outlined to this point, there was simply no way it could have detected the formation and the actual execution of a surprise enemy attack against the United States anywhere in the world. With its lack of resources, poor direction, fragmentation, obsessiveness with domestic security, and general inability to properly understand the larger world, American intelligence was in no position to detect anything, much less a surprise attack. That intelligence structure continued to exist as though nothing had changed in the world since 1914, a year that just happened to be the last time any belligerent nation bothered to issue a formal declaration of war before attacking. Since then, nations had adopted the practice of falling upon unprepared enemies without warning—witness Nazi Germany's two great surprise assaults that changed the map of Europe: the attack on Poland in 1939 and the invasion of the Soviet Union in 1941, the latter when a formal peace treaty was still in effect.

Thus, American intelligence's first great failing: although the evidence was there for all to see, the Americans failed to understand that the speed of modern communications, the power of air bombardment, the extended reach of naval forces using carrier-borne aircraft, and the mechanization of ground forces had combined to give nations unprecedented offensive military power. A surprise attack with such power was capable of overwhelming an opponent within days or weeks. And it was a power that nations clearly were tempted to use—most clearly in the case of Japan, whose surprise attack on China was the real beginning of World War II.

This conceptual failure was shared by the entire U.S. Government, and although Pearl Harbor is most often described as an intelligence failure, it was a military failure as well; there is more than enough blame to go around for everyone, from Franklin D. Roosevelt himself, on down. Just to cite a few of the failures:

• The Navy ONI's OP-20-G, a code-breaking outfit, was working hard on Japanese naval codes before Pearl Harbor, and had managed to crack JN-25, the main code. But just before the attack, the code was abruptly changed—an almost certain indication that a major operation was underway. OP-20-G was suddenly blind, and could not read the coded orders dispatching the Japanese Navy task force toward Pearl Harbor. Worse, the Navy code-breakers failed to attach any significance to that change.

• Although another code-breaking operation had managed to break high-level Japanese diplomatic codes, a number of whose messages pointed unmistakably to some sort of major Japanese military move in the Pacific, there was no central coordination of this and other code-breaking efforts, and no analysis of what the various intercepts might mean in the context of other intelligence. A restricted circle, including President Roosevelt, was authorized to see the raw intercepts. But without proper analysis, most of the intercepts were simply fragments that made no sense. Moreover, the circle of those authorized to see the intercepts was too small; many military leaders, particularly those concerned with the defense of Pearl Harbor and the Philippines, were unaware of the code-breaking, and therefore did not know of Japanese intentions to strike southward.

• The American cryptanalytic effort was too widely dispersed, and the Navy's operation was hampered by intense personal bickering among the officers involved. There was also intense inter-service argument; even as late as 1943, Army and Navy code-breakers spent much of their time in internicine warfare with each other.

· Uncertain of Japanese intentions, the White House and the War Department issued ambiguous "warning" orders to military commanders in the Pacific that essentially told them to do something or nothing. The commanders chose to do nothing. At Pearl Harbor, the U.S. Pacific Fleet rested in peacetime formation, with no torpedo baffles, no barrage balloons, and no long-range air reconnaissance patrols. On the ground, Army anti-aircraft guns were situated in gun parks, their ammunition stored in magazines—requiring several hours to move guns and ammunition to firing positions. New Army radars were being used only intermittently, for training by inexperienced crews. Planes were parked wingtip to wingtip.

· In February 1941, State Department intelligence officials were told by a source in the Peruvian embassy in Tokyo that Japan was planning an attack on Pearl Harbor. The information was discounted, because American officials believed that such an attack was contrary to Japanese doctrine. Although Roosevelt believed that Japan would attack the United States at some point, American intelligence kept telling him that Japan lacked the military capability to do so.

· Without agents and sources in Japan, American intelligence had no insight into either Japanese military developments or Japanese strategic intentions. Both Army and Navy intelligence tended to denigrate Japanese military capability, and there were ONI officers who actually believed that Japanese eyesight was inferior to American eyesight, so that Japanese pilots were unable to fight in the dark.

And so on and on it went, a recitation of disaster. The resulting shock would appear to have galvanized American intelligence, for in the wreckage of Pearl Harbor and the cry "never again!" a new American intelligence was born.

But, as things turned out, it did not fully understand the lessons of December 7, 1941.

THREE

"We Cannot Afford
to Be Sissies"

OBVIOUSLY, it was the proverbial "something big": General William Donovan himself was there, along with his aide, E. Edward Buxton, and J. M. Scribner, deputy director of Strategic Services Operations. The brass heavyweights of the Office of Strategic Services (OSS) had been gathered for a meeting, ostensibly to discuss the agency's operations in Burma.

Colonel Carl F. Eifler had the sense that Burma was not the real reason he had been summoned to this high-level convocation at OSS headquarters in Washington, D.C., that hot June day in 1944. Possibly, he thought, they wanted to create a new partisan unit behind German lines in Europe—similar to the Detachment 101 organization Eifler had commanded in Burma a year before.

One thing was clear: despite the fact that the OSS was supposed to be an intelligence agency, the meeting would not discuss spying. Fundamentally, the OSS was an agency dominated by action. Eifler himself was pure action; one of the OSS's most

famed operatives, he was an ex-Army officer, Los Angeles policeman, and Customs agent, and among Donovan's earliest recruits.
No small judge of talent, Donovan had just the right job in mind
for this tall, broad-shouldered, brawling man in love with action.
Early in 1943, Eifler, who had been recalled to active Army duty
after Pearl Harbor, was sent to Burma with twenty-one handpicked men to organize, train, and direct Kachin tribesmen behind Japanese lines to operate as guerrillas against the Japanese
occupiers, whom the Kachins hated. Called Detachment 101—in
part to create the illusion of many other such units operating—it
was brilliantly successful. But Eifler had been badly injured in
one of the detachment's operations, was sent home to recuperate,
and by mid-1944 found himself on temporary assignment to OSS
headquarters. Now the OSS was ready, apparently, to tell him his
next assignment.

The meeting with Donovan and his two top aides began routinely enough, Donovan asking about Detachment 101's operations. Eifler assumed that he was to organize a similar operation
somewhere else, but Donovan told him he was about to be let in
on a secret—one so sensitive, it did not even have a code name.

"It is one of the biggest items of the war to date," Donovan told
him solemnly. "We cannot even tell you much about the men you
will be working with."

Donovan then began briefing Eifler on something that was indeed momentous. The Allies and Germany were in a race to develop a new, ultimate weapon called the atomic bomb. The Germans, so intelligence indicated, had made major scientific
breakthroughs; they might be very close to a weapon that would
destroy an entire city with one blast—in other words, a weapon
that would allow Adolf Hitler to win the war. Such an eventuality was unthinkable.

Donovan got to the point of why Eifler had been called in. Key
to the German atomic bomb project was its director, the world-
famous nuclear physicist, Dr. Werner Heisenberg. Donovan proposed that Heisenberg be "eliminated" in order to cripple the
German program.

"His brain must be denied," Donovan said.

At first, Eifler thought Donovan meant an assassination, but
the OSS director said instead that he wanted Heisenberg kid-

napped, then brought to the United States. The OSS had learned that Heisenberg occasionally visited Switzerland's large German colony to deliver scientific lectures. The idea was for Eifler to lead an OSS team into that country, kidnap Heisenberg during one lecture, and then somehow spirit him out of the country. Could it be done?

"Yes, I can do it," Eifler replied, unhesitatingly.

Someone in the room loudly banged his hand on a table. "By God, I knew it!" Buxton shouted. "Everyone else said it's impossible!"

Not impossible, Eifler noted, but still fraught with many difficulties, not the least of them being what to do with Heisenberg if the kidnap operation was suddenly interrupted.

"As I said," Donovan said quietly, "Nazi Germany must be denied his brain." A moment of silence settled over the room.

As things turned out, the kidnap operation never took place. For five months, Eifler put a plan and a team of men together. The plan was relatively simple: Eifler, operating under cover as a U.S. Customs official, would go to Switzerland for meetings with top-level Swiss customs officials to discuss what their American counterparts could learn from the Swiss experience. At the proper moment, they would snatch Heisenberg, then spirit him out of the country aboard a plane waiting at a nearby airport. The rest would depend on luck and how fast they could get out of Swiss airspace.

But in late 1944, when Eifler was in OSS Algiers headquarters, jumping-off spot for the kidnap plan, he was visited by Donovan and Colonel M. Preston Goodfellow, one of Donovan's chief aides. Apparently fearful that the room might be bugged, they took Eifler outside.

As the busy Algiers traffic bustled around them, Donovan said, "Carl, there's a change in your orders; your mission is scrubbed. We beat the Nazis." Donovan did not explain further, but Eifler could figure it out: the American project was close to perfecting the ultimate weapon—or already had done so.*

---

* Eifler spent the remaining year of the war training Korean exiles for operations against Japanese-occupied Korea. Now retired, he lives in California.

However extraordinary, this incident remains only as an obscure footnote to a war in which it played no part. And yet, there is much worthy of attention in the operation that had no name, for it reveals a great deal, both about the personality of the man who dreamed up the idea, and the curious organization he headed, America's first flirtation with the idea of a central intelligence agency.

It reveals, first of all, the man Donovan: shrewd, daring, direct, totally pragmatic, and totally ruthless as the occasion demanded. And his organization: equally daring, in love with action, and convinced that the solution to any complex problem was a risky operation. Where the devil feared to tread, the OSS would jump with both feet.

The idea of solving the problem of the German atomic bomb by kidnapping its top scientist was prototypically OSS. No real thought seemed to have been devoted to the considerable impact of such an operation.

Why was an intelligence agency making such a momentous decision?

This question is important, for it goes to the very heart of how agencies like the OSS operated in the context of American democracy. It is a question that arose first during World War I, as we have seen, and arose again during World War II—this time, even more urgently, for the decision to create the wartime OSS carried with it the seeds of trouble. And that trouble was to recur later, this time in OSS's descendant, the Central Intelligence Agency.

The problem was that however compelling the reasons for creating a centralized intelligence system, it would not work in America without the proper controls. From the moment of its creation, the OSS did not have clear guidelines or controls. It grew misshapenly, fastening on to anything not denied by bureaucratic rivals in the FBI and the military intelligence agencies. Mostly, "anything" involved covert political action and large-scale commando operations, the two main areas with which the rest of the American intelligence community did not want to bother. Those are precisely the two areas that cause the most trouble for democratic systems, for they involve critical questions of policy being decided by a particular agency of the government whose actions are not accountable. Mission-oriented agencies like the OSS—and, later, the CIA—tended to be the arbiters of their own plans and actions.

Once described by McGeorge Bundy of the OSS (and later national security adviser to President Kennedy) as "one half cops and robbers, and one half faculty meeting," the OSS was a curious organization difficult to describe. Its real roots lay in the organization Roosevelt and Donovan most admired, the British Secret Intelligence Service (SIS), a poor model for an American intelligence agency. The SIS was cloaked in near-total secrecy, operated strictly as an arm of the British Government, incestuously recruited only among a relatively small group of upper-class men who shared similar views, and conducted operations free of parliamentary oversight.

"In an age of bullies, we cannot afford to be sissies," Donovan often said as the OSS was being created, by which he meant the United States had to play by the same rules as her ruthless enemies, Nazi Germany and Japan. The argument, made as the OSS came to life in June 1942, was familiar, made during the previous world war by men who cited the menace of the Kaiser's Germany. In Donovan's case, he had much greater resources than his World War I counterparts (the OSS budget in 1945 reached $57 million) to carry out the kind of operations he thought necessary to prove that America was not a sissy.

For the most part, they concerned what OSS operatives came to call "boom and bang," commando-type operations behind enemy lines that created or supported indigenous guerrilla movements. The objective, logically enough in wartime, was to tie down as many enemy troops as possible trying to suppress the threat to their rear areas. But many of these operations had political objectives, for they also involved creation of various "exile" entities whose American support had a secondary agenda: their role in the postwar government of their nations.

And that is where the OSS commando operations began to run into trouble, for decisions on whether to support an anti-Communist or Communist guerrilla organization—most notably in Yugoslavia—involved important foreign policy questions. They were not the kinds of questions that an intelligence agency could answer alone, yet the OSS inevitably found itself making political decisions, often with severe consequences. There was trouble in Indochina, where an OSS team that aided Indochinese guerrillas under Ho Chi Minh supported Ho's call for independence from France—to the fury of the French, who decided the United States had no business deciding the future of French territory. There was trouble in Spain, where the poorly conceived Operation Banana—infiltrating ex-Spanish Republicans into that country to blow up German facilities—caused grave problems with the delicate issue of Spanish neutrality. There was trouble in Hungary, where Operation Sparrow, designed to take Hungary out of the war, led to a German seizure of the government.

The OSS was ultimately to become dominated by the men of "special operations," covert actions that represented, at least in theory, shortcut answers to complicated problems. This was the most striking heritage of the British SIS, along with a tendency to consider political assassinations as an even quicker solution to problems.†

The OSS also copied the British technique of "black propaganda," carefully prepared disinformation whose source is concealed. Among the best practitioners of this art was the British SIS station in New York, misleadingly called British Security Coordination. Run by Donovan's close friend and mentor, William Stephenson (code-named Intrepid), the BSC was part of a secret arrangement between the British and Roosevelt allowing British intelligence to conduct operations on American soil against Germany. To the fury of J. Edgar Hoover and the Justice Department, it was discovered that the arrangement included allowing BSC to carry out kidnappings, break-ins of consulates and embassies, and other wholesale violations of American law.

Roosevelt ignored the complaints, including specific instances of the BSC disseminating propaganda in the United States on behalf of the U.S. interventionist political movement, which advocated greater preparedness and more aid for Great Britain. One classic example was the appearance, in late 1940, of a widely distributed (and very successful) pamphlet under the byline of the

† There were at least two OSS assassination plots against Hitler and other Nazi leaders: Operation Freiheit and Project Skipper, both of which foundered when the anti-Hitler (and politically divided) German exiles could not be properly organized to carry them out. Additionally, the inexperienced OSS operatives discovered that a large network inside Germany itself would be needed to support so complicated an operation as killing Hitler—a network the OSS neither possessed nor had any hope of developing.

famous mystery writer Rex Stout. Entitled *The Uncensored Story: How Your Dimes and Quarters Pay for Hitler's War*, it claimed that German companies with American branches were raising money in the United States for Hitler. Actually, Rex Stout never wrote a word of it; the pamphlet was prepared by the SIS.

The OSS did differ from its British SIS model in two important respects. Unlike the British, the OSS did not separate its intelligence-gathering and "boom and bang" operations, and second, it created a very powerful Research and Analysis Branch. The R&A, as it was known, marked the first attempt of a normally isolationist U.S. Government to take a serious measure of the outside world. Much of their information, quite ordinary, was gleaned from the reading stacks of the Library of Congress and other public institutions. The OSS maps in particular became prized possessions for their accuracy, even for Winston Churchill, who showed them off to Roosevelt during one conference. The R&A also set the pattern for the later CIA habit of written intelligence "estimates," a uniquely American idea of having academics and other experts read through all open and secret intelligence, then formulating sometimes-voluminous studies on what it all meant—and, occasionally, an estimate on the probable future course of events.‡

Eventually, the OSS was to have three distinct "cultures": the "boom and bangers," the analysts, and the secret agents. It was the latter category that handled what might be called The Case of the German Atomic Bomb.

If there was one piece of intelligence during World War II that surpassed all others in importance, it was the question of how close Nazi Germany was to making a nuclear weapon. On the answer rested not only how much effort the Allies would need to expend on their own atomic bomb program, but also the very course of the war; it did not require much imagination to consider what a man like Hitler would do with nuclear weapons.

---

‡ Included was an American habit of "psychological studies" of world leaders, prepared by psychiatrists who had never interviewed the subject. The OSS hit rock bottom with one of its studies, a "psychiatric portrait" of Hitler, which depicted the German leader's rise to power in terms of a seduction, then went on to say he had only one testicle and liked to have women beat him, then urinate and defecate on him.

The OSS SI (secret intelligence) branch devoted great effort to tracking the German program, but was handicapped by the lack of good sources in occupied Europe.

The OSS was also hampered by the compartmentalization of the atomic bomb project, which was under the control of the Army's Manhattan Engineering District—a secret the Army would not share. The Army project had its own intelligence operation, which was running operations in Europe—unbeknownst to the OSS. When OSS and Army agents began to stumble across one another, a truce was arranged: OSS agents would be restricted to neutral countries in Europe.*

The truce solved nothing, for neither agency was getting much in the way of hard information. Since nuclear fission had first been achieved in Germany in 1938, it was fair to deduce that the Germans obviously were trying to develop nuclear weapons. But aside from a heavy-water plant in Norway and reports of Germany amassing uranium ore, there was no trace of the German program. OSS and Army intelligence officials were besieged with volumes of contradictory reports from inside Europe, among them wild accounts of vast underground atomic factories. Finally, a curious intelligence deduction was formulated: Germany had a massive and efficient atomic weapons development program underway. What was the evidence for it? None: the fact that no concrete evidence could be found was considered solid evidence that the program was so secret, no trace of it could be found.

Therefore, the Germans had taken extraordinary measures to hide it; the high priority such a massive undertaking required indicated that the Germans were close to the bomb.

A myth began to grow during this intelligence hunt: there was a specific "secret" of the atomic bomb, like some mad scientist's secret formula in the movies. One of the main reasons for the OSS's plan to kidnap Heisenberg was the conviction that this "secret" reposed somewhere in his head; remove him, and the entire German effort would collapse. Army intelligence agents also shared this myth, and believed that if the United States could

* Among the OSS agents working on attempting to uncover the German program was Moe Berg, the former baseball player who had spied in Japan in the 1930s. Recruited by Donovan early in 1941, Berg set about trying to trace the key man in the German project, physicist Werner Heisenberg. Berg was to have been part of the aborted Eifler mission to Switzerland to kidnap Heisenberg.

protect its own dark secret of the bomb, then no one else would be able to develop it for years.

In fact, there was no such thing as the "secret" of the bomb. The principle of fission and the more general principles of how that fission could be harnessed to a weapon of great destruction were well known to the world's scientists—and had been known since at least the 1920s, when scientists from all over the world, Russian included, journeyed to Germany to study nuclear physics. What only the Manhattan Project was close to realizing in 1944 was the *technical* aspect of actually taking that fission process and putting it into a practical bomb.

Curiously, it was British intelligence that discovered the Germans, despite their prewar scientific leadership, had taken a fatally wrong turn in their atomic weapons program. The British, unlike the Americans, had a key source inside the German scientific establishment. That source was able to tell the British that the Germans had built their own atomic pile and understood the principles of a fission bomb, but could not figure out how to convert that pile into a weapon—not realizing, as scientists in the Manhattan Project did, that the pile was used to make plutonium, which in turn was used in the actual bomb. But the intelligence was not shared with the Americans, with whom the British were feuding at the time. As a result, the American intelligence verdict remained: the Germans were on the verge of producing an atomic bomb. The conclusion had the effect of accelerating the Manhattan Project to produce a bomb to be used against Germany. In one of history's ironies, Nazi Germany surrendered before the bomb was developed. The awesome weapon was instead used against Japan, whose own nuclear weapons program remained moribund for lack of resources.

Army intelligence teams that later fanned out across Germany, seeking to round up German nuclear scientists and deny their skills to the Russians, discovered how badly behind the Germans really were. The Germans were aware of the Manhattan Project, since the sudden cessation of all scientific papers on nuclear physics and equally sudden disappearance of the world's top nuclear physicists clearly indicated that they had been taken for a big project (a nuclear weapon, obviously). But the Germans lacked the resources for such a project, and, to make matters worse, atomic weapons research was split up among several of the competing fiefdoms of Nazi Germany. Indeed, the Germans came closest to a real bomb in a small scientific unit attached to the German Post Office, of all places. A scientist working there figured out that uranium could be converted into a fission weapon. When Hitler was informed of this development at a cabinet meeting in 1944, he replied, to guffaws from everybody else in the room, "Look here, gentlemen! You are all racking your brains to discover how we are going to win the war, and lo and behold, here comes our postmaster, of all people, with a solution to the problem!"

The OSS knew nothing of what was going on in the German atomic bomb program, a glaring failure—although, to a certain extent, it might be argued that the OSS was *meant* to fail. From the moment William Donovan was appointed Coordinator of Information, the FBI and the military intelligence agencies sought to cut him off at the knees. The history of the OSS is dominated by the succession of bureaucratic struggles that raged constantly among these protagonists. They were not only fighting for their turf in wartime intelligence, they were also looking ahead to the postwar world, when, Donovan believed, centralized American intelligence would become a fact—thanks to the record established by his agency. The FBI and the military intelligence agencies were just as determined that no such thing would ever happen.

All sides were playing for high stakes in this game, but Donovan always had the fifth ace: Franklin Delano Roosevelt. So long as Roosevelt was President, Donovan and his organization were safe, because Roosevelt regarded Donovan as his personal intelligence officer—much as he regarded Hoover as his personal internal security officer. Like Hoover, Donovan did much to foster that relationship, sending the President intelligence on subjects in which, he knew, Roosevelt had particular interest. In late 1944, Donovan prepared a memorandum on postwar American intelligence, which outlined the general shape of what was to become the CIA. Donovan carefully did not mention a specific name of the man he thought ought to head that new organization, but no one reading the memorandum could fail to get the point: Donovan was proposing himself as the new czar of American intelligence.

It might have worked, except that Roosevelt died in the spring of 1945, and Donovan suddenly was left without his chief protector. He had one last hope: there was a chance that the new president, Harry Truman, would be receptive to the ideas outlined in the 1944 memorandum. But Truman, not especially fond of Donovan, was beginning to look elsewhere for a solution. And one of the things that struck him as he took an overview of American intelligence's performance during World War II was how generally poor its performance had been. Yet, there was one bright spot, a glittering achievement by an agency no one would have expected to perform so well: the FBI.

The man who stepped from the gangplank of the passenger ship in Havana, Cuba, the morning of September 1, 1941, seemed to be just who he said he was: Heinz August Luning, Jewish refugee from Hitler, one of the lucky few who had managed to buy his way out of Germany and Nazi persecution.

But the two men watching from a distance as Luning made his way through Cuban immigration knew differently. They knew him as a German *Abwehr* agent code-named A-3799, dispatched to Cuba to reinforce a network of German spies who were collecting intelligence on ship movements for the U-boats. And from the instant Luning set foot on Cuban soil, his every movement was watched and recorded. For the next twelve months, every one of the forty-seven letters he sent to mail drops in Spain and Portugal was surreptitiously opened, and its contents read.

Not much more is known about Luning; the following year he was arrested and shot by Cuban authorities, taking to his grave what must have been his own remarkable story. Luning was in fact Jewish, but he never revealed whatever Faustian bargain he made with the Nazis to trade the certainty of death in a concentration camp for the brief life of a spy.

Luning's espionage career was brief because the two men who watched his arrival in Havana and who, with other men, knew his every move, were part of a remarkable American counterintelligence effort that completely neutralized all German intelligence efforts in South America before and during World War II. Little known to this day, the operation was run by the FBI, which assigned 360 agents to an effort whose success was equaled only by the British intelligence operation that rounded up every single one of the several hundred agents German intelligence sent to Great Britain during the same period.

In June 1940, concerned about growing reports of Nazi infiltration among the large German colonies in South America, Roosevelt gave the FBI exclusive authority to run intelligence and counterintelligence operations in that continent. Roosevelt's action was extraordinary for a number of reasons, particularly considering that the FBI had no real authority to operate outside the United States. Again, however, Roosevelt could use that handy State Department loophole in the FBI appropriations legislation.

Roosevelt's precise motives for choosing the FBI are not clear, but they undoubtedly had a great deal to do with the FBI's vaunted public reputation at that point. The highly publicized "gang-busting" of the 1930s, the "G-man" ethos, and the Bureau's presumed omniscience (in the public's perception, anyway) on the matter of enemy spies had made Hoover's Bureau almost sanctified. Thus, there may have been shrewd political calculations behind Roosevelt's choice.

The President could not have looked at the FBI's counterespionage record too closely, for a detailed examination would have disclosed that Hoover's reputation as a great spy-catcher was not entirely deserved. The fact is that between the time of Roosevelt's inauguration in 1933 and the outbreak of World War II in 1939, there were a total of ten German or Japanese agents caught, plus two agents of the Soviet NKVD (the KGB's predecessor). One of the NKVD agents was discovered after he foolishly left some important documents in a coat delivered to a dry cleaning business. Two Japanese agents were caught because ONI agents detected the flamboyant behavior of their source, a corrupted ex-Navy officer. One German agent was caught after his briefcase, stuffed with incriminating documents, was found lying on the street after an auto accident.

Both *Abwehr* and Japanese intelligence ran inept operations in the United States, and were so inefficiently directed, British intelligence experts tended to deride the FBI counterespionage efforts against them. "Dillinger mentality," was how they summarized the FBI's overall effort, and they were not impressed with Hoover's boast that no act of enemy sabotage was carried out in the United States before and during the war.

Nevertheless, Japanese intelligence managed to obtain plans for the most up-to-date U.S. battleships, and German agents scored a major coup, stealing the specifications for one of America's most closely guarded military secrets, the Norden bombsight.†

This would appear to represent a relatively paltry number of espionage cases, but they served to create the beginning of another spy mania in the United States, similar to the one that had occurred only two decades before. This time, a new phrase entered the language, one signifying the perfidy of internal threat fomented from without: the "fifth column." One of the period's most durable myths, it served to explain why so many European countries had fallen to the Nazis. The explanation was that they had been infiltrated by a silent enemy within, an enemy that, like termites, silently and unobserved ate away the structure until only a small push from the outside caused it to come crashing down in defeat.

The term came from the Spanish Civil War, and although Ernest Hemingway took credit for it, "fifth column" was first mentioned by an anonymous Nationalist general, who claimed to have the conventional military formation of four columns of men marching on Madrid, and "a fifth column already inside Madrid." As a piece of propaganda, it had the advantage of explaining why such powerful nations as France had fallen, even with superior numbers and the Maginot Line.

The "fifth column" myth had an invidious impact in the United States, especially in the more extreme reaches of the American political spectrum. Representative Martin Dies of Texas urged Americans to hunt down "internal enemies," while Georgia Governor E. D. Rivers actually had the state issue a declaration of war against "aliens."

The hysteria also began to grip the military intelligence agencies. In 1941, Captain Alan G. Kirk, chief of ONI, who for some years had been obsessed with "domestic security," claimed that the United States was "crawling with fifth columnists and alien agents and labor unrest", that, along with the Communists, were now part of a massive plot to take over the country.

Once again, the perceived threat of an outside, alien force ig-

† The Japanese managed to obtain their own copy of the bombsight in 1942, when they found it aboard some B-17s abandoned in Java. To their surprise, the Japanese discovered that the vaunted American technology was not very impressive; their own bombsight was superior.

nited demands that the Constitution be stretched (or ignored altogether) to combat the danger. Early victories by Japan in the Pacific sharpened those demands, and finally, the Constitution gave way, creating one of the darkest days in the history of constitutional rights.

The victims were the Japanese-Americans, the bulk of whom lived on the West Coast: at the time of the attack on Pearl Harbor, there was a total of 126,947 people of Japanese descent in the United States, 112,935 of them on the West Coast. Of that latter figure, all but 41,089 were American-born. A full-fledged panic broke out on the West Coast, which took the form of demands that the Japanese-Americans be "relocated" to the interior of the United States so that they would not function as "fifth columnists" for the Japanese military invasion of California expected at any moment.

This forced relocation ultimately removed over 100,000 loyal Japanese-Americans and imprisoned them, under armed guard, in what the U.S. Government described as "resettlement centers." They were in fact virtual concentration camps. Not one Japanese-American was ever proved guilty of disloyalty to the United States.

Interestingly, one of the strongest opponents of the relocation was J. Edgar Hoover, who saw no justification for it. His Intelligence Division, which had increased manifold during the 1930s, maintained Hoover's favorite weapon, the files and card indexes of "known internal security threats to the United States," and since none of the Japanese-Americans were in those files, then Hoover saw no threat. The files concentrated on domestic Nazis and an old concern to Hoover, the American Communist Party.

Communism was an abiding Hoover obsession, but his concern focused on the overt Communists, the domestic, garden variety party member Hoover was convinced was everlastingly plotting to take over the United States. His agents spent much of their time with this menace, and not enough time with the real menace that was growing every day: Soviet intelligence operations in the United States. These operations, which utilized a special underground network of Communist Party members who had suddenly dropped out of party activities, by the late 1930s had managed to infiltrate nearly every government department.

The Russian appetite for intelligence was insatiable, and even their official representatives made no attempt to hide espionage activities. Shocked U.S. Navy officers told stories about the first Soviet naval attaché to be posted to Washington: he immediately demanded access to U.S. Navy ships and bases, along with blueprints for the new fast battleship *North Carolina* and specifications for the aircraft carrier *Saratoga*. Shortly thereafter, two Russian diplomats showed up at the Norfolk naval base, demanding a limousine to "inspect" the facility.

But it would be some years before the real extent of Soviet intelligence's penetration became known, and longer still before the full measure of Hoover's myopia was understood. Before then, however, Hoover achieved the pinnacle of his career and popularity, not to mention his close relationship with the President. Even an occasional slip—such as his attempt in 1940 to prosecute veterans of the Abraham Lincoln Brigade, American volunteers in the Spanish Civil War—failed to dent his public reputation. The brigade was one of Hoover's pet obsessions, and the FBI harassed the veterans for years on Hoover's firm belief that they were all Communist agents.

The FBI's brilliant performance in South America made Hoover not only politically unassailable, it also gave him a long lead in his real dream, heading up all American intelligence. His chief competitor, William Donovan, had slipped badly since Roosevelt's death, and by 1945, the OSS was fighting for its life. It fought back by trying an old Hoover trick: build up public support. Quickly, a spate of books, magazine articles, and even comic books appeared, all of them with a common theme of OSS hair-raising adventures, agents outwitting the Gestapo, and entire nations apparently saved from the Nazi yoke by brave OSS agents.

The campaign, organized by Donovan and his aides, did not work, for however fascinated the American public was with these tales of derring-do, nobody in the White House or Congress was. The truth was that the OSS's record was not that sterling, and no amount of publicity would conceal that fact. The final blow to Donovan's hopes came in early February of 1945, when the Chicago *Tribune* caused a sensation with an article saying that Donovan was trying to create a "super-spy agency." The article quoted Donovan's 1944 memorandum nearly verbatim, indicating that one of Donovan's bureaucratic enemies had leaked it. (Suspicion fell on Hoover, but the evidence suggests that officials of the Bureau of the Budget, infuriated at the OSS's free-spending ways and lack of accountability, had done the leaking as a means of getting Donovan out of the government.) It was the end for Donovan; that September, in a barely polite letter, President Truman curtly informed Donovan that he was ordering the OSS closed down.

And that, Hoover assumed, left only himself for the czar's job. But it didn't happen, for gradually a consensus was building in both Congress and the White House that something quite different was required—an entirely new structure, in fact. That consensus had concluded some time before Donovan's departure that American intelligence in general—and OSS in particular—had not been very effective during the war. Clearly, the entire problem would have to be rethought, for the Cold War had already begun; a new, and much more threatening enemy had appeared, and the threat required something more than the old structure, with its inefficiencies, its failings, its inability to work in concert.

Also at stake in this decision was a great prize: an intelligence secret that dwarfed all secrets. Whoever obtained this prize would be armed with a priceless intelligence resource—and the very soul of American intelligence itself.

PART TWO

Toward an American Colossus
1946–1960

FOUR

Black Jumbo in the Ether

IT WAS, one of the men who worked there later recalled, like living in the middle of the jungle, with all the cries, shrieks, and growls of creatures announcing their presence in a merciless world of death and danger.

The simile was more than apt, for the radio-interception station at Coonawarra, near Darwin in Australia, in late 1944 existed in an electronic jungle. Around the clock, a group of American, British, and Australian technicians monitored the sounds of a world at war. They listened for the sounds of that war's most critical link, coded radio transmissions—the high-pitched whines of signals moving through the ether, the staccato *da-dit-da-da-dit* of telegraph keys, the flutter of high-speed transmissions. Those signals were taken down, and immediately broadcast elsewhere, to men who could read the meaning that lurked among the columns of four- and five-digit number ciphers.

Very few people knew about Coonawarra, and fewer still knew

that the men who worked there were on the front line of two of history's most successful espionage operations. Known as Magic and Ultra, the operations had managed to peek into the high-level codes of Nazi Germany and Japan. The men of Coonawarra—and several dozen other, similar, interception stations—played a critical role in the operations. They sat hunched over their receivers, earphones pressed to their heads, slowly twisting the dials across the radio spectrum, paying special attention to the transmissions from major military command posts.

Coonawarra was especially critical to the interception operations. Because of a combination of curious geological features and unique ionospheric conditions, the Coonawarra station could intercept an amazing amount of traffic, even from transmitters many thousands of miles away. Any one of those interceptions could have an important impact on the war. A Japanese Navy message, rerouting a merchant convoy, would alert American submarines that could wait in ambush. A German Army message, ordering the movement of a Panzer division, would lead to an Allied thrust into the area the Germans had just vacated.

Coonawarra had sprung into life some months after Pearl Harbor, at first concentrating on the flood of radio traffic that accompanied the Japanese military movement southward in the Pacific. Later, after Coonawarra's technicians discovered that the area's unique geology allowed them an astonishing range, they began to tap into a widening circle of transmissions, including those of Germany.

But in late 1944 came the first intercepts of the strangest transmissions the technicians had ever heard. Contrary to standard practice, the radio operators sending these transmissions sometimes stayed on the air for hours at a time; the transmitters seemed to work around the clock, sending vast oceans of material to a central receiver, which, technicians deduced, was located in Moscow.

The men of Coonawarra dutifully transcribed this vast pile of material, day after day taking down the seemingly endless rows of numbers. They did not know that they were participating in the first real battle of the Cold War.

The intercepts were code-named Venona, and from the first moment it was clear that something very big was afoot. To begin with, the most powerful of the transmitters beamed toward Moscow were located in Washington, D.C., Switzerland, and London —none of which sites contained operating Soviet military forces. So the transmissions were not military orders. Secondly, the transmitters in London and Washington were located in the Soviet embassies; the volume of traffic was much more than usual for an embassy, even in wartime. Thus, the transmitters were sending important material on a crash basis—material so vital, it could not wait for the diplomatic pouch. Almost certainly, then, it was intelligence. But there was so much of it; did the Russians have armies of spies?

Possibly, judging by the sheer volume, but initially, it was not known exactly what the intelligence amounted to. American and British cryptanalysts who examined the Coonawarra intercepts noticed that the transmissions were cloaked in a cipher reserved for only the most important intelligence: the "one-time pad," the mainstay of the modern spy. Spies, in order to transmit their intelligence as quickly as possible, had to use radio as replacement for such time-honored techniques as sewing messages into the lining of clothes or using relays of couriers. That solved one problem, but created others: clandestine radios can be tracked down with radio-detection gear (hence the idea of staying on the air as little as possible), and the transmissions can be intercepted. Those intercepts, in turn, are attacked by cryptanalysts. If the codebreakers succeed, then the enemy spy and his transmitter can be "played"—fed misleading data, and allowed to continue operating.

The solution was the "one-time pad," a cipher used once, then discarded, allowing cryptanalysts no chance to read an extensive series of messages and divine the system. The "pad" was actually two pads containing columns of groups and random numbers, with the sender and receiver each having one copy. The sender, using his codebook, would encode the word "troops," say, into 3652. He would then go to the first sheet of his "pad," and finding 1749, would add that to 3652, arriving at 4391 (numbers greater than nine were not carried forward). He would continue with the message until all the numbers on the first sheet of the "pad" were exhausted, then destroyed, and on to the next page. The receiver would follow precisely the same procedure.

Such ciphers, which amounted to what the cryptanalysts called "double encipherment," were virtually unbreakable, for each message was using, literally, a new cipher. Even if the cryptanalysts managed to obtain the codebook, they would still be stumped without knowing the numbers on the "one-time pad."

The Soviet transmissions intercepted at Coonawarra were in "pad," meaning they offered no real hope of encipherment. But in carefully examining them, the code-breakers at the innocuously named Government Communications Headquarters in Great Britain and the equally bland Signal Security Service in the United States made an astonishing discovery: the Russians, normally security-obsessed (especially in their communications), had made colossal errors.

The errors were almost beyond belief. Code clerks, pressed by heavy traffic, in some cases had used the same one-time pads repeatedly. In other cases, apparently out of pads, they resorted to sending vital intelligence in ordinary (and easily breakable) commercial code. And in still other instances, they had been sloppy, repeating too many phrases and committing other errors that allowed the American and British cryptographers their first look inside the transmissions. And what the code-breakers began seeing caused grave shock.

In a word, the West was hemorrhaging. Judging by what the Russians were transmitting back to Moscow, virtually every secret was an open book. There were top-secret telegrams between Winston Churchill and President Roosevelt transmitted verbatim. There were the details of virtually every military development project in which the British and Americans were engaged. There were transcripts of decisions reached inside British intelligence and the OSS.

There were even greater shocks to come, because as the cryptographers began to peel away the ciphers, they were turning up the sources for this flood of intelligence, the code names of Moscow's spies. From the London signals came the names Stanley, Hicks, and Johnson, three officials of the British Government, apparently, who were providing high-level information from the very heart of British intelligence itself.* Another source, code-named Homer (later identified positively as Donald Maclean of

* These were later deduced to be H. A. R. (Kim) Philby and Anthony Blunt of British intelligence and Guy Burgess of the Foreign Office. The real persons behind five other cryptonyms were never completely identified, although one of

the Foreign Office), was providing high-level intelligence from his post at the British embassy in Washington, D.C. And from the Washington intercepts also came reports from an NKVD source at the highest levels of the American government: Agent 19, who was feeding the Russians the most secret decisions of President Roosevelt, the State Department, and Roosevelt's inner circle of advisers. (Agent 19 was presumed to be State Department official Alger Hiss, although no firm proof was ever adduced.)

The transmissions of material from Agent 19 and Homer were among a torrent from Moscow's transmitters in Washington, a flood whose beginning no one knew. Tapping into this huge volume in 1944 revealed a Soviet intelligence operation that apparently had been cranked up quite some time before—perhaps coincidental with the German invasion of Russia in 1941. Or perhaps earlier, for decryptions of the Washington messages revealed that the Russians had been using no less than *eight hundred* sources in the United States, sources that must have required years to develop. The sources covered the entire spectrum of the U.S. Government, including at least sixteen employees of the OSS and five government officials.

As a result, there apparently was no American secret that Moscow did not know—including the greatest American secret of all, the Manhattan Project. The decryptions showed that one of the high-ranking scientists attached to the project was providing information on its progress, and a man and wife team of agents had penetrated its most important technical secret, the bomb's unique "implosion" process.†

The decryptions of Venona—known as Black Jumbo among the British and Bride among the Americans—represented brilliant feats of the cryptographer's black art. The Soviet NKVD had spent many years perfecting ciphers that it believed were unbreakable: one-time pads were used for all important transmis-

them was suspected to be a high-level mole in MI-5, the British counterespionage agency.

† The scientist was positively identified as Klaus Fuchs; the man and wife team was Julius and Ethel Rosenberg, although the cryptographic evidence was sketchier in their case. To the relief of British intelligence, Fuchs confessed his guilt before trial, while the Rosenbergs were convicted on other evidence. Both the British and Americans decided that Venona was too valuable a secret to be used as court evidence.

sions, and its basic codebooks were multivolume, using random numbers. It was like looking for the proverbial needle in a haystack. The attacks on Venona lasted for nearly thirty years from the day the men at Coonawarra first detected the messages, and only portions of the messages were ever solved, even with the most advanced computers.

But it was enough to cause a profound change in the way American intelligence regarded the Soviet Union. There, in black and white, was incontrovertible evidence of the size and power of an old—but now much more dangerous—enemy, which had created, virtually unnoticed, an internal security threat of the first order.

Much would flow from the perception of the new threat, but that would come later. In 1944 and 1945, when Venona began to yield its secrets, the Soviet Union was officially an ally. The tiny circle aware of Venona knew better, but for the moment, they were in possession of a secret too great to reveal. Cryptography always seemed to run ahead of history. And no one grasped that truth better than two Americans who really made Venona possible—and yet, ironically, played no role in it.

As a man looking for some excitement in his humdrum job as a nine-hundred-dollar-a-year telegraph clerk at the State Department in the torpor of pre-World War I Washington, Herbert O. Yardley certainly had come to the wrong place. Nothing even remotely interesting seemed to happen in the huge Victorian mausoleum that housed the State Department (along with the War and Navy departments). Although the world seemed to be in some ferment across the two oceans that sheltered an isolationist America in that year of 1913, very little of that turmoil penetrated the seat of government.

A man with an active mind, Yardley sought to slake his restless mental energy with a hobby: cryptography. He haunted the Library of Congress during his off-duty hours, studying everything he could about the field. And the more he learned, the more he realized that the American diplomatic codes he saw every day in his job were hopelessly antiquated, just so much child's play for anyone with a rudimentary cryptographic knowledge. One day, spotting a long coded message from an American diplomat who had just concluded highly sensitive talks with the German kaiser,

Yardley sat down and solved the message in two hours. Yardley, quite logically, reasoned that if he could decipher the message so easily, then so could more professional cryptographers elsewhere —such as in Germany, France, and Great Britain. (He turned out to be quite right: the British were in fact reading all American diplomatic messages, having easily cracked the simple ciphers in which they were supposedly hidden.)

Yardley had found his true calling. Spending every spare hour in a self-education in cryptography, he discovered a natural flair for the ancient art, along with an important insight: the American code system had to be changed at once. Clearly, Yardley argued unavailingly to his superiors, American secrets were now open books. All American communications with Europe were routed through Great Britain, known to be actively developing a first-class cryptographic capability. The odds were good that they were reading all of the American diplomatic messages they were not supposed to see.

But Yardley got nowhere. To prove his point, he then spent the next several months solving every single American code currently in existence, and wrote up a report entitled *Exposition on the Solution of American Diplomatic Codes*, which he presented to his immediate superior—who happened to be the man who devised the codes in the first place. The superior's mood was hardly improved when Yardley coolly opened the man's safe, having decoded the combination based, amusingly enough, on the telephone number of President Woodrow Wilson's fiancée.

With what must have been a sigh of relief among his beleaguered superiors, Yardley was shipped off to the Army when America entered World War I in 1917. Made a lieutenant, Yardley was put in charge of a small Army Signal Corps outfit that concentrated on German ciphers for agents dispatched to France. Yardley made a name for himself by solving the ciphers, leading to the capture of virtually all the agents.

Yardley's outfit, known as MI-8, was among the scheduled victims of the postwar cutbacks. But Yardley's feats had become well known in the upper echelons of Army intelligence and the State Department, so an unprecedented arrangement was worked out: Yardley and MI-8 would continue functioning, but now in greatest secrecy, using State Department funds. Yardley set up shop in a four-story brownstone in New York City, grandly christening the operation the "Black Chamber," a tribute to the famed French code-breaking outfit known as *Chambre Noir* during the war.

At first, Yardley concentrated on Cheka ciphers used to dispatch agents and orders around the world, but in July 1919, was diverted toward a growing concern of American intelligence: Japan. Yardley and his small team of seven cryptanalysts went to work on the Japanese diplomatic ciphers, the task further complicated by the intricacies of the Japanese language. The team solved sixteen ciphers, but the last, and most important, resisted all efforts at solution. Yardley attacked the cipher around the clock, and according to his own later account, the solution finally came to him one December night in a deep sleep.

Two years later, the solutions provided American diplomats at the Washington Naval Arms Limitation Conference with a critical advantage: given the texts of secret instructions to Japanese negotiators, the Americans were able to anticipate every Japanese move, and imposed a shipbuilding ratio highly favorable to the United States.† Meanwhile, Yardley's men expanded their horizons, breaking the codes of a dozen other countries.

Only a handful of people in the entire United States knew of Yardley's operation and its brilliant successes. Such anonymity was crucial to the success of the Black Chamber, which relied on the other side's permanent delusion that its codes were safe; obviously, so much as a hint that the codes might be compromised— or even under severe attack—would force a revamping of those codes, requiring the cryptanalysts to start all over again.

The Black Chamber's achievements were astonishing, but only a handful of officials understood the real significance that lay behind the yellow flimsies hand-delivered to them from Yardley's operations, the ones that began, "We believe from a source considered reliable that . . ." (followed by the text of an intercepted communication). As Yardley argued, to little avail, cryptography had become the cutting edge of all intelligence.

Behind it all was the growth of electronic communications, hastened by World War I, which ushered in the new age of mass

† Key to the conference's limitation agreement was the question of "ratios": each major nation would be permitted construction of warships in proportion to size of population, and so forth. The Japanese wanted a 10:7 ratio (700,000 tons of Japanese ships for every 1 million American), but secretly instructed their delegates to accede to an American demand of 10:6 "to avoid a clash."

armies and movements across great distances, a military revolution that could only be controlled electronically. The same applied to diplomacy: in a world where space and time had suddenly become compressed, the bulk of diplomatic traffic now had to be sent via radio or telegraph.

But what was sent into the open air was therefore available to be read by anyone who wanted to take the trouble. So was born modern espionage, which, Yardley insisted, had become a race between code-makers and code-breakers: nations seeking to protect their most vital communications would create large establishments to balk the efforts of enemy eyes and ears. Those efforts, in turn, would have to be overcome by equivalent establishments that kept pace with ever more complex code systems. And which side won that race, Yardley concluded, would win the single great struggle of modern espionage.

Yardley advocated such a large-scale code-breaking establishment for the United States, but despite the successes of his own minor establishment, the example created little support for the scale of his proposal. First of all, Yardley was proposing a large centralized intelligence operation, and central intelligence, long an anathema in American political thought, was not a possibility. Secondly, an increasingly isolationist United States saw no need for the type of complex (and expensive) organization Yardley advocated.

Nevertheless, Yardley's view of the new world of espionage was quite correct. The Americans failed to fully heed the lessons of World War I, when code-breaking operations had a momentous impact on the course of the war. Indeed, one operation, carried out by a British naval intelligence operation known as Room 40, was responsible for an incident that led directly to the entry of the United States into the war. Room 40 cryptographers managed to crack the most important German diplomatic cipher, and on January 16, 1917, deciphered a bombshell, the telegram from German Minister of Foreign Affairs Arthur Zimmermann to the German legation in Mexico City.

The telegram announced that Germany was about to begin unrestricted submarine warfare, and that if the United States did not remain neutral, Mexico would be offered a deal to join with Germany as an ally, in exchange for which Mexico would be encouraged to reconquer former Mexican territory now comprising the states of Texas, New Mexico, and Arizona (assuming, of course, that Mexico would be capable of such a military feat). The British, armed at last with a potent propaganda weapon to induce American entry into the war, slipped a copy of the decoded telegram to American diplomats. On March 1, 1917, news of the German perfidy appeared in American newspapers; it undercut any remaining American support for Germany.

Eager to conceal the cryptographic break, the British spread the false story that their operatives had managed to steal a deciphered copy of the telegram from a careless German diplomat, a patently absurd story inexplicably believed by the Germans—who continued to use a compromised code the British read with ease the remainder of the war.

Yardley suspected that the telegram was more likely the result of a large-scale cryptanalytical effort, and in August 1918, sent to London by the U.S. War Department to see what the British might teach him about cryptography, he tried to find out how the British code-breaking operations were organized. The British were unfailingly polite, but conspicuously vague on how they had managed to break virtually all the German ciphers. Those ciphers, Yardley realized, were considerably more sophisticated than the American ones, leading to the inescapable conclusion that the British were probably still reading American diplomatic messages, too. Clearly, the British had an extensive cryptographic operation underway, one whose true dimensions they wanted to conceal from Yardley.

After the war, while the United States was keeping Yardley in business in a New York brownstone, the Europeans set about creating large, centralized cryptographic establishments. In 1919, as the French *Chambre Noir* reorganized for peacetime operations, the British collected all their cryptographic efforts and set them to work under a new agency, the Government Code and Cipher School (later Government Communications Headquarters). The Soviet Cheka, aware that its codes were compromised, was working to create a new agency that would control both code-making and code-breaking establishments.

However, the most impressive postwar code-breaking establishment was in Poland. Polish intelligence recruited the top mathematicians from the famed "Warsaw school" of mathematical theorists and turned them loose on the most difficult foreign codes, particularly those of Poland's mortal enemies, Germany and the Soviet Union. (Given an "unbreakable" German army cipher, the mathematicians broke it in three hours.) The code-breakers' efforts saved the young Polish state in 1920, when a Soviet invasion was decisively defeated, largely because coded Red Army offensive plans were deciphered almost as soon as sent, allowing Polish forces advance warning of major attacks.

However impressive these accomplishments, they had no impact in the United States. The Navy's ONI, despite its knowledge of the British Room 40's critical role in breaking German U-boat ciphers, did not even form a code-breaking unit until 1924. Serious work did not begin until four years later, when ONI agents broke into the Japanese consulate in New York and photographed the current Japanese Navy codebook. The break-in, undetected by the Japanese, afforded a temporary peek into Japan's codes (which were later changed). This initial success had its down side, however: ONI pointedly did not inform its Army counterparts of the Japanese decipherments, omen of a future recurring problem, interservice rivalry.

Had he known about it, Yardley would have been furious, for the incident underscored his argument about the necessity of a centralized American code-breaking operation. Another man would have been equally upset, for like Yardley, he was a vigorous proponent of the centralization idea.

But there the similarity ended, for Herbert O. Yardley and William F. Friedman were two very different sorts of men.

Although Yardley has passed into American history as its most famous code-breaker, in fact the less-publicized Friedman was not only his superior in cryptanalysis, but the real father of American code-breaking—and the colossus today known as the National Security Agency.

Originally a geneticist by training, Friedman drifted into cryptography by a side door. Hired by an eccentric millionaire to decipher old Francis Bacon manuscripts and prove that Bacon was the real author of Shakespeare's plays, Friedman became hooked on the subject of cryptography in general. He and a small group of similarly self-trained code-breakers joined the U.S. Army Signal Corps' Code and Cipher Section when the United States entered World War I.

Sent to France, Friedman encountered Yardley, and from the first moment, felt a distaste for him. The differences between the two men were both personal and professional. An intense, reticent man, Friedman disliked Yardley's personal flamboyance; Yardley, an inveterate womanizer, was a self-aggrandizer who liked to boast of his prowess as a code-breaker and poker player. Friedman also disliked Yardley's organizational style, which consisted, mainly, of egocentrism. Friedman, an organization man, believed that only organizations of anonymous men, working in the deepest secrecy, could effectively run code-breaking operations—such as Great Britain's Government Code and Cipher School.

And it was Friedman's concentration on organization that ultimately contributed the most to America's cryptographic capability. His emphasis was on recruiting, then rigorously training, new generations of cryptanalysts to create a self-perpetuating organization.* (Yardley did not conduct such training.) Friedman was also a strong believer in the team concept of cryptography, in which teams of code-breakers would be assigned specific targets, working under a "team leader," who would channel their efforts into what he regarded as the most promising areas.

Like Yardley, Friedman decided to stay in code-breaking after the war. He shared Yardley's concern about the large cryptographic organizations growing in Europe while the United States seemed unable to comprehend the necessity for creating its own organization. In 1921, Friedman joined the War Department as a civilian on a one-year contract for cryptographic work. (The contract was renewed annually for the next fifty years; during the 1960s, the NSA discovered, to its horror, that Friedman had never received a security clearance.)

In 1929, Friedman was named head of a new Army organization, the Signal Intelligence Service, which amounted to the grand total of seven people and a $17,400 annual budget. It operated parallel with Yardley's Black Chamber, meaning that by 1929, the United States, along with the Navy's ONI, had three different

* Several of the graduates of Friedman's training courses went on to glittering careers years later in the National Security Agency, among them Frank Rowlett. Although unknown to the general public, Rowlett's contributions were so great, he was given a special award of $100,000 by Congress in 1964 for what were described only as "cryptographic activities."

cryptological organizations—the very thing both Friedman and Yardley had long argued against. But the three organizations suddenly were reduced to two that year when a curious event took place.

It was not until May 1929 that the new Secretary of State, Henry L. Stimson, got to see the source of those reports on yellow paper that seemed to come straight from foreign chancellories. A gentleman of the old school, a shocked Stimson directed the State Department immediately to "cease any further activities of such nature," summing up his distaste in a sentence that would come to haunt his public career, "Gentlemen do not read each other's mail."

Actually, Stimson's action was largely academic, since a decision had already been made to absorb the Black Chamber into Friedman's Signal Intelligence Service. Yardley's operation was technically a joint function of the State and War departments, but the military had become increasingly uneasy about it. Checking into the Black Chamber, Army investigators found that nearly a third of the Chamber's one-hundred-thousand-dollar annual budget was being paid to Yardley as salary—a princely sum at the time—and that Yardley was suspected of working privately on commercial company codes, along with a flourishing real estate business. (A more serious allegation, never proven, was that Yardley had approached the Japanese and offered to sell them the decryptions of their diplomatic messages of 1921 for seven thousand dollars.)

In October 1929, the Black Chamber was closed down. Yardley not only was out of a job, his real estate business collapsed in the stock market crash. Desperate for money to support his wife and two children, he prepared a manuscript on his cryptographic adventures. First serialized in the *Saturday Evening Post*, in 1931 it was published in book form as *The American Black Chamber*. The book was immensely popular, but its popularity did not extend to Friedman and the rest of the small American cryptographic establishment. They were positively horrified, for not only had Yardley revealed the existence of a highly secret intelligence-gathering operation, he had also in the process tipped off the Japanese and a number of other countries that their codes were compromised. (Yardley's subsequent work on the same subject, *Japanese Diplomatic Secrets*, was seized by the government before publication, an action upheld in a landmark court case broadening the government's power to classify intelligence secrets.)†

The chief reason for Friedman's anger at Yardley's indiscretion was how difficult it made the work of his Signal Intelligence Service. The Japanese, among others, studied Yardley's book very carefully, and concluded, correctly, that the standard diplomatic ciphers—no matter how carefully prepared—were vulnerable to attack. Additionally, as the electronic revolution accelerated, the need for fast and secure diplomatic communications was growing more acute.

The solution came in the form of one of the century's most ingenious inventions, the cipher machine. Reduced to its simplest form, the machine amounted to a standard typewriter keyboard hooked up to an electrically operated wheel or series of wheels (called "rotors"). The rotors would turn at random, striking various letters transmitted to a machine at the other end.

Without pattern, decoding such transmissions appeared virtually impossible, and promised true security of communications. Given the randomness of the rotors, there was no way to deduce the unciphered message—unless, somehow, the cryptanalysts could recapture all the electrical currents precisely.

Some time after the appearance of Yardley's book, the Japanese began using their first cipher machine, which Friedman's cryptanalysts code-named RED. The machine was quite formidable, but by 1935, the American teams began breaking into *Angooki taipu A*, the cipher used for Japanese naval attachés stationed abroad. The race was on: just as fast as the Americans were solving messages, the Japanese were introducing new, more complex codes as they further refined their machine. Both sides were about neck and neck when, in 1937, the Japanese introduced what they called *97-shiki O-bun In-ji-ki*, an advanced cipher machine code-named Purple by the Americans, who suddenly found themselves in the dark: the machine's messages were absolutely unreadable.

Japan's invasion of China that year and its increasing bellicosity fixed the attention of the American cryptanalysts on Japanese intentions, for Friedman believed that some sort of war with Ja-

† Yardley subsequently worked for Chinese intelligence, and, later, the Canadians. Following Pearl Harbor, he tried to join William Donovan's organization, but was rejected on the grounds of "security violations." After the war he wrote a classic treatise on poker. In 1958 he died, virtually forgotten.

pan was inevitable. He was convinced that a major code break against Purple—used to transmit the most secret of Japanese diplomatic communications—would provide early warning of a hostile Japanese move against the United States. To that end, he dropped whatever else he was doing, and devoted all his time to the Purple problem.

The task was skull-cracking: essentially, Friedman and his men had to carefully analyze every single interception of the Purple messages, and use them to divine how the machine was constructed. The only way to solve Purple, Friedman decided, was to actually build a replica of the machine—the technical equivalent of cloning a human being without ever seeing the twin.

Friedman suffered a nervous breakdown in the process, but by August 1940 the Americans had achieved their first break. A month later, they read, for the first time, an entire Purple message. Now, Japanese intentions—at least as communicated to the diplomats—were an open book. A small circle of high-level officials, including President Roosevelt, began to receive visits from solemn military couriers who handed them documents code-named Magic, verbatim transcriptions from Purple messages. The officials were required to read a transcripted message, then hand it back to the courier. Security was extraordinarily tight.

Magic, Friedman thought, would provide America with warning of threats arising in the Pacific. The next step was to cover the other side of the world. In the spring of 1941, four of the best American cryptanalysts went to Great Britain bearing a precious gift: a model of the Purple machine. In return, the British let the Americans in on an even more astounding secret: they had begun reading messages dispatched by the German cipher machine, known as Enigma. Code-named Ultra, the British code-breaking operation actually began in Poland, where code-breakers managed to crack some German Army ciphers sent via Enigma. The decryptions were of little help in the flood of the German onslaught in 1939, but the Polish code-breakers had put together a replica of Enigma, and after fleeing their homeland, made a gift of the machine and their knowledge to British intelligence.

By December of 1941 it appeared that the United States, in cryptographic terms, was very near something like intelligence omniscience. To the east, it had an agreement to share in the fruits of Ultra, which guaranteed access to high-level German military and diplomatic decisions dispatched over the Enigma machines. Toward the west, the United States was in the position of looking over the Japanese leaders' shoulders as they conveyed their most secret plans to their diplomats—most importantly, to the Japanese ambassador in Washington. No secrets were ever guarded more closely than Ultra and Magic.‡

Yet, Pearl Harbor happened. "But they knew! They knew!" Friedman cried out in rage and frustration when he heard the news, forgetting that however astonishing his technical achievement in defeating Purple, its result was raw intelligence. Without a centralized operation to interpret the data, they were fragmentary, selected insights shown to a small group of people who often did not understand their context or broader meaning. On top of that, the American cryptologic establishment was divided, with the Army and Navy running their own separate operations and barely talking to each other.

Pearl Harbor changed all that, for although there was never a Magic intercept which specifically conveyed an order to attack Pearl Harbor, postmortems revealed that the clues pointing unmistakably toward the attack were scattered all over the fragmented American intelligence structure, especially its cryptological arms. The U.S. Navy had learned a bitter lesson, but it had learned. The military advantage to be gained from Magic intercepts, ignored at Pearl Harbor, proved a critical factor in the decisive Pacific battle at Midway in June 1942 when American Naval intelligence again brought advance warning of a Japanese attack. The information was heeded, and this time it was Admiral Isoroku Yamamoto, architect of the Pearl Harbor attack, who was surprised and defeated. One year later, Yamamoto was himself to be a victim of Magic when U.S. Navy code-breakers learned of his precise flight schedule while on an inspection tour of Japanese forces in the Pacific. American fighter planes were there to meet him and shot him out of the sky.

Besides strengthening Naval intelligence, Friedman's once-mi-

‡ The British kept Ultra secret for nearly thirty years after the war. One reason for that secrecy was the fact that the British captured large numbers of Enigma machines, which they generously offered to a number of small nations around the world—forgetting to mention that anything sent via Enigma might just as well have been printed in a newspaper, since the British had unlocked the machine's secrets long before.

nuscule agency was transformed into the Signal Security Agency, which by V-J day, had seven thousand employees. At the same time, the British-American cryptological partnership was nurtured, resulting in the 1947 pact known as the "UKUSA Agreement." Still classified, the agreement joined the United States, Great Britain, Canada, Australia, and New Zealand in a vast, worldwide net of listening posts that attempted to vacuum up every signal they could detect.

The network was the result of an important lesson of World War II, when it was discovered that the vital key to cryptologic success was thoroughness: *everything* had to be collected, in order to gain enough traffic on which to work. One of the deep secrets-within-a-secret of both Ultra and Magic was that despite the wonder of cipher machines, human beings operate them—and human beings make mistakes. Code clerks get tired, undertrained operators make foolish mistakes, and ordinary men make extraordinary errors (such as the Japanese clerks who would transmit diplomatic documents with routing numbers, an important "crib," or attack point, for a cryptanalyst seeking routes into a cipher).

It was human error that had led to the Venona code-break at one of the UKUSA network stations, the Coonawarra installation. No one could have anticipated such an intelligence bonanza, nor could anyone have anticipated that in 1945, a disaffected GRU (Soviet military intelligence) code clerk would defect from the Soviet embassy in Ottawa with a priceless list of GRU codes and cryptonyms.

His name was Igor Gouzenko, and his little treasure trove confirmed what Venona had already revealed: the United States and its allies faced a new enemy whose dimensions had been badly underestimated. Among other things, Gouzenko provided details on Operation Candy, a crash intelligence operation mounted by both the NKVD and GRU to ferret out secrets of the Manhattan Project. Judging by the results revealed by Gouzenko, the operation had been a spectacular success: a British scientist named Alan Nunn May was providing technical secrets to the GRU from the Canadian end of the project, and matched up with information collected by Klaus Fuchs and the American sources run by the NKVD, Moscow knew everything there was to know about the American atomic bomb.

But the Soviet operation—and others like it—had an Achilles' heel: everything collected had to be transmitted to Moscow Center by the fastest route, radio. It was Moscow's lifeline everywhere; tap into that lifeline, strip the ciphers of their protection, and Moscow would be as open a secret as Washington and London apparently were to the Russians.

The specter of Pearl Harbor, Venona, and the revelations of Igor Gouzenko all combined to create the basis for the great postwar cryptologic expansion, now aimed at the new enemy. To William Friedman, the pioneer who did more than anyone to create what would become a vast clockwork, far greater than he could ever have imagined, it all represented the culmination of his longtime dream. He saw it come to ultimate fruition in 1952, when President Truman signed a document, *National Security Council Directive 6,* creating a new agency called the National Security Agency. Although the document remains classified, it is known that the new agency was to collect the raw intercepts produced by the UKUSA network of listening stations and the military intelligence agencies, attempt to crack any ciphered material, and produce ciphers to protect American coded communications.*

But in the rush to confront the new enemy, there were a number of important questions that had escaped attention. They centered on the relationship between the vast new apparatus and the democratic system in which it operated. The new NSA's "vacuum cleaner" approach might get all the Soviet signals it sought —but it would also pick up a lot of signals that had nothing to do with the Soviet Union, such as private transmissions by Americans. What was to guarantee that their rights were not violated in the name of national security? And more importantly, as the NSA's technical power grew, what was to prevent the government from using that capability against domestic targets?

Legally, not much, for from the very beginning, the crypto-

---

* Nevertheless, there are recurring attempts to slice pieces from the NSA's monopoly. For some years, the CIA ran its own communications interception operation, known as Staff D. The FBI also ran its own operation, called the Special Security Section. Neither these attempts, nor efforts by the military intelligence agencies along similar lines, ever got very far, because they were never able to get the kind of funding (in the multibillion-dollar class) NSA receives.

logic part of the American intelligence apparatus had been sidestepping the law. In 1927, Congress passed a law flatly prohibiting divulging or intercepting any radio communications in the United States. That law presented a serious obstacle to men like Friedman and Yardley, who were busy intercepting telegraphic messages dispatched by American companies. The law seemed to put an end to the informal practice of telegraph and radio-communication companies providing copies of dispatches to the cryptanalysts—except that certain key executives of those companies were approached and convinced to break the law. (Vincent Astor, President Roosevelt's friend and private spy, was on the board of directors of the Western Union Company. He ordered the company's traffic made available, despite the law; David Sarnoff, head of the Radio Corporation of America, issued a similar order.)

Several years later, the Federal Communications Act of 1934 contained an even stronger prohibition, and when the communications companies demonstrated increasing nervousness about providing further copies of communications, Friedman's agency and the other cryptanalytic outfits solved the problem by simply forming their own interception stations—all of them illegal.

Meanwhile, FBI Director J. Edgar Hoover, involved in domestic security operations, faced an even more serious legal problem. A U.S. Supreme Court decision in 1939 prohibited wiretapping, a sweeping ruling that appeared to balk further FBI taps, which were operating without benefit of warrants. Hoover was leery of running afoul of the ruling, but received dispensation from President Roosevelt himself, who told Hoover that the court ruling did not apply to "grave matters involving the defense of the nation." Further, Roosevelt, by executive order that ignored the Supreme Court, authorized Hoover to wiretap anyone "suspected of subversive activities" without warrant, an authority so broad as to practically invite abuse.

The abuses would come, inevitably, for history had demonstrated that the American intelligence apparatus would at some point turn inward during a future crisis. Meanwhile, however, there was that great threat looming outside.

FIVE

Admiral with a Wooden Sword

PROMPTLY AT NOON on January 24, 1946, President Harry S
Truman strode into the White House dining room and greeted
the two military officers seated at the table: Admiral William
Leahy, the President's chief of staff, and Rear Admiral Sidney W.
Souers.

With mock solemnity, Truman proffered a black hat, a black
cloak, and a wooden sword, which he handed Souers to put on.
Then Truman placed a large black false mustache on Souers' lip.

The antics of the ceremony were matched by a subsequent
memo Truman wrote about the significance of the occasion: "By
virtue of the authority vested in me as Top Dog," Truman wrote,
"I require and charge that Front Admiral William D. Leahy and
Rear Admiral Sidney W. Souers receive and accept the vestments
and appurtenances of their respective positions, namely, as Personal Snooper and as Director of Centralized Snooping."

And with this droll ceremony and memo, the United States

took one of the most significant actions in its history, for Souers had just been inducted as the country's first Director of Central Intelligence. He was now head of a new organization called the Central Intelligence Group, the first real attempt to centralize all American intelligence in one organization.

Ironically, Souers—who had a modicum of experience in U.S. Navy intelligence during the war—was the one intelligence official in the United States who absolutely did not want (nor had he sought) the job of running the new organization. A personal friend of Truman, Souers was a Missouri businessman most noted for heading the regional chain of Piggly-Wiggly stores, the very mention of which caused people to smile. He had reluctantly taken the job only because his friend had requested him to; asked what he wanted to do, Souers replied simply, "Go home."

Even if he wanted the job, Souers would have had very few resources to do much of anything. He was an emperor without an empire: his organization was a bureaucratic nightmare, a paper entity that was supposed to draw on the resources of the other components of American intelligence. But since those agencies had a deep antipathy toward the idea of a central intelligence organization—or sought to dominate it for themselves—they were not about to cooperate with Souers.

After five months of savage bureaucratic warfare, Souers resigned, having decided to return to what must have seemed a much more genteel world of cutthroat business competition. He was only the latest victim in a back-room struggle for control of postwar American intelligence, a struggle that finally resulted in an organization very much to Truman's liking.

But Truman himself was to become a victim in that struggle—although from a direction he never expected.

"You're the one in trouble now," Eleanor Roosevelt warned the new President of the United States. Harry Truman, within fifteen minutes of being sworn in after the sudden death of President Roosevelt, was plunged into a world of ferment during the spring of 1945.

History records that no other President has been confronted with so many momentous foreign policy decisions all at once as was Truman: the war, the shape of the postwar world, the atomic bomb, and the beginning of the Cold War. Aware of his moment in history, Truman early in his presidency decided that the press of world events would no longer permit the loose, informal conduct of foreign and military policy that Roosevelt preferred. A methodical man, Truman wanted a more formal system of organization, with the departments of state, war, and navy given a much greater role in decision-making. Uneasy about Roosevelt's often slapdash style of deciding foreign policy, Truman wanted a structure that would compensate, to a certain extent, for his own lack of experience in managing foreign policy.

One of Truman's particular concerns was intelligence. He had no experience in the field, but as a veteran of the Washington political wars Truman was no fool, and had a good grasp of the general dimensions of American intelligence. He was also aware of its weaknesses, and quickly decided that the fragmented nature of that structure was inadequate to meet postwar realities. But what kind of new structure would replace it?

The man who provided the answer was Secretary of the Navy (and, in 1947, Secretary of Defense) James V. Forrestal, in Truman's view among the most impressively talented men in the government. An ex-bond trader who had made his fortune on Wall Street, Forrestal directed the Navy's mobilization during the war, and decided to stay in government. It was said of Forrestal that his view of the postwar world was fixed at Iwo Jima, where, watching the slaughter of Marines on the beaches, he decided that never again would American young men die because the country was militarily unprepared.

A full-fledged Russophobe obsessed with communism, Forrestal predicted a postwar world dominated by a titanic struggle between the United States and the Soviet Union, with the very fate of the world at stake. With the memories of Munich and Pearl Harbor still fresh, Forrestal argued that only a fully prepared America could withstand that challenge. And a whole new structure would be necessary for the coming battle: a centralized military and foreign policy apparatus, under the direction of the President and fully informed by a central intelligence agency through which all intelligence would flow.

Forrestal's vision ultimately resulted in the National Security Act of 1947, which created the modern American national security structure—including the Central Intelligence Agency. But in the intervening two years before the CIA's creation, Truman hesitated; like many politicians of his generation, he retained the fear of an "American Gestapo." Others, especially Forrestal, had no such fear; in their view, the developing struggle between the United States and the Soviet Union was just this side of Armageddon, and America had to be armed militarily and organizationally, tradition be damned.

Truman's initial hesitation was shared by another government official whose abilities he admired, Harold D. Smith, head of the Bureau of the Budget. Shortly after the end of the war, Smith prepared an extensive analysis on the state of American intelligence, and found it deficient in almost every regard, especially Smith's major concern, how the millions of taxpayers' dollars were spent. Most of the money was wasted by duplication, and intense rivalry among the intelligence agencies, Smith concluded, but added that a centralized intelligence agency (which he called a "superagency") might be more trouble than it was worth.

But while Truman was trying to figure out what to do, he was being besieged by crises—all of which demonstrated some severe failings of the intelligence agencies. Eager to demonstrate their usefulness to the new president, they bombarded him with often-contradictory "hot poop" from the latest crisis. (During his first several months in office, Truman often found himself awakened in the predawn hours to be informed of some "vital" intelligence tidbit, which more often than not was wrong or premature.)

Truman needed good intelligence, for there seemed to be a foreign policy crisis every day: Communist-led strikes in France, civil war in China, threats of Communist insurrection in Greece, Soviet pressure against Turkey, a threatened Soviet military invasion of the Azerbaijan area of Iran, political unrest in Eastern Europe. And the more unsettled the world became, the less American intelligence was able to tell him about it. Even the simplest questions somehow seemed to be fumbled: asked to estimate the size of the Soviet military machine that Stalin clearly had no intention of demobilizing, Army intelligence claimed that the Soviets had an army of 5 million men—60 percent higher than the number of men actually under arms.

In January 1946, Truman ordered creation of the Central Intelligence Group. That act precipitated intense opposition from the military intelligence agencies, a back-room struggle fought mostly in the closed hearing rooms of congressional committees.

The committees, especially the powerful House Military Affairs Committee (which decided military budgets), had been concerned for quite some time about the state of American intelligence. There was a gradually emerging consensus for a centralized intelligence organization, for congressional investigations of the Pearl Harbor attack and other military disasters revealed a consistent pattern of intelligence inefficiency. The result was that Congress and Truman were of the same mind on two things: one, a centralized intelligence system was the only answer; and two, the first experiment in that direction, the Central Intelligence Group, was not the kind of central intelligence organization that would work. What was needed, it was agreed, was an organization that would function independently of the military intelligence agencies and the FBI, under the direct control of the President.

The director of this prospective agency, of course, would have to be a powerful man, with the kind of experience and skill necessary to maintain his agency's independence; a man with the full confidence of the President. Two potential candidates came immediately to mind, but they were men who Truman had already decided would not fill that job.

One was William Donovan, head of the wartime OSS. The OSS was a doomed organization: by July 1945, its death knells were already sounding. The Joint Chiefs of Staff, the White House, and the Bureau of the Budget were all taking hard looks at America's most highly publicized intelligence organization—and concluding that OSS was not nearly worth its cost, and provided no effective model for a postwar central intelligence agency. The Joint Chiefs surveyed the major theater commanders in 1945 on what they thought about the OSS's contribution to the war effort, and discovered that the responses about OSS were mixed. Dwight Eisenhower, head of the European Theater of Operations, said that short-range (tactical) operations of the OSS were "of valuable assistance," but that longer-range OSS penetration operations were "not consistently effective." Army commanders in Italy pronounced OSS generally effective, but pointedly noted that the organization could be reduced to 20 percent of its strength. General Albert C. Wedemeyer, chief of the China-Burma-India Theater, reported that OSS had played a "minor role" in his theater, but diplomatically added that OSS's "potential value" was high.

Hardly ringing endorsements, but even OSS veterans shared

some reservations about the OSS record. Ray Cline, an OSS officer who later became one of the CIA's deputy directors, was critical of what he regarded as the OSS's legacy of "boom and bang" operations. William Colby—a participant in such operations who later became CIA director—was among many OSS veterans who could recite stories indicating that the agency's paramilitary operations were sometimes less than efficient. (One of Colby's favorite such anecdotes concerned the time he was to parachute into a deserted far field; actually, he wound up being dropped into a German-occupied town swarming with troops.) Other OSS veterans were critical of the agency's occasional tendency to hurriedly mount major infiltration operations. Several such operations, directed by a young OSS officer named William Casey, aimed to create large networks of spies inside Germany by the simple expedient of hastily recruiting some volunteer exiles, then dropping them deep inside the enemy's lair. Most of the ill-trained spies were rounded up and killed. Only in the last few months of the war was Casey able to infiltrate with any effectiveness.

Overall, the OSS was a managerial nightmare; Donovan, not interested to any degree in managing his sprawling empire that by the end of the war included over sixteen thousand people, operated out of his pocket. His real preference was action, and he liked to spice his deskbound existence with occasional forays into the field, where he often demonstrated total recklessness. In Burma, he ordered his agents to fly him to an OSS base deep behind enemy lines. On other occasions, he wound up perilously close to danger in North Africa and Italy—to the horror of the White House and senior military commanders, who imagined what would happen if a man like Donovan and the secrets he carried with him were to fall into enemy hands. (Not all his secrets were recorded: after the war, it was discovered that Donovan had a habit of occasionally approving highly sensitive operations without bothering to tell his staff in Washington.)

In his perception of a future centralized intelligence agency, Truman had in mind an intelligence collection organization that would be very different from the one created by Donovan. It would be concerned exclusively with intelligence collection and evaluation, the two areas in which Donovan had demonstrated the least ability. Truman conceived of no further need of the "boom and bang" capability of the OSS, and in his view, commando operations were properly the function of the military. And as far as military intelligence was concerned, Truman subscribed to Forrestal's view that it should concentrate on the traditional military intelligence role of collecting tactical intelligence —the "bean counting" function of measuring the enemy's military capability.

If neither Donovan nor any military intelligence chief was to run the new centralized intelligence organization, that left only one remaining figure whose persona and organization enjoyed immense popularity with the public, and who had also demonstrated the requisite bureaucratic skills to survive in the Washington jungle. Nevertheless, Truman had no intention of appointing FBI Director J. Edgar Hoover as director of central intelligence, the post Hoover most desired.

Hoover had made his move in that direction in late 1945, submitting to Truman, via Attorney General Tom Clark, a plan for a postwar central intelligence agency. Hoover cited the success of the FBI's South American operations during the war, then proposed that a "policy committee" be set up to run similar operations, this time on a worldwide basis. And domestically, too: Hoover claimed that "foreign and domestic civil intelligence are inseparable and constitute one field of operation." The point was, of course, that there was only one organization extant that had combined overseas intelligence and domestic security operations, the FBI. Hoover did not specify who was to head this "policy committee," but even a cursory reading of his plan made it clear the man he had in mind.

An extremely shrewd politician, Truman for many years had kept his eyes and ears open, and as a result, had a fair idea of what was going on in the corridors of power. He was close to Eleanor Roosevelt, who often told him that the FBI was a "Gestapo." Truman also heard other stories about some of the activities of Hoover that did not reach public attention: his compilation of secret files on the weaknesses and assorted peccadilloes of members of Congress and the White House staff; his wiretaps on a wide range of domestic dissidents; his currying of favor with presidents by providing them with reports on political opponents; and, most of all, his drive for power.

All in all, Truman decided, Hoover was not the kind of man

who should be given the vast power represented by the post of director of central intelligence. Besides, Truman perceived Hoover as hopelessly provincial, a man who had never traveled overseas (save Caribbean vacations) in his life—and had no desire to.

The man who did finally become the new Director of Central Intelligence was Rear Admiral Roscoe Hillenkoetter. The choice reflected a number of factors Truman considered, not the least of them being politics. Aware of the military intelligence agencies' still-smoldering resentment against the whole idea of centralized intelligence and their conviction that no "civilian" would ever be competent enough to evaluate intelligence dealing with military matters, Truman selected a military man.

Judged politically, "Hilly" Hillenkoetter was a good choice. A man of amiable disposition, he was well liked within the military establishment, thus ensuring smooth relations with the often nettlesome military. Further, he had strong intelligence credentials. In 1940 and 1941, he had served as naval attaché at the U.S. embassy at Vichy, where he secretly helped the French underground spirit fugitives from the Gestapo to safety. Later in 1941, he was executive officer of the battleship *West Virginia*, and was wounded at Pearl Harbor when the ship was sunk in the Japanese attack. During the war, he set up an ONI network in the Pacific.

Not surprisingly, Hillenkoetter was a man obsessed with his Pearl Harbor experience, one he vowed would never happen again to the United States. No job seemed more guaranteed to prevent such a recurrence than the one of Director of Central Intelligence he accepted in May 1947. Created by the National Security Act that year, the post, at least as conceived, seemed a guarantee that policymakers would no longer be given fragmentary and conflicting intelligence. There would be one intelligence chief only, one man who would tell the President each day the shape of the world and its lurking dangers.

According to the National Security Act, Hillenkoetter's mandate was quite clear. Section 102(d) of the act, covering "powers and duties" of the new Central Intelligence Agency, prohibited the agency from any "internal security functions," and went on to specify how the Director of Central Intelligence (DCI) was to collect and coordinate foreign intelligence. But the act also contained a huge loophole, one that contained the potential for disaster.

Buried in paragraph five of the CIA's functions was a statement that the agency would also be called on "to perform such other functions and duties related to intelligence affecting the national security as the National Security Council may from time to time direct." Since "other functions and duties" were not otherwise defined, that meant that the president—who headed the National Security Council—was now being handed a virtual blank checkbook.

The implications of this loophole escaped attention, for most of the controversy surrounding the National Security Act was concentrated in the military services, busy squabbling over organizational and other changes wrought by the new law. The military generally paid little attention to the act's intelligence provisions, since its parochial concern—the continued existence of military intelligence agencies—was virtually unaffected. More importantly, the new act did not affect the crown jewel of military intelligence, the one great asset it was not prepared to give up: signals intelligence. (This broad term covered signal interception, cryptography, and cryptanalysis.)

No aspect of intelligence was so jealously guarded as Sigint—as the military preferred to call it—and one reason why Donovan never succeeded in becoming a true czar of intelligence was the military's refusal to cede any part of Sigint. But left strictly in military hands, signals intelligence was a problem. Despite the lessons of Pearl Harbor, the Navy and the Army insisted on running their own Sigint operations; to complicate matters further, the new U.S. Air Force—created as a separate military service after the war—also set up its own Sigint operation. The conflict over Sigint was an even more intense backstage struggle than the one over centralized intelligence, and Truman was not able to achieve a final solution until his last year in office. On October 24, 1952, he signed *National Security Council Directive 6*, a seven-page document that eliminated the first, failed attempt at uniting all the military Sigint operations—the Armed Forces Security Agency—and replaced it with the new National Security Agency.

To this day, Directive 6 remains classified, and the *U.S. Government Manual* says only, "The National Security Agency performs highly specialized technical and coordinating functions relating to the national security." It was to be many years before most

Americans learned about the sprawling apparatus that lay behind that bland phrase. There were those "training" or "weather collection" flights that were occasionally shot down near or just across the Soviet borders—in fact NSA planes, jammed with electronic interception gear. There was a fleet of converted World War II merchant ships, also crammed with interception equipment, which sailed in waters near world trouble spots, collecting signals for the NSA.* There were U.S. Navy submarines, equipped with special gear, tapping—on behalf of NSA—into underwater communications cables used by the Russians. The support for this apparatus was buried in the recesses of the federal budget, hundreds of millions of dollars in concealed appropriations for the NSA (in one instance, some of the money was listed as funds to buy light bulbs for Air Force installations). Much of the money was being used to buy "crunchers," huge state-of-the-art computers that could process millions of bits of information in seconds.

The United States had created an awesome data-collection organization that could sweep up virtually every single transmission within its reach, from ordinary telephone conversations to super-secret enciphered transmissions. Among those who knew, no one yet fully grasped the implications of that capability.

Unknown to most Americans, the postwar American code-breaking operation had grown rapidly. The growth was spurred by the memories of World War II and its code-breaking triumphs that had done so much to win the war. Key to that success was sheer volume: the code-breakers discovered that the more that was collected, the better their chance of cracking the ciphers. The cryptanalysts called it "traffic analysis," the process of poring through thousands and thousands of messages, looking for the slips by code clerks or the repetitious pattern that would offer

---

* This highly secret operation burst into public view in June 1967, when one of the NSA's "snooper" ships, the USS *Liberty*, was attacked by Israeli planes while on patrol off the coast of Sinai. Although the Israelis described the attack as an "error," in fact they were attempting to prevent the *Liberty* from discovering a deep secret: Israel had broken all Arab codes, and was using that information to broadcast false orders to Arab military forces. Seven months later, another NSA spy ship, the USS *Pueblo*, was captured by North Korea. The ship's secrets were conveyed to Moscow, and that was the end of the NSA spy ship operations.

insights into ciphers. The process needed volumes of traffic, and what could not be picked up by interception stations had to be collected by more dangerous means: "ferret" planes that would slip across Soviet borders for a short while to collect transmissions, then flee for their lives as Soviet fighters closed in; or so-called "Holystone" submarines that worked their way into Soviet harbors and naval installations. (Later, special "ferret" spy satellites would replace these hair-raising missions.)

The reason for this exponential growth in American intelligence was the new menace of the Soviet Union, a threat that dwarfed anything the United States had ever confronted. Neither German nor Japanese militarism had ignited so great a fear within the American psyche, for the Americans now confronted an enemy that spanned nearly half the globe, and despite severe losses in the war, had a military machine much more vast and powerful than the Nazis or the Japanese had, even at the height of their power.

Further, the Soviet Union's intentions were unmistakable. Stalin had told Yugoslavian Communists in 1944, "This war is not as in the past; whoever occupies a territory also imposes his own social system." And that is precisely what the Russians set out to do: Soviet aggression in Eastern Europe, Asia, and the Near East clearly signaled Moscow's intention to dominate the postwar world. Or perhaps more; so long as the Soviet military machine, still at its wartime strength even after the surrenders of Nazi Germany and Japan, stood poised for offensive action (at least potentially), there remained the threat of a Soviet military attack against its enemies in the West. This possibility assumed even greater dimensions after the Soviet Union ended the American monopoly over atomic weapons in 1949 by developing its own atomic bomb.

The first alarm bells had rung several years before, in 1943, when several OSS operatives based in Europe warned that the Russians were already working to shape the postwar world in their own image. Allen Dulles, among others, pointed to Moscow's creation of the "Free Germany Committee," a collection of German Communist Party exiles, pro-Communist German war prisoners, and assorted other elements. The committee, which downplayed Communist rhetoric, was making propaganda broadcasts to Germany, urging Germans to surrender. To officials in Great Britain and the United States, the committee was a standard propaganda operation. But, Dulles claimed, the committee was in fact intended to be the governmental and organizational nucleus of a communized Germany after the war. (Dulles turned out to be right: virtually all of the committee's top echelon later became the leading officials of the new state of East Germany a decade later.)

Dulles, considered a "rightist" within the OSS's senior leadership, did not have much of an impact with his warning, nor did other OSS agents who delivered similar warnings. Moscow, they reported, was creating "national committees of liberation" all over Europe, part of a massive operation to take over all partisan and resistance organizations. Such committees already dominated anti-German resistance in Eastern Europe, and there were extremely active Communist factions seeking to dominate the resistance movements in Italy and France.

The most infamous example of how the Soviet operation worked was in Poland, where the Soviets created the Polish National Committee as a counterweight to the resistance organization run by the exile government headquartered in London. The Communist group gradually took control of the resistance movement, in some cases giving up non-Communist partisans to the Germans. The non-Communists suffered a disaster in 1944, when their uprising in Warsaw was crushed while Stalin cynically ordered his forces—just outside the city—to do nothing to help them.

All of this was obscured by an elaborate deception plan organized by Moscow. The Communist International (Comintern), the ruling body of international communism that ran propaganda and political action operations worldwide (the organization long before had been taken over by the Soviets), ostentatiously was dissolved in 1943 as a gesture to "Allied unity." But, as Dulles and others argued, to no avail, the dissolution was not simply a propaganda move; the Russians had decided to replace the Comintern with something else much more dangerous.

That perception was especially acute in a branch of the OSS which had the first encounters with the intelligence arm of the resurgent Soviets. Known as X-2 (counterespionage), the branch in 1943 was already engaged in a struggle with the NKVD, racing all over Italy to seize German intelligence files (and their precious lists of assets) before the Russians could. The head of the X-2 branch, James R. Murphy, aware of growing NKVD operations all over Europe, had begun to think of ways his branch could "double" (turn) NKVD agents and assets.

Murphy and the OSS quickly learned this would be no easy task—certainly not as easy as the doubling of German *Abwehr* agents. Compared with the NKVD, the Germans were rank amateurs. They had dispatched to England one agent who did not speak any English, another who had a previous arrest record in Great Britain for espionage, a man who was parachuted into the country wearing jackboots and carrying his World War I medals, an Indian-born agent who arrived in England in a straw hat and a bright silk suit, and an agent sent to Canada who was outfitted with outdated currency. To make matters worse for the Germans, the British and Americans had cracked the *Abwehr* ciphers, meaning that they could not only read orders dispatched to the German agents, they also had a perfect check on how well doubled agents' reports were received in Germany. (Every one of the more than 150 *Abwehr* agents sent to England was caught.)

No such weapon existed against the NKVD, for the Venona code break, for all its value, was a temporary victory. One of the NKVD moles operating inside British intelligence—probably Kim Philby—tipped off Moscow about the code break, and the Russian codes were completely overhauled. By 1948, the Russian codes for NKVD operations were rendered totally impenetrable. In addition, the NKVD was a thoroughly professional organization; its agents, veterans of decades of underground work, represented a corps of seasoned professionals of unrivaled experience.

Among the NKVD's greatest strengths were elaborate deception operations. During the war, it developed a large network of ex-White Russians, headed by an agent code-named "Max." Recruited by the Germans, the network established its *bona fides* by providing advance warning on major military moves by the Russians—who actually sacrificed thousands of their own troops to solidify Max's credentials. When the Germans were completely hooked, the Russians then began feeding false information via the network, leading to several important German military defeats.

The NKVD demonstrated the same tactic when it turned its attention to the OSS and British intelligence operations that in

1945 were refocused eastward. In Poland, the NKVD reconstituted the Polish Home Army (actually wiped out earlier by the Russians), and convinced the British and Americans that a huge, anti-Communist network now existed. The large-scale deception, complete with bogus guerrilla units supposedly fighting the Russian troops, and radios broadcasting false information, lured London and Washington into sending agents and several hundred thousand dollars into Poland to support this fictitious network. (It was not finally closed down until 1952, when the CIA became suspicious and began asking awkward questions.)

Similarly, early American operations in Romania, Finland, and Hungary also were stymied by the NKVD, whose task was considerably eased by a common American habit: trying to do everything at once. In a hurry, the OSS men who after the war stayed in American intelligence were trying to build networks overnight. Among them were such later CIA luminaries as Allen Dulles, Richard Helms, and Frank Wisner, who learned the hard way that there was no shortcut to creating the kind of structure the NKVD needed several decades to accomplish. Wisner had run OSS's first major operation against the Russians, slipping into Bucharest, Romania, in 1944 with a team that snatched German intelligence records before the Russians arrived. But a year later, other OSS agents trying to create an anti-Communist organization to prevent a Communist takeover of the government were stymied by the NKVD—which discovered that the Americans had foolishly kept written records of all their human assets, making the task of arresting them that much more simple.

Operations against the Soviet Union itself were out of the question. There were no networks of assets to be recruited, for the Soviets had constructed an internal security apparatus that dwarfed the world's most notorious police state, Nazi Germany. The Nazis were never able to achieve the system the Russians put into place: an interlocking web of administrative procedures, police controls, passport restrictions, prohibited zones along borders, scarce transportation facilities to and within frontier zones, and strict document checks at airports, highways, and railroad crossing points. To American intelligence, the Soviet Union was a closed book.

But by the end of 1945, the full dimension of the new threat was easy enough to discern. In Eastern Europe, the Russian military presence stretched from the Baltic to the Black Sea; in its shadow, the new governments of Czechoslovakia, Romania, Hungary, and Bulgaria were struggling to survive in the face of relentless Communist pressure. In Western Europe, France and Italy were on the edge of civil war between Communists and non-Communists. In the Balkans, Greece was already in a civil war between those two ideologies; further east, Turkey and Iran were under strong Soviet pressure. In Asia, civil war had broken out in China, and the rest of the continent was in ferment, especially Indochina, where an independence movement dominated by a veteran Communist named Ho Chi Minh vowed to remove the French colonial regime.

All these developments were perceived as of one piece: the international Communist monolith, directed by Moscow. That monolith was now on the march everywhere—including the United States. Venona had demonstrated the depth of that threat, but for the vast majority of Americans who knew nothing of the code break, there was sufficient evidence for concern. The cases involving Klaus Fuchs, the Russian spy inside the Manhattan Project, and others, combined with the deepening chill of the Cold War, created a dramatic shift in American public opinion: the wartime ally had suddenly become the greatest enemy.

What resulted was a series of developments remarkably similar to the "Red Scare" of 1919 and the "fifth column" panic two decades later. Again, it took the form of a major interal security crisis, a tremendous burst of political energy turned inward, almost tearing the country apart. In the process, the Constitution suffered grave, but not irreparable, damage.

The series of events has been called many different things, usually "McCarthyism." But that is a misnomer, for the man who was most responsible for what happened was J. Edgar Hoover.

There were a number of anomalies in the career of Hoover, and among them was his attitude toward communism. From the very beginning of his career, he was a man clearly obsessed with that question; yet, for all his experience in dealing with it, he never seemed to quite grasp what the political phenomenon was all about.

One problem was that Hoover was focused almost exclusively on the domestic variety Communist, and throughout his life he never could understand why an American would subscribe to what he considered the most alien of all alien ideologies. He arrived at the conclusion that the American Communists were not really Americans at all; actually, they were "aliens," unthinking puppets of Moscow, blindly following orders. Thus, he spent most of the FBI's time divining the meaning behind the utterances and assorted political machinations within the American Communist Party, believing these provided important clues to Moscow's thinking. They did nothing of the kind, and led Hoover into some gross miscalculations—such as his assertion, in a 1945 intelligence report to Truman, that the purging of American Communist Party leader Earl Browder meant Stalin had been deposed, and that Soviet Foreign Minister Vyacheslav Molotov had taken over the government.

The onset of the Cold War in 1945 caused a pronounced new edge in Hoover's reports to the White House, which were now full of dire warnings of domestic Communists and the danger they represented to America. In Hoover's view—a virtual reprise of his view during the 1919 "Red Scare"—domestic Communists, armed with a "new militancy," were the "internal enemies" who would aid the Soviets during the approaching war between communism and capitalism in taking over the United States.

However, this was not the real internal threat. The real threat had been spelled out by a stuttering magazine writer named Whittaker Chambers in 1942, when he began telling the FBI about something only suspected: a vast underground Communist apparatus in the United States, run by the NKVD, that had infiltrated the government from top to bottom. Chambers himself had been a member of that apparatus, later broke with it, and was now revealing the depth of the apparatus's penetrations.

Some years later, Chambers's revelations—along with those of other defecting former members of the underground apparatus—would set off the great Rashomon dramas of the Cold War: prominent public officials, most notably Alger Hiss, accused of being Soviet spies. But in 1942, Hoover seemed barely interested in what Chambers had to say, probably because he sensed that the White House, firmly committed to helping Soviet Russia in the war, was in no political mood to hear anything about Soviet infiltration of the government. (Chambers had not yet mentioned the microfilms of purloined government documents he had hidden away, so for the moment, his allegations were totally unsupported by any other evidence.)

Whatever the reason, in 1945, Hoover suddenly found Chambers's revelations vitally important, and the FBI was reoriented toward uncovering the depth of the penetrations. One NKVD asset mentioned by Chambers and others was no less a personage than the Assistant Secretary of the Treasury, Harry Dexter White. Hoover cited the White case and other similarly shocking examples to Truman, but discovered that the President did not seem particularly alarmed. Indeed, in the case of White, Truman ignored Hoover's contention that the Treasury official was a Soviet spy, and named him to the International Monetary Fund.

Hoover was infuriated, and Truman's continued refusal to share his alarm over the "Communist menace" began to cause an estrangement between the two men. Truman had little use for Hoover's obsessions. Convinced that Truman was naïve about the Communist internal security threat, Hoover made a fateful decision, allying himself with the Republicans. In the 1946 congressional election campaign, the Republicans, sensing the public's alarm over communism, rode the issue for all it was worth, declaring that the election amounted to a choice between "Republicanism or communism." The campaign was accompanied by an FBI publicity blitz that concentrated on a number of undercover operatives inside the American Communist Party, FBI informants who supported Hoover's view that the party was simply a tool of Moscow—and a grave internal security threat.

Full-scale hysteria was underway. Too late, Truman realized his political opponents had taken over the nation's hottest political issue. In an attempt to retake that ground, Truman in early 1947 announced a new "loyalty program," under which all government employees would be investigated; those found to be Communists would be fired. The program set off a witch hunt: within a few years nearly fifteen hundred employees of the State Department were fired.† The loyalty of physicist J. Robert Oppenheimer, the scientific leader of the atomic bomb project, was

† Including, unfortunately, nearly all the department's China experts—primarily because they had criticized Chinese leader Chiang Kai-shek and thus "lost China" to the Communists under Mao Tse-tung. Their expertise would be sorely missed a few years later, when there were no experts around to understand the signals from China warning that they were about to intervene in the

questioned (he was ultimately denied a security clearance), largely on the grounds that he had doubted the wisdom of proceeding with the H-bomb project. Oppenheimer and many others were prominent victims, but the loyalty program's reach extended everywhere, even to an archery club in California, whose members were required to prove their loyalty to the United States before being permitted the privilege of using a bow and arrow.

Hoover wanted "all subversive or disloyal persons" to be removed from the government. The FBI would have the major role in such a purge, Hoover insisted; those accused would not be permitted to confront their accusers, and the FBI files which contained charges (however unsubstantiated) against anyone would not be revealed. Truman publicly called such clearly unconstitutional procedures a "witch hunt," a characterization that further widened the rift between himself and Hoover.

As a demonstration of just how wide that rift had become, Hoover made a highly publicized appearance before the House Un-American Activities Committee in 1947, during which he propounded a view of communism and the American democratic system that was nothing short of extraordinary. Among other things, Hoover insisted that domestic Communists were the greatest threat to the United States, and that their menace came not from what they did, but what they *actually* were saying. Hoover explained that Communists adopted an "Aesopian language," in which their real revolutionary message was cunningly concealed. Only an expert—by which, obviously, Hoover meant himself—could decode that language. Further, Hoover said, there was now "one Communist for every 1,814 persons in the United States." Those who doubted such statistics or who openly questioned just how serious this domestic Communist was (Hoover described these people as "liberals and progressives") had been "hoodwinked" by the Communists.

Hoover began covertly slipping information to the committee, and its quasi–Star Chamber proceedings became the center of a furious political controversy. Truman had sought to dampen the uproar by calling the search for Communists hiding everywhere "red herrings," an unfortunate phrase that only made things

---

Korean War. The missed signals led to one of the worst military defeats in American history.

worse. Truman was in serious political trouble, and the American intervention in Korea didn't help; the plain truth was that a full-fledged public panic was underway, and the President could not think of anything to dampen it.

The issue was largely out of his hands. Hoover and the House Un-American Activities Committee had set the agenda, and were busy riding the issue for all it was worth. Hoover saw it as the perfect opportunity to achieve a long dream, destroying the American Communist movement by having it declared illegal. In 1940, Congress had approved the Smith Act, which made it illegal to advocate the overthrow of the government by force or to organize or belong to a group with such a goal. The Justice Department had always been uneasy with the law's constitutional problems. But Hoover, riding the crest of his public popularity, convinced the department to dust off the largely unused statute, and in 1948 eleven top leaders of the American Communist Party were convicted—largely on the testimony of undercover informants. (Later, over 100 other Communists were prosecuted.)‡

What it all amounted to was a pile of combustible political tinderwood, requiring only a match to set it off. That came in February 1950, when the junior senator from Wisconsin, Joseph McCarthy, made a speech in Wheeling, West Virginia, in which he claimed he had the names of 205 Communists in the State Department, all of them protected by Truman and his administration. He unleashed a firestorm.

The events of the next several years, popularly known as "McCarthyism," represent a low point in the cycle of occasional American obsessions with internal security. Truman himself—along with many others—was consumed in its fires, and out of office, sadly read the accounts of J. Edgar Hoover telling a Senate committee that the country was engaged in a battle to the death against "the godless forces of communism," and that those who had failed to demonstrate sufficient ardor for the battle—he clearly hinted that Truman was one of them—were helping Moscow. Hoover went on to impugn Truman's loyalty, and stopped

‡ Sixteen years later, the Smith Act died when federal courts, reviewing the convictions, ruled that no one could be convicted for simply talking about revolution; there would have to be *proof* of a concrete plan to undertake a violent revolutionary act. That proof never existed; the American Communists were great talkers, but not much in the way of doers.

just short of calling the former President of the United States a Communist.

No more ironic event occurred during this postwar American internal security convulsion, for although Hoover did not know it, Harry S Truman was the man who set in motion an even greater conflagration, far beyond America's borders.

It was one whose effects were much more long-lasting—and much more dangerous to American democracy.

SIX

The Nine Lives
of the Yellow Cat

AS USUAL, there were no security guards. Generalissimo Rafael L. Trujillo Molina—*Benefactor de la Patria y Padre de la Patria Nueva, el Supremo* of the Dominican Republic, commander in chief of the Dominican armed forces, owner of nearly 60 percent of his country's economic wealth—believed that his people really loved him.

So when his distinctive 1957 Chevrolet with the two large silver horns rushed along the deserted country road just outside Ciudad Trujillo the night of May 30, 1961, Trujillo was accompanied only by his chauffeur. The dictator sat relaxed in the rear seat, idly gazing out the window.

He did not hear another Chevrolet pull up behind his own. The shotgun blast blew out the rear window and smashed into Trujillo's back. "Fuck!" he shouted. "I've been hit!" Ordering the chauffeur to stop the car, the wounded Trujillo got out, drawing a pistol. He stood in the car's headlights as four assassins closed in on him. Before he could get off a shot, they riddled the gaudy green uniform and the chestful of equally gaudy medals with submachine guns. One of the killers rushed to the body and applied the *coup de grâce* with a pistol shot into the generalissimo's mouth. Then he and the three other assassins picked up the body, dumped it into the trunk of their car, and roared off.

It was no coincidence that Arturo Espaillat was the first person to arrive on the scene just minutes after the assassination. Espaillat, one of the top officials in SIM, Trujillo's intelligence service, was perfectly aware that Trujillo was to be murdered that very night at that particular spot, for Espaillat had done a great deal to set up the assassination. He had taken this step not for the reasons the assassins did—to rid the country of an infamous dictator and create a "new Dominican Republic"—but to carry out the wishes of his most important client, the United States Central Intelligence Agency.

How and why the CIA came to be involved with a man like Espaillat—and, more importantly, how it came to be involved in the murder of the head of a sovereign state with whom the United States was at peace—represented a very disturbing development in the history of American intelligence.

Somewhere, deep in the bowels of the CIA's records, there was a thick file on Espaillat. He was listed under "asset," agency argot for people who agree secretly to provide help to the agency, usually for pay. Espaillat was among several hundred such assets who had been recruited in Latin America, and to a certain extent, he fit the standard pattern of most of them.

Almost universally, they were officials of assorted secret police agencies who didn't mind playing both sides of the street. As human beings, they ranged from the relatively benign to the truly horrendous—such as Colonel René Chacón, head of the secret police in El Salvador during the 1960s, whose favorite activity was torturing the ruling regime's political opponents by feeding them, piece by piece, into a meat grinder; the result was fed to his dogs. Espaillat was somewhere in the middle: he had been a secret policeman for Trujillo for nearly sixteen years by 1961, but unlike other of his contemporaries in the dark world of Latin American secret police operations, he was not brutal, and did not like to torture people.

He was, as he preferred to describe himself, an "operator," a slender man of almost feline grace who delighted in intricate plots, double crosses, and triple crosses. Smooth and deadly, he had been involved in the murky espionage world of a half-dozen nations on behalf of the generalissimo, and took delight in his nickname of "the yellow cat" (a tribute to his close escapes in several operations and to his ability to survive the intricate palace intrigues around Trujillo). His supreme loyalty was to the game; despite Trujillo's fondness for him, Espaillat regarded *el Jefe* as simply a client, to be betrayed if the need arose.

That need arose, surprisingly, in the United States, which since 1930 had been propping up Trujillo as a rabidly pro-American bulwark in the Caribbean. In the words of President Roosevelt's Secretary of State, Cordell Hull, on the subject of Latin American dictators, "He's a sonofabitch, but he's *our* sonofabitch."

But after nearly thirty years in power, Trujillo was becoming a liability in American eyes. Increasingly erratic as the old autocrat approached the third decade of his dictatorship, Trujillo in 1956 had a falling-out with fellow dictator Fulgencia Batista of Cuba. Trujillo actually came to believe that Batista, of all people, was a Communist, and provided training sites and a launching pad for one of Fidel Castro's early, failed forays into Cuba. Trujillo also began picking fights with other Latin American leaders, and by 1959 he had become a real problem.*

Castro's revolution in 1959 caused deep alarm in the American government, which believed that Trujillo's Dominican Republic was the next domino to fall to the outbreak of Latin American revolution. Sometime in early 1960, President Eisenhower decided that Trujillo would have to go.

Whether Eisenhower ordered (or agreed to) an assassination of Trujillo is not known. What is known is that in June 1960, following extensive contacts with the anti-Trujillo underground, the

---

* Trujillo was also accused of a crime he may not have committed. In 1956, anti-Trujillo activist Jesús de Galindez, head of the Spanish Basque exile movement in North America, was kidnapped off a New York City street and disappeared. Trujillo was openly accused of ordering the kidnapping, but recent evidence suggests that Galindez may have met an untimely end for other reasons: a CIA asset, he had been entrusted with $1 million in CIA cash for the Basque movement—which eventually saw only half the money. Galindez was suspected of stealing the other half. Who was responsible for his death remains a mystery.

CIA began providing arms. Some of them were smuggled into the country inside shipments of groceries ordered by an important CIA asset in the Dominican Republic, the American owner of the Wimpy's Supermarket. Another shipment came via the American diplomatic pouch.

There could not have been any question in anyone's mind what the anti-Trujillo forces planned to do with these weapons; right from the beginning, they made it clear they intended to kill Trujillo, the only way, in their view, of checkmating the *Trujillista* forces inside the military and secret police who ran the country and were fanatically loyal to *el Jefe*.

Espaillat, the "yellow cat," was to play a key role in the plot to get rid of Trujillo. First, he was to divert the secret police away from the high-ranking military officers who had agreed to join the plot (one of them was to head up an interim government after Trujillo's demise). Second, after ensuring that Trujillo really was dead, he was to shepherd the generalissimo's successor through the first hours of the difficult task of suppressing any counterreaction. The CIA did not know that its important asset had no intention of doing anything of the kind; the cat, as usual, was playing his own game.

By April 1961, everything seemed to be ready. But during that month, there was disaster at the Bay of Pigs, and a suddenly cautious CIA—apparently at President Kennedy's direction—ordered the plotters to hold off on any assassination. Things were complicated enough in the Caribbean without a revolution in the Dominican Republic.

But the anti-Trujillo forces had waited long enough, and now they refused to halt the assassination. Using the CIA-provided weapons, they murdered *el Jefe* the following month. A panicked CIA ordered its men to burn all records, then flee the country to avoid any connection to the slaying and the convulsions of the revolution to come.

But there was no revolution. Immediately following Trujillo's assassination, Espaillat took the Dominican Army's top general, Pupo Roman, for a ride in his car to "protect" him—at the very moment the anti-Trujillo plotters needed the general the most. Roman was supposed to declare martial law and take control of the government; when the plotters could not find him, they stood around, uncertain what to do. Precious time was lost. The *Truji-*

llistas rallied, Ramfis (the generalissimo's son) returned from Paris to take over the reins of power, and within a short period the plotters were in big trouble. They were rounded up by the hundreds; many were hideously tortured to death in a nationwide bloodbath.†

Meanwhile, many miles away, the CIA, in a postmortem on the Dominican operation, pronounced it a "success." Looking back it is difficult to imagine what the agency could have meant; the operation to dispose of Trujillo set off his supporters' bloody purge, followed by years of unrest. (An actual civil war did break out in that unfortunate land a few years later, and U.S. troops were sent into the country in 1965 to intervene in a struggle that threatened to engulf the entire region.)

Still, by the standards of 1961, the CIA may have been justified in calling the Dominican mess a "success." The definition was an operational one, and demonstrated the extent to which the agency had become dominated by an operations ethos. But there was something even more disturbing at work: how did an agency, created to collect intelligence, wind up in the business of shipping arms, involvement in assassinations of world leaders, and deciding who would rule what country?

The reason was a serious mistake made thirteen years before, a mistake whose full implications were lost in the first great battles of the Cold War.

It began with an odd question.

One morning in January 1948, Secretary of Defense James V. Forrestal asked Director of Central Intelligence Roscoe Hillenkoetter: what was to stop the CIA from spending money covertly to help defeat the Italian Communist Party in the upcoming Italian elections? Hillenkoetter was uncertain; it didn't sound like anything within the new CIA's mandate. He sent a query note to the agency's general counsel, Lawrence Houston.

Houston's reply was clear. He could find no specific authority in the National Security Act to undertake covert action. That was

† Espaillat did not escape unscathed. When he discovered that the "yellow cat" was trying to take over the government himself, Ramfis Trujillo threw Espaillat in jail, had him tortured for a month, then ordered him out of the country. Espaillat had an unhappy exile: after suffering crippling injuries in an automobile accident, he shot himself in 1969.

not the answer Hillenkoetter wanted to hear, for at the moment, the government was in something of a panic. The problem was Europe, where the military menace of the Soviet Union was accompanied by a sudden resurgence by the Communist parties in Western Europe. The first threat could be deterred by the American monopoly on the atomic bomb, but there was no real weapon at hand, seemingly, for the second. That threat was invisible, a silent war for men's minds, the relentless quest for power led by men whose skills had been honed in lifetimes of underground struggle.

At hand was the terrifying example of Eastern Europe. The Soviets needed only fourteen days to install a Communist government in its occupation zone in Germany. A Communist minority in Hungary was already in the process of seizing control of the government, and a similar coup was underway in Romania. In Czechoslovakia, the Communists and anti-Communists were locked in a struggle for control of that nation's government (in March 1948, Jan Masaryk, popular leader of the anti-Communists, was found dead after falling—or, more likely, being pushed—from a five-story window). To the alarm of Washington, the Communist minority then staged a parliamentary *Putsch* and seized control of the government.

The course of events in Czechoslovakia, especially, underscored the Communist political threat in France and Italy, where Western Europe's two largest Communist parties were extremely active. The most immediate threat was in Italy, where parliamentary elections were scheduled to be held in April 1948, postwar Italy's first national election; there was a real possibility that the Communists would win and take control of the government.

In the view of Forrestal and Truman, the only way to forestall that possibility was to strengthen the non-Communist political organizations. But such aid would have to be rendered clandestinely, for any hint that the Americans were intervening in Italian politics would backfire. Further, neither Forrestal nor Truman wanted to submit the plan to Congress; that would not only take too long, it would also possibly ignite a foreign policy debate about just what the Administration was doing in Europe.

Under increasing White House pressure, CIA Director Hillenkoetter sent a second note to Houston, asking his in-house attorney whether there were "any further considerations" on the subject of the CIA undertaking covert activities. Houston picked up on the inner meaning, and promptly issued a revised opinion, concluding that if the President authorized a covert act and Congress paid for it, then the CIA could be deemed to be within the legal restrictions of its charter. Immediately, a large-scale covert political operation was cranked up for the Italian election, with $10 million budgeted to bankroll anti-Communist politicians, "black propaganda" against the Communist Party candidates, bribes to election officials to ensure that the results in certain election districts came out the right way, enlistment of key Vatican officials to invoke higher authority against Communist candidates, creation of front groups—and even an operation that enlisted Italian-Americans to write to relatives back home, pleading with them to vote against the Communists. The operation, which was finally to spend another $20 million, was a brilliant success. The Christian Democrats, the main centrist opposition to the Communists, won 307 of the 574 seats at stake.

So Italy had been saved from communism, but at what cost? The CIA had taken the first step on a very slippery slope: Congress knew nothing of this foreign policy adventure, the American ambassador to Italy was not informed, and the State Department, although it had hints something strange was going on, did not know. And, most significantly of all, the American people did not know.‡

The very success of the operation lured Truman further; the CIA had demonstrated an ability to block the Soviet political offensive in Europe, so it was but a short step from there to the idea of a counteroffensive against the Soviet Union itself. The result was the creation of a CIA division that really wasn't a CIA division. The new organization was given the misleadingly bland name of Office of Policy Coordination. OPC represented an odd

‡ Some years later, Truman was to claim in a newspaper interview that the CIA had "overstepped its mandate" in carrying out covert political operations. That brought a sharp rejoinder from former Director of Central Intelligence Allen Dulles, who pointedly reminded Truman in a six-page letter that it was President Truman who had insisted on the operation in Italy—and a number of others in the postwar years. Later, the two old cold warriors had a private meeting at Truman's home, during which Truman admitted that Dulles was right.

bureaucratic structure: funded by the CIA, it was attached to the State Department.

Which meant, of course, OPC was largely free of any oversight, since the organization had no real higher authority—except for the President. In fact, OPC became the White House's agency for action, equipped with an overly broad mandate that allowed it to conduct *any* covert operation that would have a deleterious effect, however vague, on the Soviet Union. The mandate, contained in the National Security Council order creating OPC, authorized OPC to conduct "political warfare, psychological warfare, economic warfare, and preventive direct action." In 1950, another National Security Council order authorized OPC to "reduce and eventually eliminate dominant Soviet infuence in the satellite states." In other words, a secret war was to be conducted against the Soviet Union without bothering to seek a declaration of war from Congress.

The man picked to head OPC, Frank Wisner, was a man totally convinced that no barrier, constitutional or otherwise, should exist when it came to a battle with the Soviet enemy. An ex-Establishment lawyer who had served in the OSS—largely in the Balkans—Wisner was bored with civilian life after the war. He leaped at the postwar chance to get back into the fray; a classic example of the OSS heritage of action, Wisner recruited similarly minded men. Together they built what Wisner was later to call his "mighty Wurlitzer": underground guerrilla armies in the Baltics; Russian exiles parachuted into their motherland to form armies-in-being for the inevitable Soviet-American world war; a huge propaganda apparatus beamed eastward (notably Radio Free Europe); covert funding of anti-Communist political leaders; formation of CIA-funded student groups and other such organizations; and a wide range of similar activities designed to put the Soviets on the defensive.

OPC's growth was remarkable. In 1949, Wisner had a staff of 302 people and a budget of $4.7 million; only four years later, he had a staff of more than 3,000 and the budget had reached $82 million. There were virtually no restraints on OPC's activities, and in an organization dominated by action—"Don't just sit there; *do* something," some of its agents would joke—that meant action was really the sole determinant. It was an atmosphere guaranteed to cause trouble, best illustrated by Wisner's plan in 1950 to form a "second front" against mainland China to relieve pressure on American troops in Korea.

The plan called for the signing up of several thousand Chinese Nationalist soldiers as American mercenaries. They were taken by OPC to an old OSS stomping ground, northern Burma, which was to be used as a launching pad for raids into southern China— the theory being that the Chinese, forced to divert troops from Korea to snuff out the threat, would be rendered militarily weaker in Korea.

The idea was poorly conceived. In the first place, Korea and southern China are several thousand miles apart, so what happened in one area would hardly affect the other. Second, the Nationalist raids would amount to pinpricks, at best, and would not serve to divert any Chinese troops, much less those fighting in Korea. Even more serious were the political implications of the operation. Truman had already publicly vowed he would not widen the war in Korea, and vetoed the idea of "unleashing" Chinese Nationalist forces; sending Nationalist troops into southern China (too noisy an operation to keep secret) would undercut the President's own public vows. Then there was the matter of Burma's neutrality being violated.

Characteristically, OPC had not thought through these implications, nor had it asked a simple question: did the Nationalists have the military capabilities to carry out such raids? It turned out that they did not: the Nationalists instead settled into a comfortable existence in northern Burma, spending most of their time in the profitable pursuit of opium-growing. (Free-lance pilots working for OPC agreed to fly the opium to Thailand, the real beginning of the "golden triangle," a narcotics problem that persists to this day.)

There were even more serious reverberations from OPC operations in Europe, where Wisner's organization had the unfortunate habit of recruiting *anyone*, regardless of background, if he demonstrated sufficient anti-Communist zeal. As a result, there was a long roster of Nazis enrolled in OPC operations, including Otto Albrecht von Bolschwing, a former aide to Adolf Eichmann; Franz Albert Six, who directed the killings of Soviet commissars in German-occupied Russia; and Friedrich Buchardt, who commanded an infamous SS *Einsatzgruppe* (killing squad) that slaughtered the Jews of Smolensk. These Nazis, enlisted for their presumed expertise on Eastern Europe, had their records expunged and were protected from war crimes prosecutions.*

Such recruitments demonstrated a severe moral myopia, for the United States and its allies in 1943 had jointly pledged to bring all Nazi war criminals to justice after the war. How such men were to provide the cutting edge of OPC's offensive against the Soviet Union remains somewhat obscure. Their expertise was strictly concerned with genocide—against Jews, mostly—and their recruitment left OPC with a Nazi taint. The Nazi war criminals could hardly have served as much inspiration to oppressed Eastern Europeans, whose memories of Nazi atrocities were still quite fresh.

The Eastern Europeans were not impressed by a rainbow of other OPC front organizations that attempted to inspire the loyalty of oppressed peoples, including the Kalmuk-Tibetan Defense Society, and the Free Ukrainian Committee of Byzantine Rite. Even less impressive were OPC-recruited groups of pro-Nazi Russian collaborators who had cooperated with the Nazi invaders during the war; whatever Russians might have thought of Stalin, they retained a deep hatred for the collaborators who had participated in the killings of so many of their own people.

To make matters worse, the NKVD had penetrated all the assorted exile groups from which Wisner's OPC drew most of its assets. Pressured to volunteer for missions inside the Soviet Union and receive dispensation for war crimes, many of the exiles received a modicum of training, then were parachuted in to a certain fate at the hands of the NKVD. Similar operations in Albania and Romania ended in even greater disasters.

Yet, all the while, Wisner's propaganda radios at Radio Free Europe and Radio Liberty continued broadcasting eastward the appeals to resist and throw off the Soviet yoke. Interspersed with "coded messages" to alleged networks of anti-Soviet partisans operating behind the Iron Curtain, the broadcasts vowed that the United States would aid such uprisings. But Wisner was speaking

* The OPC recruitments of Nazis ran in tandem with a similar program of U.S. Army Intelligence, whose recruits included Klaus Barbie of the Gestapo, known as the "Butcher of Lyons." Army agents in 1951 smuggled Barbie to sanctuary in South America to keep him from French war crimes prosecutors. Barbie many years later was extradited to France, convicted of war crimes, and is now serving a life sentence.

for himself; not only hadn't he received any authority to make his own foreign policy, there was never any intention by the United States to risk World War III by militarily supporting an uprising anyplace in Eastern Europe. However, the East Europeans who took the broadcasts seriously did not know that. Some of them bravely became involved in a Wisner brainstorm, code-named Operation Red Cap, in which arms were stockpiled at secret locations, waiting to be used to conduct guerrilla operations against Soviet troops in the event of a Soviet-American war. That war did not break out, but when East Europeans revolted—East Berlin in 1953, Poznan and Hungary in 1956—they discovered, tragically, that the much-heralded promise of U.S. aid was only propaganda hot air.

The smashing of the East European revolts was the end of OPC and Wisner;† clearly, the great secret offensive against the Soviet Union had failed. True, Soviet expansionism had been halted in Western Europe, but the Iron Curtain was stronger than ever, and there remained other Soviet threats elsewhere in the world. How those threats were interpreted was a matter of some controversy, for even the slightest political tremor could be (and often was) deduced as part of a Soviet master plan for world conquest.

Whatever the interpretation, it was clear that the American struggle with the perceived threats would be largely covert, conducted by the CIA. Indeed, by 1953 the CIA was much more than just an intelligence agency, since the bulk of its manpower and budget were preoccupied with covert political operations. To be sure, the agency ran conventional intelligence-gathering operations, but the record was decidedly mixed. Most notably, the agency's inability to anticipate the North Korean invasion of South Korea brought back disturbing memories of Pearl Harbor. With a hot war in progress, Admiral Hillenkoetter was shipped off to sea duty in Korea.

His replacement was the extremely intense General Walter Bedell Smith, Eisenhower's World War II chief of staff, nicknamed

† Following the failure of OPC, Wisner's mind snapped. Believing he was pursued by Soviet agents, he suffered two nervous breakdowns, and committed suicide in 1965. James V. Forrestal, the real progenitor of OPC and the secret offensive against the Russians, was also pursued by demons; he committed suicide in 1949 while he was hospitalized after running through the streets shouting, "The Russians are coming! The Russians are coming!"

"Beetle." Smith's short fuse was due to the near constant pain in which he lived; half of his stomach had been cut away because of severe ulcers. Despite his knowledge of the mixed appraisals of the OSS espionage operations during the war, Smith surprisingly turned out to be a pronounced enthusiast of covert political operations. One reason was the experiences he underwent before taking the intelligence post: a three-year stint as U.S. Ambassador to Moscow during the early period of the Cold War. As a result, Smith developed an abiding dislike for Stalin and other Soviet government officials—along with a deep concern for what these men would do if they were able to achieve their dream of world domination. Smith became convinced that every possible measure must be used to stop what he perceived as a very dangerous group of men. One of his first measures was to merge OPC into the CIA.

Smith's enthusiasm for covert action against the Soviet Union did nothing to address the increasing unhappiness at the White House over the CIA's performance in the intelligence area, and a year before Smith took the DCI job, there were continuing rumbles about the necessity for a "shakeup" at the agency. In an attempt to discover just what needed shaking up, an outside review panel by men experienced in intelligence (but who were not employees of any intelligence agency) was appointed by the National Security Council to examine the CIA from top to bottom.

One of the group's members—and its most active—was Allen Dulles, the ex-OSS officer who had become a prominent lawyer. But Dulles, among the great romanticizers of espionage, had never quite lost his taste for intelligence; as a private citizen, he kept in close touch with ex-OSS colleagues who had enlisted in the CIA. In 1951 he decided to practice what he preached, giving up his law career to join the CIA as one of its deputy directors.

Although the 1949 review of the CIA's problems concentrated on intelligence collection, Dulles as CIA official plainly cared most for covert action. He was barely interested in intelligence analyses and other such essentials of the espionage business, much preferring to spend hours in his office discussing details of covert political operations, occasionally breaking out in his famous Santa Claus-like laugh. An avuncular figure, Dulles most often gave the impression of a kindly old uncle.

But he had a hard edge, and it concerned his view of the world. Like many other former OSS officers, he was fixated on the idea that World War II happened largely because the democracies had failed to take action early enough against the threat of Hitler and fascism. That would never happen again; Dulles was convinced that the Soviet Union and the United States were locked in a climactic struggle that could not be decided militarily because of the mutually destructive power of nuclear weapons. Therefore, the outcome would be decided by clandestine means, with the entire world the battlefield. Whichever side won the battle for political domination would rule the world.

It was a view shared by his brother, John Foster Dulles, and, more significantly, President Dwight Eisenhower. When Eisenhower took office early in 1953, "Beetle" Smith was granted his wish to become a State Department official, John Foster Dulles was appointed Secretary of State, and Allen Dulles became Director of Central Intelligence.

It was a cozy triumvirate. Three men, of remarkably similar worldview, now controlled the wellsprings of foreign policy. While none of them believed there was any hope of a "rollback" of the Soviet "empire" as envisioned by Wisner and the OPC, they were convinced the United States could keep Moscow contained within the borders of its military and political conquests. And that containment idea contained one important piece of strategy: any Communist virus which escaped the isolation ward would be firmly stamped out, primarily via clandestine means. The CIA would be the chief instrument, confirming the agency's main role as a covert political action organization.

Underlying all this was a broad public consensus, without many questions as to means. "The day of sleep-walking is over," the New York *Times* proclaimed editorially as Eisenhower took office, as though the United States had been in a deep slumber the previous decade. ". . . The policy of vigilance replacing the Pollyanna diplomacy is evident." The *Times* meant public diplomacy, of course, for it knew nothing of the huge clockwork of CIA covert political operations.‡ Neither did Congress and the American people—nor did they know that the new Administration was about to dispatch the CIA on two covert foreign policy adven-

‡ Nor did the KGB (the renamed NKVD). In 1948, when Italian Communists complained to Moscow that U.S. intelligence agents were pouring millions into the Italian election campaign, the KGB initially dismissed the reports as alarmist nonsense.

tures that ended in brilliant successes. But the triumphs carried the seeds of later disaster.

The citizens of Teheran, accustomed to noisy street demonstrations in the politically turbulent nation of Iran, had never seen anything quite like it. This was a demonstration to end all demonstrations: thousands of angry people, carrying banners and placards, surged through the streets on a hot August morning in 1953, waving their fists, shouting slogans against the man who had apparently infuriated them: Premier Mohammed Mossadegh.

The shouts of "Down with Mossadegh!" seemed odd; only a year before, Mossadegh was an immensely popular figure, having led the Iranian drive to nationalize the Anglo-Iranian Oil Company, which had a stranglehold on Iran's sole natural resource. In fact, he was so popular, he had openly defied the country's young ruler, the Shah Mohammad Reza Pahlavi, forcing the Shah into political exile.

Despite their vehemence, the crowds now demanding Mossadegh's ouster could have cared less about who ruled the country. They were hired hands recruited from all over the city and paid handsome sums for the simple task of marching through the streets, holding placards and banners prepared by others. They were under firm instructions to shout "Down with Mossadegh!" the loudest whenever they were in range of a news camera. The "demonstrators" represented the final stage of a British-American plan to depose Mossadegh, return the Shah from exile, and establish a pro-Western regime in Iran.

The acute sensitivity to events in Iran stemmed from geopolitics: Iran not only had vast reserves of oil, it shared a long border with the Soviet Union. A recurring American nightmare that persists to this day concerned a Soviet takeover of Iran, which would lead to access to the Persian Gulf, and warm water ports for the Soviet Navy. Mossadegh ignited that concern in 1952, when he accepted the support of Tudeh, the Iranian Communist Party (and perceived by the United States as a stalking horse for Moscow's master plan to penetrate into the Persian Gulf).

Mossadegh's nationalization of the British-owned Anglo-Iranian Oil Company didn't help matters, and when he announced that Iran would sell oil to the Soviet Union, his fate was sealed. It was jointly decided in Washington and London that Mossadegh would have to go.

The plan was to undercut Mossadegh's popular support by fomenting opposition within the armed forces (which did not like him) and certain segments of Iranian society by portraying him as a pro-Communist tool of the Moscow-controlled Tudeh. Code-named Ajax, it was a joint operation of British and American intelligence. Mossadegh's government, fairly shaky to begin with, soon found itself battered by a political opposition that suddenly seemed to have acquired large sums of money. On August 19, 1953, following a massive street demonstration by irate Iranian citizens (in fact mobs of people paid by the CIA), Mossadegh's government fell. Three days later, the Shah returned from exile and retook the reins of government.

And just like that, Iran and its oil fields were made safe for the West. This momentous change, which was to have significant impact on the entire Persian Gulf region for decades to come, had been accomplished with astonishing ease. It required the services of only a dozen CIA agents, and approximately $10 million—a trifle, considering the results.

The entire operation also required something else: secrecy. From the first moment of its conception, Ajax was decided by a small group of people in the deepest secrecy, all of whom agreed that Mossadegh represented a threat.

The cheap and quick success of Ajax blinded Eisenhower and the Dulles brothers—the men who made the decision to intervene —to the very real dilemmas such operations were creating. Chief among them was the intelligence on which the operations were based. It had been collected by the CIA, the very agency that would carry out the covert political action. In other words, the agency was the arbiter of its own intelligence.

Also obscured were some fundamental questions about the role of such operations in the context of American democracy: Should American foreign policy be conducted clandestinely with neither Congress nor the American people aware? Who should exercise control over covert operations? Should the United States even conduct such operations in the first place? What kind of commitments were being created as a result?

These questions were not addressed, the prime reason being that the Eisenhower administration believed it had a mandate for an aggressive foreign policy and a public consensus to contain the Soviet Union. Covert operations required quick decisions, speed, and complete secrecy, none of which could have been achieved in a congressional debate.

And besides, the covert political operations were working. Iran was one good example. Guatemala was another.

Although they were two very different countries on opposite sides of the world with very different cultures, there were strong similarities between the political situations of both countries: Iran and Guatemala were politically unstable, had a large foreign economic entity in control of their greatest natural resources (in the case of Guatemala, the United Fruit Company), and were led by men whose politics made the United States very nervous.

The man who made the Americans nervous in Guatemala was Jacobo Arbenz Guzmán. Arbenz, an ex-army officer, was suspected of Communist connections prior to his election as president of the country in 1950. Subsequently, he brought Guatemala's tiny Communist Party into his ruling coalition, a move that caused alarm bells to ring in Washington. Early in 1953, newly elected President Eisenhower dispatched his brother Milton, an extremely conservative anti-Communist, to Guatemala on a fact-finding tour. Milton returned to tell his brother, "One nation has succumbed to Communist infiltration," and he went on to say that "timely action was desirable to prevent communism from spreading seriously beyond Guatemala."

Translated, that meant Arbenz would have to go. Accordingly, the CIA was once again cranked up to accomplish the task. As in Iran, the task proved to be almost a cakewalk. By early 1954, the CIA had created an anti-Arbenz opposition centered around the figure of Guatemalan Army Colonel Carlos Castillo Armas, who was living in exile in Honduras. Gathered around him was a motley force of 150 other exiles and mercenaries whom the CIA proclaimed to be a "government in exile," complete with its own CIA-operated radio station.* Meanwhile, the Guatemalan armed forces' loyalty to Arbenz was undermined with cash bribes and "evidence" that he was a secret Communist, along with promises

* The radio operation was under the direction of a CIA agent named E. Howard Hunt, later to achieve dubious fame in the Watergate scandal.

that the American arms embargo—which had been in effect since 1948, when the U.S. first became concerned about the drift of Guatemalan politics—would be lifted, once Arbenz was gone.

PB/Success, the CIA code name for the operation, switched into high gear in March 1953, when Arbenz made a bad mistake: he sought to evade the American embargo by asking the Soviet Union to provide arms. The CIA later claimed to have evidence that a Czechoslovakian ship actually delivered some arms, but whether such a delivery actually took place remains questionable. In any event, on June 18, 1954, Castillo Armas's men "invaded" Guatemala (actually, they simply walked across the border), preceded by air strikes carried out by CIA-provided P-47 fighter planes flown by mercenary pilots. The Guatemalan army sat on its hands, Arbenz was deposed, and there was a new government of Guatemala.

It was that simple. With the services of two dozen CIA men, a modest outlay of somewhere around $15 million, and a few old World War II planes, the CIA had managed to overthrow a government without major bloodshed.† The agency had even managed to hush up a potentially serious "flap" that resulted when one of the CIA planes sank a merchant ship thought to be carrying Soviet arms. Unfortunately, the ship was actually a British vessel carrying a load of cotton. The infuriated British were mollified with a cash payment of $1 million, plus generous compensation for the crew.

CIA agents involved in the operation, including a young agent named David Atlee Phillips (later the head of the agency's Latin American operations), basked in the glow of Eisenhower's admiration and gratitude. Eisenhower gathered many of the CIA men together at the White House for a briefing for senior government officials, a meeting that had to be moved to the East Room because there were so many participants.

Turning to one of the CIA agents involved in the military side of PB/Success, Eisenhower asked, "How many men did you lose?"

Informed that only one man—lost during a training accident

† Arbenz and members of his government fled the country. Among Arbenz's departing entourage was a young economic adviser, Che Guevara.

on a mountain trail—had died, Eisenhower was astounded. "Well, that's just dandy," he said.

Perhaps so, but it was a judgment that many Guatemalans, discovering that another country had decided what kind of government they should have, might have questioned. So might have the people of the Congo, subject of an even more extensive CIA covert operation to determine their political future.

The former Belgian Congo, which had the misfortune to be the site of some of the world's richest mineral deposits—including high-grade uranium—in 1960 was the target of every major and minor world power seeking to dominate the newly independent country. The United States was directly involved, and was keeping an eye on a charismatic and leftist Congolese politician named Patrice Lumumba. In the May 1960 parliamentary elections, Lumumba and his party won a plurality.

Things became complicated when Moise Tshombe, tribal leader in Katanga province, seceded. Belgian and United Nations troops were sent to stabilize the situation, while Lumumba committed a serious political error: he asked the Soviet Union to "watch the situation" in Katanga, and "send help" if the revolt did not end.

The CIA station in the Congo, run by chief of station Lawrence Devlin, now perceived Lumumba as a Soviet stalking horse in Africa. By August 1960, Devlin was cabling headquarters: "Embassy and [CIA] station believe Congo experiencing classic Communist takeover government."

Devlin's frantic reports of Soviet subversion via Lumumba led, finally, to a decision by Eisenhower that Lumumba must be overthrown. A CIA-arranged coup took place only a month later, but Lumumba, a highly popular politician, was still loose and threatening to form a new government.

The CIA at this point took a dangerous step, one that went far beyond anything it had done before: the agency planned to kill Lumumba, the easiest and most convenient way of disposing of a nettlesome problem. Devlin himself was involved, first trying to poison Lumumba by having an agent slip a toxin into the Congolese leader's toothpaste. Devlin, who knew little about Africa, was unaware that Africans do not use toothpaste, and instead clean their teeth with a "chew stick," a piece of soft aromatic wood. Next, Devlin asked CIA headquarters for a shipment of high-powered rifles with telescopic sights. Before they could be used, Tshombe's soldiers solved the problem by capturing Lumumba in November, later beating him to death.

Again, the Congo was listed as another CIA "success," but a review of just how far the agency had come at this point would have inspired alarm. Its Clandestine Service, the division responsible for covert operations, as early as 1952 was already swallowing up 74 percent of the agency's budget, and about 60 percent of all CIA personnel; the trend since then had been steadily upward. Dominated by "action men," the CIA existed in an atmosphere of little oversight; operational considerations decided operations.

Directed by presidents who found the option of covert action extremely useful in carrying out American policies, the CIA had a benign relationship with Congress, which exercised virtually no oversight functions. Allen Dulles' relations with Congress were distinctly clubby, for in an institution ruled by the seniority system, he found he had to deal only with three mossback Southern conservatives who autocratically ruled the fiefdoms that decided appropriations and military policy. Carl Vinson, chairman of the House Armed Services Committee, Clarence Cannon, chairman of the House Appropriations Committee, and Richard Russell, reigning power in the Senate and chairman of the Senate Armed Services Committee, would conduct desultory and irregular chats with Dulles on CIA operations. Dulles would tell them details— if, as Dulles noted pointedly, "they want to know."

Mostly, they didn't, and the CIA, virtually unnoticed, constructed a massive, secret apparatus. The empire included a long list of foreign politicians who were regularly bribed; propaganda radio stations; subsidized books; the secret underwriting of newspapers, magazines, television and radio stations; covert support of labor unions; a small army of "contract agents" to carry out paramilitary operations; political front groups; and a network of "proprietaries" (air charter companies and other businesses secretly owned by the agency, but operating under corporate fronts).

All of it was directed in a manner that had become almost slapdash. On the basis of a vague suspicion or presumption, governments were overthrown. The intelligence on which some of these decisions were based could also be slapdash, since the roster of secret police chiefs and other dubious sources providing intelligence to the CIA tended to tell the agency what they thought the Americans wanted to hear—mostly scare stories about Communists everywhere. Further, CIA largesse, ostensibly for the purpose of financing intelligence organizations to keep track of Communist agents, was instead largely used to underwrite the machinery of repression against a particular regime's political opponents.

It could not go on forever, of course. The CIA's operations, haphazardly planned and directed in the conviction that the agency's workers of political and paramilitary miracles could do no wrong, were bound to fail at some point. The failure, a spectacular one, occurred in the one location where failure was unthinkable: Cuba.

PART THREE

America Agonistes
1961–1973

SEVEN

Seeking the Third Force

FROM THE OUTSET, it went terribly wrong. The boat, dangerously overloaded with eighty-two exile soldiers and supplies, grounded on a reef several hundred yards offshore. Many of the soldiers had nearly drowned making their way to the landing beach—which turned out to be more swamp than beach, with solid ground over a mile away. And now, after four miserable days, the small invading force was in total disarray. Three of the survivors—hungry, exhausted, and low on ammunition—were pinned down by the automatic rifle fire of government troops while above hostile planes circled. The glorious invasion was a rout.

Prior to the landing, the exiles had made a pledge to live in Cuba as free men or die trying. Hiding beneath a canopy of sugarcane leaves, barely daring to breathe, two of the three Cubans feared their lives rested decidedly with the second option. But not the third man. He was the expedition's leader, a young lawyer with no formal military training, who, remarkably, whispered, "We are winning! Victory will be ours!" It seemed hardly the time for a pep rally. The other two soldiers, incredulous, simply stared at their comrade wondering if he had gone mad.

For five days the men would remain on their backs, gnawing on sugarcane for nourishment, licking the morning dew off plants for water, and listening to plans of future battles that would remove the yoke of despotism from their country. It was December 1956. The thirty-year-old commander, Fidel Castro Ruz, was intensely optimistic—a necessary requirement for any good revolutionary.

Government troops eventually gave up hunting for the rebels, and announced, in a moment of wishful thinking, that Castro and over half of his landing party had been killed. Far from dead, Castro, with his two companions, crawled out of the sugarcane field and fled into the Sierra Maestra to form a new guerrilla army. Just over two years later, on New Year's Day 1959, Castro led a triumphant procession of that army into Havana. A few hours before, dictator Fulgencio Batista had fled into exile, carrying nearly $300 million in cash with him, the proceeds of bribes paid by the owners of Havana's Mafia-run gambling casinos.

Passions ran deep in the Cuban civil war, and the American intelligence community seemed perplexed by events on the turbulent island. The confusion mainly centered on the Cuban revolution's central dynamic, Fidel Castro himself, a charismatic, engaging, voluble, and intelligent man whose political outlook seemed rather vague. Throughout his years in the mountains, when he was often portrayed in the American media as a dashing guerrilla leader, Castro had been careful to fudge his political agenda.

Sensitive to the political persuasions of Latin American revolutionaries—especially those operating in a country only ninety miles from the American mainland—the CIA made several assessments of this curious figure, which generally concluded he was not a Communist. Overlooked, somehow, was Castro's extensive involvement with Communist revolutionary organizations in Venezuela and Mexico during his two decades of political exile from Cuba. Also missed were Castro's numerous avowals to friends during that period proclaiming himself a Communist.

During an executive session only a few days after Castro took power, Allen Dulles informed the Senate Foreign Relations Committee that the new leader of Cuba did not have "Communist leanings." Yet only weeks earlier, the CIA Director had dropped off at the White House an intelligence report that greatly upset Eisenhower. "Communist and other extreme radicals appear to have penetrated the Castro movement," the report warned. "If Castro takes power, they will probably participate in the government." The CIA, unsure as to Castro's *bona fides*, was emitting mixed signals. But events in Cuba in the months following Castro's victory confirmed the worst fears.

First, Castro told the moderates in the July 26th Movement coalition that he would not restore the 1940 Cuban constitution and civil liberties—as he had promised to win their support during the war against Batista. Less than two weeks after taking power, Castro relegalized the Cuban Communist Party; in March, promised national elections were postponed. Amid arrests and executions, upper- and middle-class Cubans began fleeing the island to Miami; by 1960, over one hundred thousand Cubans had left. Finally, the nationalization of American businesses on the island, worth millions of dollars, caused a distinct frost on already chilly U.S.-Cuban relations.

Castro was openly thumbing his nose at the United States. Eisenhower, with few options, could only sit still and take it. South America, as Eisenhower observed, judged Castro as "a champion of the downtrodden and the enemy of the privileged" and would be up in arms at the thought of United States interference with this new Latino hero. Castro's seething revolutionary ideas, Ike feared, might spread through the economically parched nations south of America's border.

In vivid contrast to Castro's popularity was the Vice President's recent trip to Latin America. In Lima, Peru, Richard Nixon and his wife were greeted by rocks and spit. Even more unfriendly was Caracas, Venezuela, where the windows of Nixon's limousine, stalled in the midst of an anti-American demonstration, were shattered by rioters carrying placards and heavy rocks.

Eisenhower's concern over the safety of his Vice President led to the assemblage of a sizable invasion force to physically extract him if necessary. "We could get no reports from the outside," the

President explained at the time, "and not knowing whether the Venezuelan Government might not want some aid from us, we simply put it at the places where it would be available in reasonable amounts . . ." The "reasonable" force consisted of an aircraft carrier, a missile cruiser, six destroyers, and a helicopter detachment, assembled thirty miles off the Venezuelan coast, plus four companies of Army paratroopers and Marines, numbering some one thousand troops, which were rushed to quick-striking bases at Ramay Air Force base, Puerto Rico, and Guantánamo Bay, Cuba.

Clearly Latin America was a volatile and unpredictable place, where the popularity and politics of a man like Castro might spread quickly. Something would have to be done; what was needed, as Eisenhower put it, was "a third force," a solution other than Castro's obvious communist leanings or the brutal despotism of Batista. But what could be done? And who to do it?

Not surprisingly, Eisenhower in March 1960 turned to the CIA to formulate a plan to get rid of Castro. The CIA concocted a reprise of the plan that had worked so well in Guatemala. A small cadre of several dozen carefully chosen Cuban refugees from among the Cuban exile community in Miami would be trained at the U.S. Army's Jungle Warfare School in Panama. These men would then train a larger group of approximately one hundred and fifty other Cubans, who would be infiltrated into Cuba in small groups to build up an anti-Castro underground that with American aid would rise up and depose Castro. Meanwhile, as in Guatemala, an important component of the plan, a propaganda radio station, was set in place. Called Radio Swan, it was constructed in the spring of 1960 on Swan Island, an uninhabited speck ninety-seven miles off the Honduran coast.

Radio Swan and the rest of the Cuban operation were under the command of one of the CIA's most striking figures, Richard Bissell, chief of the agency's covert operations. Standing over six feet tall, Bissell struck everyone as a dynamo of energy and ideas. An Ivy League economist and, later, government bureaucrat, he had never been a spy in his life, but Allen Dulles sought him out in 1954 because he was known as a bureaucrat who actually got things done.

Bissell's rise in the CIA was meteoric. Although he was not, like most in the agency's hierarchy, a veteran of the OSS, he took

William F. Friedman, America's pioneer cryptanalyst, at a telegraph cipher machine in 1919 (Harris & Ewing)

Herbert O. Yardley, head of the famed "American Black Chamber" (AP/Wide World Photos)

Moe Berg—linguist, baseball player, spy—as catcher for the Washington Senators, 1933 (UPI/Bettmann Newsphotos)

Ernest Hemingway, amateur spy, aboard his fishing boat (UPI/Bettmann Newsphotos)

William ("Wild Bill") Donovan of the OSS, father of American central intelligence (AP/Wide World Photos)

General Walter Bedell Smith, the man who did most to shape the modern CIA (UPI/Bettmann Newsphotos)

Castro at the front during the Bay of Pigs Invasion (AP/Wide World Photos)

The avuncular Allen W. Dulles, America's most famous spymaster (AP/Wide World Photos)

Arturo Espaillat, the CIA's point man in the Trujillo assassination (UPI/Bettmann Newsphotos)

President Kennedy, Attorney General Robert Kennedy, and the man who knew dark secrets about both of them, FBI Director J. Edgar Hoover (UPI/Bettmann Newsphotos)

Mafioso John Roselli arrives in Washington to testify—testimony that would cost him his life (UPI/Bettmann Newsphotos)

Godfather Sam ("Momo") Giancana, another mobster whose testimony resulted in his death (UPI/Bettmann Newsphotos)

CIA Director William Colby, who saved his agency from destruction (UPI/Bettmann Newsphotos)

Senators Church and Tower with the CIA's infamous poison gun
(UPI/Bettmann Newsphotos)

James Jesus Angleton, mysterious head of CIA counterintelligence
(AP/Wide World Photos)

CIA head Richard Helms prepares to take the oath for the Senate Watergate Committee hearings (AP/Wide World Photos)

Admiral Stansfield Turner, devotee of spy technology (UPI/Bettmann Newsphotos)

William Casey with his boss, the man who gave him cabinet rank
(Bill Fitz-Patrick/The White House)

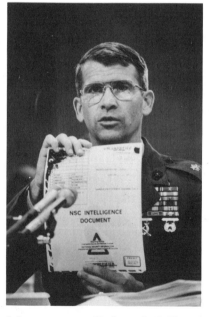

Lieutenant General William
Odom, NSA's secretive director
(UPI/Bettmann Newsphotos)

Lieutenant Colonel Oliver
North, guiding force behind the
Iran-Contra operation (AP/
Wide World Photos)

to the craft of espionage like few others. The former academic showed no fear of taking risks; quite the contrary, the professor seemed to relish them. He had been the administrator in charge of the successful U-2 spy plane, and the aura of the U-2's success, combined with Bissell's enormous energies and managerial skill, made Dulles think Bissell could run the CIA's large-scale covert operations.

Bissell took to the Cuban assignment with the same frenetic energy given to the building of spy planes, but quickly discovered the building of an underground movement would take longer than expected. "Their mission," Bissell later recalled, "would have been to build a fairly professional underground [such as] existed in France under German occupation." But the French underground's enemy was a foreign occupying power; in Cuba, the opponent was a leader who was solidifying his position every day, building a large military force and two-hundred-thousand-man militia with Soviet arms, making it much more difficult to overthrow him.

As Castro grew stronger, the CIA's plan became larger and more varied. Much attention was focused on various schemes to undermine Castro's authority, or make him look ridiculous. The schemes were hatched by the CIA's spy lab, the Technical Services Division. One idea, designed to disrupt Castro's long-winded television speeches, was to spray the broadcasting studio with BZ, an LSD-like hallucinogenic drug. Another was to inject a similar drug into a box of Castro's favorite Cuban cigars, and still another was to cause his beard to fall out by exposing him to a strong depilatory chemical. All of these comic plots were eventually abandoned, but they set a train of thought in motion: once the CIA began thinking about ways to make Castro's beard fall out, it was but a short step to the next question—why not kill him and solve the whole problem?

By July of 1960, Allen Dulles and others were now wondering aloud about what would happen if Fidel, his brother, Raúl, and Che Guevara all suddenly disappeared. The agency approved a payment of ten thousand dollars to a Cuban to arrange an "accident to neutralize" Raúl. The attempt was never made. By mid-August the CIA had focused again on Castro's ubiquitous cigar; what had been fraternity house pranks dreamed up by the Technical Services people became serious: instead of soaking the cigars with an LSD derivative to temporarily disorient Castro, the new plan called for dipping them with a deadly toxin that would kill Castro the minute he took a puff.

However exotic these gambits, Richard Bissell was not satisfied. He wanted more options, more ways to get at Castro. The CIA now reached out in another direction, one that led to one of the most bizarre alliances in U.S. history: the agency went into business with the Mafia.

Accelerator pressed to the floor, the jeep careened at top speed down the Malecón, Havana's Broadway. The driver, a *barbudo* (bearded one) dressed in the standard Castro guerrilla uniform of scruffy fatigues and beret, beeped the jeep's horn repeatedly as cars and pedestrians scattered. Four other *barbudos* in the jeep somehow managed to hang on as the vehicle roared down the wide avenue, past the expensive apartment buildings, nightclubs, and gambling casinos of Havana's entertainment district.

The atmosphere was gayer than usual along the Malecón early that New Year's Day of 1959, for the imminent arrival of Castro (and the departure of Batista a few hours earlier) meant the civil war was over. Many people on the street cheered the jeep, festooned with the flag of the July 26th Movement, as it pulled up in front of the Tropicana Hotel and Casino. The *barbudos* ignored the hung-over revelers as they rushed into the huge casino's executive offices. One look told them they were too late: the safe was empty, its door wide open.

It was the same story as they rushed to the other casinos in the city: empty safes. The advance scouting detachment of Castro's army had failed in its mission to secure millions of dollars in casino money for the Cuban National Bank and its soon to be appointed president, Che Guevara. The money had been flown out of Cuba aboard several private planes the day before, all $3 million of it. Whatever the CIA might have thought of Castro, the prescient American mobsters who ran the casinos knew enough about Castro to realize that Cuba's casino business was about to end.

But a perceived convergence of interests was soon to occur: the CIA wanted to get rid of Castro; the agency assumed the American Mafia had their own grievances against Castro. The CIA's Director of the Office of Security, Colonel Sheffield Edwards, proposed that the CIA hire the Mafia to dispose of Castro. The CIA believed that the mob had the motivation and experience to get just such a nasty job done.

Edwards did not personally know of any gangsters, but he knew a man who did: Robert Maheu, an ex-FBI agent and occasional CIA asset. Maheu was chief aide to billionaire Howard Hughes and ran Hughes's operations in Las Vegas. Maheu agreed to help, and offered underworld figure Johnny Roselli $150,000 of the CIA's money to have Castro killed. Roselli, whose underworld connections dated all the way back to Al Capone, agreed to help. According to Maheu, the deciding factor in Roselli's decision to cooperate was a sudden surge of patriotism. "He said he felt that he had an obligation to his government," Maheu later recalled with a straight face, "and he finally agreed to participate."

Roselli, a small-time mobster, immediately informed his boss, Sam ("Momo") Giancana, the Mafia godfather of Chicago whose empire included Las Vegas. The involvement of Giancana was a serious mistake for the CIA, since he was the subject of an intensive FBI racketeering investigation. Giancana, no fool, saw his opportunity to win the federal government's gratitude, and indicated enthusiastic willingness to kill Castro.

The CIA first suggested a good old-fashioned gangland-style murder. Giancana, who had been behind bars some sixty-three times, declined the recommendation as too dangerous. Poison, Giancana argued, would be a much safer means of eliminating the Cuban leader. Soon a pattern emerged: various assassination attempts would be suggested or attempted, only to have Giancana regretfully report that they had failed, for one reason or another.

It was a supreme con job, and Giancana played the game for more than a year. Meanwhile, Giancana would shout to puzzled FBI agents surveilling him, "Hey, why don't you guys leave me alone? We're on the same side!" It was not long before the agents discovered what Giancana was up to, and J. Edgar Hoover prepared one of his famous masterfully phrased memos for the CIA, wondering if the agency was aware that a notorious Mafia leader was involved in an assassination plot against Fidel Castro.

Just how much specific knowledge Eisenhower had of this and other assassination activities remains unclear even today. Is it possible that the CIA would have carried out such an operation entirely on its own? It was the age of "plausible denial," and as Bissell himself later noted, almost certainly Eisenhower was not presented with what Bissell called a "nakedly labeled" assassination plan, but may have said, "I want that man gotten rid of," which meant to Bissell, "any means are legitimate."

The same ambiguity arises in connection with Eisenhower's successor, John Kennedy, whose administration was marked by other, similar assassination plots against Castro. Again, there is no known evidence that Kennedy gave direct approval for such operations. One thing is clear: Kennedy was totally committed to destroying the Castro regime. During the election campaign of 1960, he hammered hard on the issue of Cuba, accusing Nixon and Eisenhower of "tolerating a Communist regime only ninety miles off the Florida coast." By the end of the campaign, Kennedy had all but advocated open intervention in Cuba on behalf of the "fighters of freedom" (a phrase Ronald Reagan would slightly alter two decades later for his own band of Latin exiles).

A similar theme echoed through Kennedy's inauguration address on January 20, 1961. In his now famous speech Kennedy proclaimed that the United States would pay any price, bear any burden to assure liberty. He also had a special message for those south of the border: "Let every other power know that this Hemisphere intends to remain the master of its own house." Kennedy, only moments into his administration, had drawn a line in the geopolitical dirt and had dared anyone to cross it. The inaugural words came easy, but the youngest President in American history would soon learn just how heavy a price he would have to bear for them.

Before taking the presidential oath of office, Kennedy knew that the CIA had ready a plan to back up his tough talk. Allen Dulles and Richard Bissell briefed the President-elect on what was known as Operation Zapata. Bissell's classic underground World War II parachute drop operation against Castro had mushroomed. Now the plan looked more like a small version of the Normandy invasion.

The metamorphosis took place while Kennedy was still out on the campaign trail. During this time the CIA realized it had underestimated the strength of Castro's forces and overestimated the resistance to them. The few anti-Castro guerrillas still in Cuba,

Bissell concluded, were starving in the mountains, with no experience or understanding in how to build an underground.

Cuba was not to be a repeat of the CIA's successful operation in Guatemala. The quicker recourse was rather large and noisy: an invasion force consisting of a small navy and air force, an army brigade of fifteen hundred Cuban exiles, and supporting roles provided by the CIA and the U.S. Navy.

The invasion plan called for the Navy to transport the brigade from Nicaragua to the shores of Cuba where a beachhead would be established and a new government proclaimed. As with the Normandy invasion, the key to success, the CIA planners realized, was controlling the skies. Sixteen World War II vintage B-26 bombers, flown by Cuban pilots from Guatemala, would strike first, without warning, to destroy Castro's planes on the ground. With the skies belonging to the rebels and a toehold firmly secured, the fifteen hundred exiles would then engage Castro's militia of two hundred thousand.

For the scheme to really work, there would have to follow very shortly an uprising by the Cubans throughout the island. The hope was to create, in Bissell's words, a "fluid situation." E. Howard Hunt, the CIA's political officer on Zapata, tells a different story. According to him, once the beachhead was secured, a provisional Cuban government (with Hunt as the U.S. representative) was to be flown in from Miami. Shortly thereafter, fifteen thousand U.S. Marines would come ashore in support of the new government.

Either way, the invasion operation was an extraordinary inheritance from Eisenhower. "He had been astonished at its magnitude and daring. He later told me that he had grave doubts from that moment on," remembered Kennedy's adviser, Ted Sorensen. Others, even inside the CIA, were having their own misgivings. The operation, thought David Atlee Phillips, was huge and complicated. Phillips had been a part of the radio propaganda effort during the Guatemala campaign that ousted Arbenz in 1954. Then it had been so simple. Cuba and Castro, Phillips knew from firsthand experience in Cuba, were not the same as Guatemala and Arbenz. As he reviewed Bissell's invasion plans in the CIA's war room, he sensed something was very wrong: "There's a maxim in the intelligence business that you can't hide a hippopotamus with a handkerchief. You certainly can't cover a tank on a Caribbean beach with one."

Whatever Phillips's apprehensions, he wasn't sharing his hippopotamus maxims with Bissell. Not that it really mattered, for the new commander in chief already had plenty of doubts about the invasion. There was also a big problem in shutting down the operation: how to quietly disperse an army of fifteen hundred American-trained Cubans? Allen Dulles would later describe the operation as "an orphan child JFK had adopted from the Republicans. He had no real love or affection for it." Clearly, Kennedy's political instincts were warning him of the dangers ahead, no matter which way he moved. The President had not gotten a really good handle on the operation, and he sought a second opinion from the Joint Chiefs of Staff. The Cuban Brigade, trained and ready, awaiting D-Day on an isolated Guatemalan coffee plantation, passed muster with the Joint Chiefs. Dulles went even further, telling the President, "I stood at this very desk and said to President Eisenhower about a similar operation in Guatemala, "I believe it will work." And I say to you now, Mr. President, that the prospects are even better than our prospects were in Guatemala."

There were few dissenters to the plan. Capitol Hill was all but asleep on the invasion, except for Senator J. William Fulbright, an Arkansas Democrat and chairman of the Senate Foreign Relations Committee. In contrast to the public uproar a dissenting senator might create today, Fulbright's reaction was to prepare for the President a private but prescient memorandum detailing the possible consequences should the operation fail. There were few naysayers inside the White House. One of the exceptions was presidential adviser and Harvard historian Arthur Schlesinger. When his arguments against the operation were overruled, Schlesinger offered one final, closing word of advice. If the invasion was to take place, someone lower than the President should give the go-ahead, "someone whose head can be placed in the block if things go terribly wrong." Even historians understood the theory of plausible denial.

There were no realistic hopes of keeping the invasion under wraps. It was simply too massive. The invasion was certainly no secret by April 12, 1961, when, at a White House news conference, the question was put straightforwardly to the President. Kennedy, in his answer, told the truth, but not the whole truth: "There will not be, under any circumstances, an intervention in Cuba by the United States Armed Forces."

To further reduce the invasion racket, the White House had its own ideas on how to muffle the operation. The original landing site, Trinidad, was dropped in favor of a less populated area some distance away: the Bay of Pigs. In changing the site, Kennedy eliminated a critical backup plan: in the event the invasion failed, the CIA's contingency plan called for the survivors to scatter into the Escambray Mountains and carry on their guerrilla war. But the Bay of Pigs was surrounded by swamps, which meant it lacked an escape route. The invading force might land with less noise, but now it had no options.

The guerrilla air force was another problem. A whole flock of the B-26 planes suddenly carrying out bombing runs on Cuba would surely point directly back to the United States. Allowing sixteen bombers to attack Cuba simultaneously, Kennedy reasoned, strained plausible deniability far beyond its limits. The surprise first air strike, with its critical mission of destroying Castro's air force while still on the ground, was cut in half—only eight bombers flew instead of sixteen—with the result that only half of Castro's air force was destroyed.

And so the invasion force headed for disaster. On Monday morning April 18, 1961, as the force moved toward shore, the skies belonged to Castro. A single Cuban Air Force jet sank two of the brigade's ships. One of them, the *Houston*, carried two battalions of men and the brigade's entire stock of reserve ammunition. The rest of the exiles, trapped on the beach, pounded by Castro's planes and brand-new Soviet artillery pieces, fought for three days before surrendering. Brigade 2506—named after the dog tag number of a recruit killed in a training accident—was crushed. Of its 1,500 men, 80 of them died fighting, 37 drowned, 48 escaped, and the rest surrendered, later to be ransomed for cash, medical supplies, and farm tractors. The CIA's air force suffered an equivalent disaster: 12 of the planes were shot down, with 14 killed, including 4 Alabama Air National Guard fliers who had formally "resigned" from the National Guard and were flying as civilian "volunteers."

At the CIA command post 1,200 miles away, appalled CIA officers listened to the radio messages that, like the pealing of a funeral bell, tolled disaster. Among them was David Atlee Phillips, who only a few years before had participated in the celebratory gathering at the White House after the Guatemala operation. There would be no such gathering after the Bay of Pigs.

As the radio messages came in, one of the men in the room scratched his wrists nervously; Phillips noticed that they began to bleed profusely. Another CIA man, a veteran of a tank battalion during World War II, vomited into a wastebasket. As the invasion crumbled and the radio messages began to die away, one of the last was from the brigade's military commander. Standing in the shallows, he said, "I'm throwing away my gear now. There's nothing left to fight with." He cursed the CIA. Then he cursed the United States.

"There's an old saying that victory has a hundred fathers and defeat is an orphan. I'm the responsible officer of the Government, and that is quite obvious." That was John Kennedy's public response to the Bay of Pigs. In private, Kennedy confided in his brother: how could they all have been so wrong—the CIA, the Pentagon, and his most trusted advisers? And how could he have been so utterly stupid? His instincts had warned him; he had simply failed to listen.

In the wreckage of Operation Zapata, Kennedy eased Allen Dulles into retirement. Richard Bissell followed shortly after in February 1962. A quarter of a century later, Bissell recalled Kennedy's anger as rather mild, given the magnitude of the failure: "There was no pettiness in the reaction. Privately he spoke about cutting the agency down to size, but in the end really nothing was done."

The White House bitterness over the failure of the Bay of Pigs, however, would run deep for a long time to come. There was already, as one White House staffer noted, a mood of revenge in the air. Richard Bissell, in his last few months at the CIA, was called in on the White House carpet, remembered one agency official, and "chewed out in the Cabinet Room of the White House by both the President and the Attorney General, for, as he put it, sitting on his ass and not doing anything about getting rid of Castro and the Castro regime."

Getting rid of Castro, Bobby Kennedy announced, was "the top priority in the U.S. government—all else is secondary. No time, money, effort, or manpower is to be spared." As Defense Secretary Robert McNamara later put it, "We were hysterical about Castro at the time of the Bay of Pigs and thereafter." Just what the alternative, the possible "third force" to replace Castro, might be, no one seemed to know. Or care. The effort now had little to do with geopolitical issues; Castro, the man, was the target.

The response to the White House pressure was a major CIA covert program, Operation Mongoose, managed by a new set of players. President Kennedy considered installing his brother Bobby as CIA Director following the Bay of Pigs, but political expediency led to the choice of an outsider, John McCone, a wealthy Republican industrialist. McCone was named director, but Bobby was given free rein to oversee Mongoose out of the Attorney General's office. Despite their differences in politics and age, the two men came to be close allies. "Mongoose was a program of infiltrations of annoying, but not strategic matters," was McCone's assessment. "It was really operated under Bobby Kennedy. We had no problems whatsoever."

McCone may have had no problems, but not so his new Deputy Director of Plans, Richard Helms, who had been in the spying trade since the OSS days of World War II. He had been Bissell's deputy director of covert operations, and had now moved up to replace him as the chief of covert operations. Helms had carefully kept his distance from Zapata; as other CIA officers were to note admiringly, there was not a single piece of paper in connection with the operation that contained Helms's name. Now he was charged with winning back Cuba and the agency's reputation. As Helms later put it, "We wanted to earn our spurs with the President."

The CIA had not yet earned its spurs, but Bobby Kennedy was goading Helms with constant demands to do something about Castro. "Bobby Kennedy," Helms later recalled, "was very hands-on in this period. He was the one who had the whip in hand."

General Edward Lansdale, a veteran of counterinsurgency operations in the Philippines and Vietnam, was brought in to coordinate the interdepartmental effort of State, Defense, and CIA, a task which, as Lansdale described it, was to "put the American genius to work, quickly and effectively." Like Bissell before him,

Lansdale's original plan called for building up internal Cuban resistance to Castro, but just as Bissell experienced, White House pressure and impatience, combined with the slow process of building a viable underground network (plus the CIA's inherent preference for boom and bang operations), soon turned the operation, once again, into a paramilitary campaign.

Operation Mongoose became a full-court press of covert action designed to destabilize, then destroy, the Castro regime. Mongoose included no outright invasion, but just about everything short of that: hit-and-run raids by Cuban exiles against Cuban economic targets, propaganda broadcasts, and infiltration of small teams of guerrillas. Soon Miami was the largest CIA station in the world. The unit, called Task Force W, was supported by at least two hundred CIA officers and two thousand Cuban exiles.

Mongoose came to an abrupt, if temporary, halt in October 1962 with the Cuban missile crisis. The analytic branch of the CIA had previously all but discounted the possibility of Soviet nuclear missiles based in Cuba, believing that Khrushchev could not be so foolhardy. But the Soviet hopes for success rested on just such a surprise; the missiles would have to be operational before being discovered, when the United States would have no option but to live with them. But Bissell's favorite project, the high-flying U-2 spy plane, grounded for over a year from flights over the Soviet Union following the shooting down of Francis Gary Powers, was now carrying out reconnaissance missions over Cuba. A flight over San Cristóbal near Havana on October 14, 1962, brought back photographic evidence of construction of missile sites. The CIA intelligence-gathering and analysis provided to Kennedy and his advisers over the next two weeks proved critical to a peaceful resolution of the nuclear crisis. Nearly twenty years after the sneak assault on Pearl Harbor, the intelligence apparatus set up to give forewarning of any similar surprise attack accomplished its mission. It was the CIA's finest hour.

The crisis was resolved when Khrushchev agreed to remove the missiles, while Kennedy privately guaranteed to dismantle aging Jupiter missiles in Turkey. Kennedy also promised there would be no invasion of Cuba, but the highly secret CIA assassination efforts, put on hold prior to the Cuban invasion, had already been reactivated. In April 1962 the CIA was back in touch with their old acquaintances, Roselli and Giancana. But the new plot dissolved in *opéra bouffe*, caused mostly by a little problem of the heart.

In October 1960 Momo Giancana was a busy but jealous man. On the CIA payroll while still running the Chicago Mafia, he heard rumors that his Las Vegas girlfriend, singer Phyllis Mc-Guire, was having an affair with comedian Dan Rowan. Giancana, in a fit of jealousy, demanded of Maheu that something be done. Maheu, once again the CIA's contact man with the Mafia, consoled Giancana by agreeing to find proof of the infidelity. Maheu hired a private detective to bug the trysting site. But the job was botched; the technician was arrested and the FBI notified. The private detective was not about to take the rap alone, and revealed to FBI agents that he had been hired by Maheu. In turn, Maheu admitted the Giancana connection and urged the CIA to quash any prosecution for fear that the Castro assassination plot would be revealed.

With that move, J. Edgar Hoover was provided with everything he needed to know. He could scarcely believe all that had suddenly fallen into his lap: the CIA, which he still considered a hated rival, was back in business with the Mafia, and was again trying to assassinate Fidel Castro. But there was more. His agents, in surveilling Giancana, discovered that among his other mistresses was one Judith Campbell—who also happened to be involved in a relationship with President Kennedy, as the agents found out by trailing her to the White House. A check into White House telephone records showed that Kennedy called her often.

A man who recognized opportunity and knew what to do with it, Hoover had a quiet, private luncheon with Kennedy, during which he outlined the Giancana-CIA-Campbell-Kennedy connection. No record exists of what was said, but Hoover's *modus operandi* would have been to inform the President of the delicate matter and vow his "discretion." In other words, Hoover was now privy to the kind of information that would make him politically inviolable so long as Kennedy was in office; any rumors of the Kennedys seeking a new FBI chief would end immediately. White House telephone logs show that the last of some seventy phone conversations between Kennedy and Judith Campbell occurred just a few hours after the meeting with Hoover.

But the assassination plots went on. Giancana, hoping his role in the attempts to kill Castro would win him Justice Department forgiveness on racketeering charges, told the CIA that the Mafia knew a cook at one of Castro's favorite Havana restaurants. The cook, Giancana claimed, would be willing to slip some form of liquid poison into Castro's soup. The CIA prepared a liquid toxin, but then Giancana stalled further, claiming that the cook was getting cold feet.

Meanwhile, the CIA's Technical Services Division was pursuing a second track. Having struck out with the toxins, the spy lab began tinkering with new ideas. One scheme called for arming a seashell with a powerful bomb, which would explode when Castro was underwater at his favorite scuba-diving site. The lethal seashell was never built. A second plan called for using attorney James Donovan as an unwitting assassin. The former OSS agent had recently negotiated the exchange of convicted KGB agent Rudolf Abel and U-2 pilot Francis Gary Powers, and was negotiating with Castro for the release of the more than eleven hundred Cuban exiles captured at the Bay of Pigs. The CIA plan called for Donovan to unknowingly deliver a contaminated diving suit to Castro as a present. Loaded with fungus and a pathogenic tubercle bacillus, the suit would have given the Cuban leader a nasty skin disorder and a fatal lung disease. The plot was scrapped when Donovan, still unsuspecting, bought his own, uncontaminated diving suit as a genuine gift to offer Castro.

The most important CIA asset in the assassination plots was a high-ranking Cuban official, Rolando Cubela, code-named AM/Lash. He was particularly anxious to get his hands on grenades and a high-powered rifle with telescopic sights. Cubela was later offered a ballpoint pen rigged with a hypodermic needle so small "that the victim would not notice its insertion." On November 22, 1963, the CIA handed the poison pen over to AM/Lash. That same day, John Fitzgerald Kennedy was assassinated in Dallas, Texas.

Richard Bissell has lost his enthusiasm for assassination in the quarter century since he first became involved in such acts: "I think I, for one, placed too much reliance on the ability to keep things like that permanently secret after the event, but even aside from that pragmatic consideration, I think it was a mistake. I just think assassination is a weapon to be employed by a government entity only in very, very few situations, if any." Today, Richard

Helms, who took over Bissell's job, dismisses the assassination plots hatched in his department as "crazy schemes." As for the CIA's connections with the Mafia, Helms keeps his distance, knowing that much of the truth is now buried. "Roselli is now dead; Giancana's dead; I'm concerned that a fellow like Roselli is hardly the most trustworthy fellow in the world." Giancana was shot seven times in the throat while preparing breakfast in his Chicago kitchen in June 1975. Roselli was hacked to pieces, stuffed inside an oil drum, and dropped into the sea near Miami in July 1976. Both men, it's assumed, had been too friendly with the government for the mob's liking.

There has never been evidence that any foreign leader was assassinated directly by the CIA, although it was not for want of trying. The American plots against Fidel Castro were certainly the most ambitious. The attempts numbered at least eight, and Castro has claimed that there was actually a total of twenty-four CIA attempts against his life. In 1967, President Johnson decided to end what he called a "damned Murder, Inc. in the Caribbean." The assassination program was shut down, and so was Mongoose.

LBJ had other worries on his mind. Chief among them was another Third World country in danger of falling to the Communists.

EIGHT

Midnight at Khe Sanh

ON THE DAY before Thanksgiving in 1967, two young Army intelligence officers assigned to the Defense Intelligence Agency office in Saigon finished typing a lengthy document that capped months of grueling work. The result was well worth all that work, they were convinced, because they had now produced an intelligence report that would certainly prevent a disastrous American defeat in Vietnam.

In short, the officers concluded that the roof was about to cave in. After months of close study devoted exclusively to the tactics and strategy of North Vietnamese General Vo Nguyen Giap, the famed commander in chief of the Peoples Army of Vietnam, they arrived at a startling conclusion: Giap was about to unleash a huge offensive against the Americans and the South Vietnamese, an assault so massive it would knock out the political underpinnings for the war—and perhaps even win it for North Vietnam.

The support for the conclusion was daunting, consisting of

hundreds of pages of dense columns of facts and figures, a sweeping compilation of every piece of evidence extant. All of it had been marshaled to support what the intelligence officers now were convinced was a bold North Vietnamese plan to dramatically seize the initiative in Vietnam by attacking everywhere at once. At the very least, the sheer scope of the assault would belie all the official pronouncements that the Communists were losing the war; optimally, Giap's offensive might actually defeat the Americans and South Vietnamese militarily. In either event, Giap could not lose: either he won militarily or politically, but he would *win*.

At their insistence, the two intelligence officers were given the opportunity to deliver a full-scale briefing on their findings to the rest of the military intelligence complex. Like most such briefings, only those steeped in the intricacies of order of battle intelligence, radio traffic analysis, and other such esoterica of the military intelligence trade could have fully grasped the young officers' arguments. But it required no expertise to grasp the implications of what they were saying: American military intelligence had badly underestimated Giap's resources, which he had been carefully husbanding for quite some time. The conclusion was that he was preparing an all-out offensive to strategically decide the Vietnam war. He would attack when least expected, feinting toward an important target the Americans would find necessary to defend; then, he would unleash the bulk of his forces against the vulnerable cities and towns along Vietnam's coastal plain. The American and South Vietnamese forces, stretched too thin, would be unable to defend everything at once.

There was open laughter at this rather astounding conclusion. What "important target," the two officers were asked, would Giap feint toward? Almost certainly Khe Sanh, they replied, naming the advanced American fire base in the far northern reaches of South Vietnam. Giap knew that the Americans were obsessed with the prospect of "another Dien Bien Phu," the French base whose fall resulted in a Communist victory during the first Vietnam war in 1954. The moment Giap surrounded and then attacked the isolated American base at Khe Sanh, the Americans would rush reinforcements there—lured to a trap Giap had no intention of closing. And when was this great offensive supposed to begin? During the Tet holiday of 1968, three months away.

The two intelligence officers might just as well have predicted an imminent attack on Saigon by little green men in spaceships, for all the impact they made. They had encountered American military intelligence's prevailing wisdom in Vietnam, which at that moment saw no possibility of Giap doing anything, much less mounting a major offensive. He was the head of a beaten army; the enemy was on the ropes; there was light at the end of the tunnel; Giap was having trouble replacing the huge losses in his ranks; the Americans were "attriting" the enemy faster than his capability to make up the gaps; North Vietnam was being bombed into submission; the South Vietnamese forces were getting better every day; all the indicators of progress were "up."

The two officers could not get much of a hearing in Saigon, so they demanded that their conclusions be forwarded to the Joint Chiefs of Staff in Washington. Their superior, a colonel, said no. "Crap!" he exploded, in a one-word summation of what he thought of their conclusions. Then he pointedly mounted a copy of the two officers' report on a wall behind his desk.

"Your asses are on the line," he said. "I've got your professional reputations taped up here."

The paper was quietly removed less than three months later. On the morning of January 20, 1968, U.S. Marines ran into a large North Vietnamese force just north of the Khe Sanh perimeter, confirming earlier reports of two North Vietnamese divisions having been moved into attacking positions. Reinforcements were rushed north. Ten days later, a synchronized assault by the Peoples Army of Vietnam and the Vietnam Peoples Army of the National Liberation Front (popularly known as Viet Cong) erupted throughout the entire country, striking more than a hundred cities and towns—including Saigon, thirty-nine of forty-four provincial capitals, and seventy-one district capitals.

The battle raged for fifty-seven days. More than forty thousand Communist troops died, but they inflicted an immense political defeat on the United States. The remaining political support for the war evaporated as the United States Government decided it was time to wind down American participation; President Johnson announced he would not run for reelection. Khe Sanh, battered by enemy artillery fire, drew in large amounts of American resources that defended the base against an assault that never came. After the Communist offensive ended, the North Vietnamese surrounding Khe Sanh melted away. The Americans, having decreed that the base would be defended at all costs, later simply abandoned it.

The Tet offensive represented the greatest single American intelligence disaster since Pearl Harbor. Despite vast resources and a huge army of intelligence agents, the United States had failed to detect a military offensive that gathered strength right under the Americans' noses. Nearly 100,000 enemy troops, carrying supplies on their backs or on bicycles, and without using a single airplane or helicopter, planned and moved to their attack positions undetected. Fewer than 70,000 Communist soldiers attacked 500,000 American troops, 61,000 South Koreans, Thais, and other nations' forces, 342,000 South Vietnamese army regulars, and 284,000 South Vietnamese militia troops.

If Tet was a shock to the American body politic as a whole, it was an absolute trauma to the American national security apparatus. As the Tet disaster proved, absolutely nothing had gone right in Vietnam. The failure was total: when men in black pajamas and sandals made from old rubber tires could fight the greatest military power in the world to a standstill, then something very profound had happened.

What had happened, exactly, was to be a matter of some dispute. *Why* it happened was an even more complex question, but in intelligence terms, the roots of the disaster were easy enough to trace.

It had all begun only eighteen years before the Tet offensive, in a Tokyo tearoom. If there was one adjective that best described Ngo Dinh Diem, it was Mandarin. Most often dressed immaculately in a white linen suit, he spoke and moved in that languid air of *noblesse oblige* that marked the ruling oriental upper classes. Despite his airs, in 1950 he was a rootless man of no special accomplishment, eking out a living in Japan.

He had left his native Vietnam after serving as governor of Phan Thiet Province under the French colonial administration. The departure was sudden, but Diem, a Catholic mystic, believed that destiny would call him back to Vietnam some day, where he would play some great role in the country's future. Although opposed to the French, Diem did not join other Vietnamese whose opposition was more active—especially the Viet Minh organization, led by Ho Chi Minh.

Destiny arrived in Tokyo one morning in 1950 in the person of Wesley Fishel, a Michigan State University professor. Fishel, an Asian expert and liberal seeking what many of his generation called "the third way" (a non-Communist, democratic alternative to the postwar extremes of despotism or communism), was very taken with Diem. They had tea in a Tokyo tearoom, during which Diem propounded his views on independent, non-Communist nationalism.

Fishel later introduced Diem to the hierarchy of the U.S. Catholic Church, an important power base that led to contacts with such Cold War liberals as Senator John F. Kennedy and Supreme Court Justice William O. Douglas. Diem could not have arrived at a more propitious time. The Geneva Conference, convened in 1954 in the wake of the French defeat in Vietnam, was to decide the future of the country. The United States was very uneasy about the conference, for among the provisions was one mandating national elections in 1956—elections that Ho Chi Minh, the Communist leader, would certainly win. That was unthinkable, but what was the alternative?

Diem was the alternative. Backed by an influential coalition of left and right—eventually to be known as the "Vietnam Lobby" —Diem was proposed to the Eisenhower administration as the "independent nationalist alternative" who would lead a democratic and independent Vietnam. That formula was precisely the one laid out by Senator Kennedy in a speech in early 1954, just before the Geneva Conference opened: the United States would actually create its own, non-Communist Vietnam.

In July 1954, Diem became the premier of the new nation of South Vietnam. He was a national leader without much in the way of resources: he had no army, no national treasury, and a population, predominantly Buddhist, that had no faith in the ability of a Catholic leader to understand their concerns. Besides which, nobody had bothered consulting them about who would run their country.

These were minor matters to the men who now took Diem in hand to instruct him in how to build a nation. They were the men known collectively as the Saigon Military Mission, cover name for the CIA station in that city. Part of the CIA's Office of Policy

Coordination (OPC), the mission set about to create a new state in the American image. Armed with several millions of dollars in CIA funds, as first priorities they built an intelligence service, an extensive "public information" (propaganda) organization, and a coalition of mass anti-Communist organizations. Their perception was that they were operating on a new front line for the containment of communism; like men building a dike as the floodwaters rose and lapped around their ankles, the men of Saigon Military Mission were determined that monolithic communism would be stopped at the line they had drawn in the dirt.

At the same time, the CIA men were busy conducting offensive operations against the new regime of North Vietnam. Among their operatives was the ex-OSS agent Colonel Lucien Conein, who spent much of his time dreaming up "dirty tricks" to harass and disrupt the North Vietnamese—such as blowing up the largest printing plant in Hanoi, and putting sand in the gears of government trucks. In the Asian version of the OPC's Eastern European operation that concealed caches of arms to be used in revolts against the Russians, Conein arranged for similar caches in North Vietnam, including several concealed in the graves of a Hanoi graveyard. Conein was also involved in the mission's great success, a lurid propaganda campaign that claimed the North Vietnamese were torturing Catholic Vietnamese who sought to move south, claims accepted as fact by many U.S. publications.

But the real star of the mission was its head, Edward G. Lansdale. An Air Force colonel (later general), Lansdale was a former advertising executive who had drifted into the intelligence world. He was not a spy in the classic sense, but one of the new breed exemplified by his mentor and recruiter, OPC chief Frank Wisner.

A voluble man brimming with ideas, Lansdale first won fame within the CIA for his work in the Philippines during the 1950s, when he ran operations against a peasant rebellion he labeled "Communist." The operations were successful, part of a broad "nation-building" effort Lansdale directed. Actually, it amounted to an effort by Lansdale to shape the newly independent Philippines in the American image, complete with its own Abraham Lincoln—who turned out to be Ramón Magsaysay. Although Magsaysay was in fact a talented and dynamic leader in his own right, his public image was the result of an extensive Lansdale propaganda campaign to portray him as the "democratic alternative."

Lansdale decided that Diem would be the Magsaysay of Vietnam, but the Vietnamese Mandarin lacked the Filipino's talent. Diem's instincts were purely despotic: from the first moment he took control of South Vietnam, he sought to create a dictatorship. He crushed the opposition, dispensed government posts to members of his (and his wife's) family, and tried to make Catholicism the dominant religion in Vietnam, the latter goal a terribly wrong one, since only about 8 percent of Vietnam's 20 million people were Catholics. He also sought to destroy anyone in South Vietnam who had supported the Viet Minh, a repression which began to drive most of them into a new anti-Diem political organization that would come to be known as the National Liberation Front.

These actions tended to belie Lansdale's propaganda about "free Vietnam" and Diem as democratic leader in the tradition of Washington and Jefferson, but for the moment, very little of what was really going on in South Vietnam was reaching the American public. Lansdale, aware that Diem's base of power was narrow, sought to prop it up by obtaining greater support from official Washington. First, he convinced Allen Dulles that Diem was crucial to the future of "free Vietnam" as a bulwark against communism. Dulles talked to his brother, the Secretary of State, who in turn convinced President Eisenhower that maximum American support must be given to Diem in order for South Vietnam to survive. Essentially, Lansdale's argument was that Diem was the only "popular" leader the South Vietnamese had (an assertion that would have been news to the South Vietnamese).

In 1957, Lansdale arranged a visit by Diem to the United States. It was a triumph: playing his part perfectly, the diminutive (five feet, five inches tall) Diem made speeches—including one to a joint session of Congress—liberally sprinkled with democratic clichés. Traveling aboard Eisenhower's personal plane, Diem breakfasted with Cardinal Francis Spellman of New York—the most powerful Catholic religious leader in the country—and heard himself hailed by New York City Mayor Robert Wagner as the man "to whom freedom is the very breath of life itself."

Obscured in all this was a fundamental decision by Diem and the United States, which had decided the political future of millions of Vietnamese without the formality of asking them: the

Vietnamese were denied the opportunity to vote in a proposed national election of 1956, on the grounds that the Viet Minh would "dupe" the populace into voting for the Communists. Therefore, the United States would demonstrate the superiority of democracy by denying it to the Vietnamese—telling them that they were, in effect, being saved from themselves. Meanwhile, they would be shown real democracy in action in South Vietnam —an entity largely supported by the CIA, which was either unaware, or chose to ignore, that Diem's government in the countryside was perceived only as repressive.

And it was in the countryside, where the bulk of South Vietnam's population lived, that the second Vietnam war began. It is also where it was lost, for in the first few years of Diem's reign, the countryside gradually slipped toward control of his opponents, chiefly the Communists. While Diem was busy in such flashy events as public ceremonies and ribbon-cuttings, out in the countryside the National Liberation Front won the allegiance of the rice farmers, small landowners, peasants, and shopkeepers. A fortune in money and blood would later be spent by the United States trying to win back their "hearts and minds," but no amount of treasure or military power would ever recapture the South Vietnamese people who turned their back on the man they always regarded as America's puppet.

By 1961, the growing undercurrent of anti-Diem feeling in South Vietnam became a full-fledged revolt. Diem did not appear to have the first idea of what to do about it, save to order even more repressive measures. That only made things worse, and the CIA mission then compounded the error by underwriting further expansions of Diem's police and internal security apparatus. Armed revolt broke out in the countryside; how much of it was genuine reaction against Diem's repression and how much was fomented by the Viet Minh remnants under the direction of the North Vietnamese is difficult to determine. Probably, it was a combination of both, but in American eyes, the growing guerrilla resistance was Communist directed from Peking and Moscow, simply the next move in their relentless drive to take over the entire Asian mainland.

The perception led to a deepening commitment to Diem, most prominently in a U.S. military advisory mission that was creating a large, conventional army of little use against highly mobile guerrillas. Like an amateur poker player shoving in chips on a hand he feels honor-bound to pursue, no matter how weak, the Americans decided that Diem, whatever his faults, was the symbol of freedom in Vietnam. First Eisenhower, then Kennedy, concluded that the United States would prop up Diem and his government, at all costs.* Eisenhower had described South Vietnam as the first in a "row of dominos"; when that first domino fell, all the others would, too. Eisenhower was determined to keep that first domino standing. So was Kennedy, who went a step further: something would have to be done to bolster the next Indochina domino, Laos.

The Geneva Conference of 1954, which created Vietnam, also created the independent nations of Cambodia and Laos. These two former kingdoms of gentle people and striking natural beauty had never figured large in any geopolitical calculation, but the deepening struggle in Vietnam soon drew them into the vortex.

Laos had a small Communist organization supported by the North Vietnamese. Known as the Pathet Lao, it demonstrated growing strength among the Laotians, and in the 1958 national elections, won 32 percent of the vote. The electoral success caused grave alarm in Washington, and a CIA operation was set into motion. The agency created a political front, the Committee for the Defense of National Interests, and brought back a right-wing ex-Laotian military officer, Phoumi Nosavan, from his exile in France to create an entirely new political faction. That faction took control of the government. The Pathet Lao, driven from the government by the U.S.-backed faction, began a full-scale insurgency. They hooked up with their protectors, the North Vietnamese, and by 1959, a civil war was underway. The American involvement was almost entirely covert, under the direction of the CIA. It included ostensible civilian pilots flying resupply missions for U.S.-supported Laotian forces, the recruitment (for pay) of ethnic tribesmen to fight beside the anti-Communist forces,

* Kennedy would later change his mind, believing that Diem could no longer win the war. The President's assessment was passed on to Diem's senior military officers by the CIA. With White House blessings, the military staged a coup on November 1 and 2, 1963. Diem was assassinated.

and the direct involvement of American Special Forces (Green Berets).

Again, the United States had become involved in a war without the knowledge of Congress, which did not know about the deepening U.S. commitment and the secret war being waged. The war also involved Soviets, Chinese, and North Vietnamese, raising the possibility of serious consequences. A diplomatic agreement was worked out in 1962. The negotiated settlement was supposed to defuse the Laotian situation, primarily by the method of letting the myriad Laotian political factions work out their differences without outside interference.

But President Kennedy, citing North Vietnamese violations of the agreement, approved continuing CIA covert operations in Laos, mainly support for a thirty-thousand-man army of Laotian ethnic minorities,† and a bombing campaign against Pathet Lao positions by planes flown by CIA-paid pilots. The war went on, and the 1962 diplomatic agreement became just a scrap of paper.

Much of that secret war is still classified, although the Laotians were perfectly aware of the large groups of Americans in civilian clothes who flew the spotter planes directing U.S. air strikes against the Ho Chi Minh Trail; the American "civilian contractors" who operated a huge (and secret) Air Force radar complex in northern Laos; and the Americans in fatigues without name tags or unit patches who directed ground and air assaults against the Pathet Lao. Above all, they were aware of a great secret being withheld from Congress and the American people: the secret U.S. Air Force bombing of Laos, which began in 1965 and reached a crescendo during the Nixon administration. (Throughout this period, the Air Force dropped 1.6 million tons of bombs on Laos, more than it dropped on Germany during all of World War II.)

The only uniformed Americans to be seen in the Laotian secret war—although their presence was also supposed to be a secret—were the Army's Green Berets, the elite counterguerrilla force that owed its very existence to President Kennedy. The direct descendants of the OSS paramilitary teams of World War II, the

† This secret army, primarily the Hmongs, was supplied and ferried by one of the CIA's most infamous proprietaries, Air America. Unfortunately, the Hmongs for centuries had been involved in opium poppy production, and there were accusations later that they used Air America as a convenient method by which to move opium to markets elsewhere.

Special Forces had languished in an Army backwater until 1961, when Kennedy resurrected them, later approved the wearing of their distinctive green beret, and proposed them as the shock troops for America's new concern with Communist "wars of national liberation."

But when the Special Forces were sent to Vietnam in 1961 as the spearhead of Kennedy's plan to end the insurgency there, the guerrilla war against Diem was still perceived by the American Military Mission in Saigon as primarily a conventional war problem. The Green Berets were shifted into covert operations, in effect becoming the CIA's foot soldiers. They operated under an entity created that same year by Kennedy, the Combined Studies Group, a CIA operational arm that ran covert operations in Vietnam and Laos.

The idea combined intelligence-gathering and covert action functions, a mistake American intelligence had often committed. Events in Laos proved why the combination wouldn't work. Operations using teams of Green Berets and CIA-recruited ethnic tribes were successful in observing activity along North Vietnamese infiltration and supply routes in that country. But the lure of conducting some "boom and bang" at the same time, using the same men, proved irresistible. These were precisely the kind of operations which would alert the North Vietnamese that the enemy was near. So alerted, the North Vietnamese simply deployed enough forces to make security around their base camps and infiltration routes airtight. By 1964, increased North Vietnamese security made CIA-Green Beret forays in Laos, Cambodia, and North Vietnam extremely risky. Early that year, for example, a CIA operation code-named Leaping Lena parachuted thirty-two mountain tribesmen trained by the Green Berets into northern Laos to observe the Ho Chi Minh Trail. They got nowhere near the trail, and only four men managed to fight their way to safety.

The Green Beret operations had undergone a dramatic—although secret—expansion in 1962, when the CIA devised the idea of recruiting Montagnards, mountain tribesmen from Vietnam's Central Highlands area, as paid soldiers to block North Vietnamese infiltration routes and carry out clandestine operations inside North Vietnam itself. Assigned the task of arming, training, and equipping the near-primitive tribesmen, the Green Berets soon had a full-fledged private army operating a secret war.‡

But secret wars involve real problems of accountability and control, the two areas that were to cause much trouble for America's secret war in Indochina. The first alarm rang in 1964, when the secret war was expanded yet again, this time by creation of the Studies and Operations Group (SOG), which combined personnel from the Green Berets, the CIA, and the four military services in an organization that was to conduct subversion, sabotage, and other covert operations in North Vietnam, Laos, and Cambodia. It was under a broad mandate known as OPLAN 34-A, which authorized SOG to conduct "clandestine operations in denied areas." In other words, SOG commanders could do just about what they wanted.

SOG operations were largely in the hands of individual commanders, usually in isolated base camps, who were under no requirement to justify their actions. Operational necessities of the secret war dictated what was right and what was wrong, often with no thought about consequences. Not surprisingly, some SOG operations would have very serious consequences.

The most significant such consequence came in North Vietnam, where a secret SOG operation, known as Timberwork, used U.S. Navy Seal commandos and South Vietnamese Special Forces (*Luc Long Dac Biet*, contemptuously called "look long, duck back" by Americans) in a striking force that carried out raids along the North Vietnamese coast. In July 1964, according to the later accounts of confidential sources, CIA officials decided to coordinate Timberwork with a straight intelligence-collection operation run by the Office of Navy Intelligence and the National Security Agency.

That operation was known as Desoto. It was relatively uncomplicated: National Security Agency technicians, using sophisticated tracking equipment, were stationed aboard destroyers to record radio transmissions and radar signals as the destroyers

‡ The Montagnards paid a terrible price for their participation in the secret war. Left behind when the Americans pulled out, the "Yards," as the Americans like to call them, were virtually exterminated. Similarly, the Hmongs and other ethnic tribes in Laos who had worked for the CIA found themselves abandoned; less than 4 percent of the original Hmong population managed to survive Communist retribution by fleeing to Thailand.

cruised near the coasts of trouble spots. In 1964 an important trouble spot was North Vietnam, so the USS *Maddox*, with a National Security Agency crew aboard, was dispatched to sail up the coast of North Vietnam. Its particular target was the island of Hon Me, site of a large North Vietnamese radar site apparently installed to give Hanoi early warning of any air or naval attack.

For the Desoto patrol to be effective, it was preferable that the radar station be switched on to full power as the *Maddox* passed by. To accomplish that end, the idea was that a Timberwork raid would hit Hon Me as the destroyer passed to within about ten miles of the island. That would cause the radar to be switched on as the North Vietnamese searched for the attackers.

On the night of July 30, 1964, the raid took place as scheduled. The raiders were taken to the island in large, Norwegian-built PT boats known as "Nasties," then dropped into smaller boats for the actual run to the island. The raiders hoped to put the radar station out of commission, but a navigation error put them on the wrong side of the two-and-a-half-mile-wide island. Alerted, North Vietnamese troops on the island opened up with machine guns and artillery. The raiders beat a hasty retreat as the "Nasties" opened up with a covering fire from 40-millimeter cannon and machine guns.

The North Vietnamese clearly were very angered by the attack, and when another took place two nights later they decided to retaliate. Their chosen target was the destroyer they had spotted not too far from Hon Me when the island was attacked. Assuming it was a ship that had supported the raids in some way, North Vietnamese PT boats unsuccessfully attacked the *Maddox* on August 2. Two days later, joined by another destroyer, the *Turner Joy*, the *Maddox* reported she had been attacked again by North Vietnamese PT boats—although this time there was no direct sighting of any boats. The jittery radar operators were evidently seeing phantoms on their scopes.

No matter. Three days later President Johnson proposed the Tonkin Gulf Resolution, which gave him sweeping authority to use military force in Vietnam to protect American lives. In other words, a blank check. It was approved in the Senate by a vote of 88–2, and in the House by a vote of 416–0. Of course, Johnson said nothing about Timberwork or Desoto, and as far as the American people and Congress knew, the North Vietnamese had carried out purely unprovoked attacks in the Tonkin Gulf's international waters against an American ship on peaceful patrol. The following day, the first U.S. air strikes against North Vietnam were carried out.

The consequences of the secret war in this case were momentous, for they ignited direct involvement of the United States in an undeclared war that ended, finally, eleven years later. But it can be argued that something very similar to Tonkin Gulf was inevitable, for the secret war that had been underway for several years was bound to precipitate some sort of clash. The Indochina war was growing exponentially, and by the time of Tonkin Gulf there were offensive military operations in two neutral nations and a covert war in a third, a country with which the United States was nominally at peace.

However convenient presidents Eisenhower, Kennedy, and Johnson found such operations in avoiding the war-making hurdles imposed by a constitutional system of government, the price was too high. Vietnam was to prove, once and for all, the danger of allowing any President to conduct, via the intelligence apparatus, secret covert operations without the consent of Congress and the consensus of the American people.

Vietnam marked the climax of a long postwar period of secret operations by the United States to shape the political destiny of the world in the name of protecting it from the menace of communism. A laudable enough objective, but one important reason why that crusade finally failed in Vietnam, with disastrous results, was because the circle of policymakers who made such decisions was too small. There was no one outside that circle who could inform them that the United States had overreached itself; the world had changed, and the time when the Americans could figuratively snap their fingers—as in Iran and Guatemala—and effect profound political change was now gone.

The small group of men who decided on a secret war in Indochina (which later led to a more open one) lacked the kind of outside review which might have told them that the expenditure of over $352 billion to make viable the entity called South Vietnam could not succeed. No amount of money could change a political fact: to most of the Vietnamese people, South Vietnam was largely a line on a map. Their goal was a unified Vietnam, and the unalterable fact was that many of them were willing to die to achieve it. In that context, the perceptions of the United States were irrelevant.

And so were the efforts of American intelligence, which in Vietnam deployed the bulk of its energies and resources for what eventually became an American obsession. At the height of the war, there were nearly 800 CIA agents in Vietnam, along with more than 5,000 agents of the various military intelligence agencies. For SOG and other components of the secret war, nearly 2,500 Green Berets were working with 7,500 ethnic minority assets.

The CIA's secret war would become a highly controversial aspect of American intelligence's involvement in Vietnam, most notoriously in a program code-named Phoenix. The predecessors of that program were born almost coincidental with the first serious American involvement in 1962, when the CIA decided it would mobilize the assorted tribal, religious, and political minorities in South Vietnam and "nation-build" them into a cohesive political movement against the Communists.

But the Communists, who had dominated the Vietnamese nationalist movement for more than twenty years, were unaffected by the CIA campaign, which in any event was never able to break the deep roots the Communists had sunk into the South Vietnamese countryside. The next step, in 1964, was the creation of so-called "counterterrorist teams," part of a large-scale national police apparatus to isolate, and then eliminate, the Communist infrastructure. The program, which included an American-sponsored plan to provide identity cards for all South Vietnamese, foundered because however enthusiastic the Americans were for it, the South Vietnamese officials had other ideas. Almost universally corrupt, the South Vietnamese National Police hierarchy saw the new program as simply another opportunity for graft; the Americans discovered that the police were either extorting innocent citizens, or accepting hefty bribes from persons accused of being members of the Viet Cong to win official clearance.

The same atmosphere of corruption endangered the overall American pacification effort, known as WHAM (winning hearts and minds). A long series of American innovations in pacification failed, and by 1968, it was clear—especially judging by the evidence of the Tet offensive—that the Communist infrastructure was more deeply entrenched than ever. Still, the Americans persisted in believing that infrastructure represented only a minority of the South Vietnamese population; root out that infrastructure and the Communist war effort would collapse.

To that end, *Phung Hoang* (Phoenix) came into life, in effect a militarization of the internal security problem. The South Vietnamese, with American advice and support, would identify, then imprison or murder, all members of the Communist infrastructure. Judged strictly in operational terms, Phoenix seemed the most direct method of solving the problem of removing the Communist infrastructure—the "sea," in Mao Tse-tung's famous phrase, in which the "fish" (guerrillas) swam.

However, the Americans had failed to reckon on an old problem: the pervasive corruption of Saigon's internal security organizations. Again presented with an opportunity for graft, the South Vietnamese turned Phoenix to profit, extorting money from the families of those suspected of being Viet Cong operatives or supporters. In many cases, only two denunciations were sufficient to brand someone a Viet Cong. Those who did not, or could not, pay bribes were killed or jailed; a suspiciously high percentage of jailed prisoners appeared to be not members of the Viet Cong infrastructure, but political opponents of whatever Saigon regime happened to be in power at the moment. Torture of suspects was commonplace, and many prisoners found themselves in the infamous "tiger cage" jails of the Con Son Island prison, where conditions were unspeakable.

William Colby of the CIA oversaw American participation in Phoenix from 1968 to 1971 as head of the Civil Operations and Revolutionary Development Support (CORDS). During congressional hearings in 1973 on his nomination for DCI, Colby denied that Phoenix was an assassination program. He conceded that there were "abuses" by the South Vietnamese involved in the program, but added that he had worked hard to end those abuses.

Colby was sharply upbraided by another witness during the hearings, the Reverend Robert F. Drinan, who in 1969 was a member of the private U.S. Study Team on Religious and Political Freedom. Drinan, later a Massachusetts congressman, said that the interfaith team of religious leaders visited South Vietnam to investigate charges of abuses in the Phoenix program and the South Vietnamese police and prison system. Drinan said the team found the South Vietnamese were using Phoenix to stifle all political dissent, and that Colby was insensitive to "the complicity of the United States in lawlessness."

No proof was offered for that assertion, but it was clear that there was something seriously wrong with Phoenix. Admittedly, Phoenix had been "extremely destructive" to the Viet Cong (an assessment made by a North Vietnamese general), but at what cost? Anywhere from twenty to forty-seven thousand people died in Phoenix operations by 1971, yet how many of those victims were in fact members of the Communist infrastructure is impossible to say. Because the program was so badly administered and riddled with corruption, the only definitive statements are that it cost over $1 billion, and that it ultimately failed; the infrastructure retained control of the South Vietnamese countryside right up to the final departure of American forces from Vietnam in 1973.

The real significance of Phoenix, however, lay deeper. Americans involved in Phoenix were aware of the tortures routinely inflicted on suspects at the Prisoner Interrogation Centers, as they were of the horrors of the prison system, which by 1972 contained over two hundred thousand prisoners. Yet, they chose to look the other way. The methods, however deplorable, could be justified on the grounds that in the struggle with a ruthless enemy, one could not afford to play by the rules.

It was a terrible argument, and clearly indicated that American intelligence had lost its compass in Vietnam. Just how far that structure had strayed was best illustrated by the case of a man few Americans have ever heard of, Thai Khac Chuyen.

On the night of June 20, 1969, six Green Berets, dragging a drugged, smaller Vietnamese man, left Nha Trang—a village on the South Vietnamese coast—in a small boat. When they were some distance out in the South China Sea, they shot Thai Khac Chuyen to death. His body was then smeared with blood (to attract sharks), put in a sack weighted with chains, and dumped into the sea.

The disappearance of Chuyen would have remained just another statistic among countless others in a war of many such tragedies, except that one of the Green Berets on that boat went to the CIA and told the agency of Chuyen's murder. The Green Beret's motives for revealing the murder remain unclear—remorse, perhaps—but whatever the reason, CIA officials were alarmed: they shared some complicity in that murder. Even in the Vietnam of 1969, there could be nasty complications once the story got out.

The background to all this was a unit called B57, part of the SOG apparatus. It was running operations to infiltrate Communist sanctuaries in Cambodia using some Vietnamese agents, among them Thai Khac Chuyen. The operations ended in disaster, and the Green Berets who ran them began to suspect that B57 itself had been infiltrated by a double agent. Suspicion fell on Chuyen when a photograph was recovered from an overrun Viet Cong command post; one of the men in the photograph appeared to be Chuyen, who was promptly locked up and interrogated.

Convinced that Chuyen was the double agent, the Green Berets consulted the CIA: what should they do with him? "Terminate with extreme prejudice," CIA officials were later reported to have replied. Chuyen then was taken on his fatal boat ride.

CIA officials were to claim later that "terminate with extreme prejudice" was strictly a bureaucratic phrase, meant to signify firing someone with firm recommendation that nobody else hire him. Perhaps so, but when General Creighton Abrams, the commander of U.S. forces in Vietnam, heard what happened, he had Colonel Robert Rheault, the commander of the 5th Special Forces group whose unit included B57, on the carpet. Rheault told Abrams that Chuyen had gone out on a mission, and had not returned. Enraged, Abrams ordered the arrest of the six Green Berets involved in the murder of Chuyen, along with Rheault and two other Green Berets, on murder charges.

The trial threatened to be a *cause célèbre*, but it never took place. The CIA, pleading "executive immunity," refused to allow any of its personnel to testify, and it was clear that a cover-up was underway. Pentagon officials ordered the charges dropped. Except Abrams, no one, it appeared, wanted a trial that might shed some light into the murky, secret world of the CIA and the Green Berets.

The murder began to raise questions about just what the elite Green Berets were doing in the war. Green Beret supporters liked to claim that the Army establishment had always hated the Special Forces, especially in Vietnam. The antipathy was ascribed to rigid Army thinking: regular Army types distrusted unconventional soldiers like the Green Berets, who wore unconventional uniforms, were indifferent to Army discipline, often did not bother saluting visiting Regular Army officers or staff, openly lived with native women, and walked around wearing Montagnard bracelets.

But the Army's suspicion of the Green Berets in Vietnam ran deeper than that. It was in fact a healthy skepticism centered on aspects of that unit most troubling to the American democratic system. The Green Berets lacked accountability, were involved in very murky operations, and had an unhealthy relationship with the CIA (which protected them).

What American democracy needed was not the kind of covert operations empire Vietnam represented, but an intelligence apparatus that collected intelligence and gave policymakers an unbiased, honest look at the world as it really existed. That is not what American military intelligence provided in Vietnam.

Without warning, the memo landed like a thunderclap on the desks of the senior U.S. Army intelligence officers in Saigon on August 15, 1967. Brigadier General Phillip B. Davidson, Jr., the head of intelligence for MACV (Military Assistance Command Vietnam, the American high command), minced no words.

"The figure of [enemy] combat strength," Davidson ordered, "and particularly of guerrillas must take a steady and significant downward trend, as I am convinced this reflects true enemy status."

Unvarnished, Davidson was ordering nothing less than a wholesale revision in the Army intelligence's estimate of the guerrilla enemy's strength. It was no ordinary procedural change, for the order went to the very heart of the course of the entire Vietnam war. Intelligence officers who saw the memo concluded instantly that they had now being ordered to participate in an intelligence fantasy.

They were right. Behind the memo lay an intricate struggle for high stakes, centering on how much "progress" the United States was making in the Vietnam war. That "progress" was defined almost exclusively in quantitative terms: body counts, number of weapons captured, villages "secured," and so forth. Nearly 500,000 American troops under General William C. Westmoreland were engaged in a war of attrition with the Viet Cong and North Vietnamese, a war where "success" was determined strictly in attritional ratios: if the enemy, as Westmoreland claimed, was being worn down, then there should be fewer of the enemy.

Thus, intelligence conclusions on how many enemy troops were in the field served as the final arbiter. By 1967, the war had become a divisive issue in the United States, and there was growing restiveness; there was pressure on the American and military command to conclusively demonstrate progress. But to Westmoreland's dismay, the CIA concluded there was no progress at all. Despite his claim that over 100,000 enemy soldiers had been killed in combat, the CIA's studies estimated there were somewhere around 431,000 enemy troops in the field—even more than estimated only a few years before. Westmoreland wasn't winning; he was losing.

The CIA conclusion ignited anger in MACV headquarters, which refused to believe that the army they considered just about finished—an army that had been "attrited" to the tune of 100,000 casualties, an army being pounded around the clock by air power —could have recovered so fast. No, there must be something wrong. To accept the CIA's figures would be to admit that the United States was losing the war. More importantly, those strength figures, once they reached Washington, would undoubtedly cause a wholesale rethinking of the war effort.

To be sure, the task of counting guerrillas was not easy. As General Daniel Graham of Army intelligence put it, trying to quantify elusive guerrillas in the jungles was "like counting cockroaches in a dark barn with a flashlight." Still, it could be done, and the CIA figures, considered generally reliable, represented a real problem for the military. How to solve it?

Count fewer guerrillas: intelligence officials at MACV formulated a unique theory, under which all SD (self-defense) and SSD (secret self-defense) forces, the Viet Cong part-time militia, would be stricken from the total enemy strength figures, on the grounds that they were not real combat forces, anyway. With one stroke of the pen, that removed nearly 200,000 men from the totals, leaving the enemy with a total of fewer than 300,000 men—real "progress" from previous totals. Therefore, the United States was winning the war in Vietnam.

The theory was an exercise in self-deception. Many Viet Cong militia soldiers had been killed during the previous years, and Westmoreland never showed any hesitancy including them among the body counts. Now, his intelligence branch was proposing to eliminate the very same troops he once happily took credit for killing. Westmoreland was trapped by his own rhetoric announcing "progress" in the war.

The CIA at first refused to accede to this fantasy, and a full-fledged intelligence battle was underway. It was finally settled by DCI Richard Helms, who ordered his own analysts to work out a compromise. Over strong objections from some inside the CIA, the final report showed a lower figure for enemy strength, allowing both President Johnson and Westmoreland to cite it as evidence for "progress" in the war.

The Tet offensive of 1968 swept aside this illusion, and illustrated the true dimension of how badly American intelligence had become bent. The CIA, which previously had withstood the intense political heat with its assessments on the ineffectiveness of the U.S. bombing of North Vietnam, finally wilted, and compromised the one aspect of its operations that had remained sacrosanct: intelligence judgment.

Helms and his compatriots in other arms of American intelligence had no guarantee that the White House would heed any bad news, but it was their duty to deliver the news, untemporized by political considerations. Three years after the great Vietnam intelligence imbroglio, Helms did not pass on to the White House a CIA report concluding that any attempt to eliminate Communist base areas in Cambodia would have no long-term effect. The analysts who prepared the report did not know, as Helms did, that President Nixon was planning an incursion into Cambodia in an attempt to achieve a knockout blow against the Communists. Although he received the report two weeks before the incursion took place, Helms sat on it, believing that giving it to Nixon would only provoke him.

So another failure was added to all the others in Vietnam, that graveyard of American assumptions and obsessions. If the sins of American intelligence were limited to compromised intelligence reports, then the record would be spotty, at best.

But it turned out that American intelligence was guilty of much more serious sins. And these had been committed against the American people.

NINE

The War at Home

LIKE MOST bureaucratic nightmares, the Case of the Limousine That Wasn't There began with a piece of paper, in this case a memorandum in the early fall of 1956 from J. Edgar Hoover to the New York field office. Hoover ordered that the office investigate the finances of the U.S. Communist Party's national chairman, William Foster, and the party's general secretary, Eugene Dennis.

Pointedly, Hoover noted his belief that the Communist leaders were enjoying ostentatious luxury, were residing in expensive apartments, and were paid large salaries at sharp variance with the starvation wages paid most party workers. Where he got this information Hoover didn't say, but no FBI agent was about to question the source of the man known invariably in the Bureau as "The Director." As all agents understood, Hoover was fixated on the American Communist Party, and had diverted a large portion of the FBI's resources over the years into watching and infiltrating a group many FBI agents felt not worthy of all that attention.

The arrival of Hoover's order precipitated something of a crisis at the New York office, for such an order was regarded as a commandment directly from God. And like heavenly dispatches, Hoover's orders tended to carry an air of omniscience; as the FBI agents well knew, Hoover had already decided that the two Communists were living in luxury. As was his habit, Hoover was now ordering his agents to find the evidence for the conclusion he had already reached.

It was with some trepidation that a crew of agents was dispatched to conduct a major field investigation of the two Communists' finances—aware that unless they found evidence of the two men living in opulence, Hoover's wrath would descend on the agents' heads.

To their dismay, they could find no such evidence. As they reported to Hoover in November of that year, "Foster and Dennis reside in apartments located in tenement blocks, considered to range from modest to poor. The interiors of their apartments are not lavishly furnished. They have no servants. Mrs. Dennis does her own laundry. Mrs. Foster sends hers out."

As for income, the agents reported, "Foster receives a weekly salary of $70 from the Communist Party; Dennis receives a weekly salary of $67.50 . . . Neither Foster nor Dennis is known to have an extensive expense account with the Communist Party or an outside income."

As anticipated, the New York office's report greatly displeased Hoover, who complained that his agents had fallen down on the job by failing to uncover the two Communists' luxurious life style. "On an overall basis," Hoover insisted, "they [Foster and Dennis] are living much better than the average Communist member." Further, Hoover claimed, the two men went on long vacations and had chauffeur-driven limousines, all provided by the party.

Limousines? That was news to the New York agents, who started all over again, spurred by another Hoover memo ordering them to find what Hoover knew to be a fact. The agents in New York left no stone unturned: they peered into the two Communists' savings accounts (modest), their utility bills, their tax returns, their weekly expenditures at the grocery store—in short, every dime Foster and Dennis spent was laboriously traced. In the end, the result was the same: Foster and Dennis were poor as church mice, and if there were any chauffeur-driven limousines available, they didn't bother to use them (both men, a surveillance by a platoon of FBI agents discovered, preferred to travel by subway).

The FBI reports to this effect only enraged Hoover further, and several months were consumed in double-checking and triple-checking such trivialities as whether Foster tipped lavishly on the rare occasions when he ate at a restaurant. Finally, Hoover gave up, and in a final memo in a waspish series all but calling the New York office—largest in the country—a bunch of idiots, he noted, "The investigation of the New York office failed to develop sufficient information . . ."

The agents sighed with relief at this parting shot, for the assignment was finally over, and they could return to more important business. Eager to be rid of a mission they privately agreed was a total waste of the FBI's time, the agents missed the real significance underlying Hoover's order. They did not know that their boss was about to take the first step in creating a very dangerous assault on the U.S. Constitution—an assault soon joined by the rest of the intelligence community.

The hunt for the hidden wealth of two aging Stalinists was vintage Hoover, for it reflected the depth of his ideological obsession with the American Communist Party, the entity he believed represented the single most important internal security threat to the United States. Hoover's belief persisted, even in the face of incontrovertible evidence that by 1956, the party had become a political joke. In that year, what remained of the organization virtually collapsed after Khrushchev's stunning Twentieth Party Congress speech shattered Stalin's reputation.

What remained in 1957, honeycombed with FBI informers, was a pitiful remnant of 3,474 faithful. They were virtually forgotten, and as the courts began overturning Smith Act convictions, the fear of the great internal threat of domestic communism was fading. Also fading was Hoover's lifetime dream of completely eradicating the American Communist Party.

Sometime in 1956, Hoover decided on a dramatic plan to rescue that goal. It was devised in the greatest secrecy, for Hoover was perfectly aware that what he was about to do was clearly illegal. Known as the Counterintelligence Program (Cointelpro in FBI argot), Hoover's plan sought to destroy the Communist Party by a series of actions that would tear it apart. Using FBI informants inside the party, false rumors would be spread, setting off one faction against another. Anonymous charges would be made, sowing suspicion. Employers of Communists would be pressured to fire those employees. Families of Communists would be harassed. Any firm doing business with Communists would be pressured to stop doing so. Neighbors of Communists would be told how dangerous those Communists were, with suggestions that they should be forced to leave the neighborhood. Party leaders would be accused of being FBI informers.

Cointelpro had nothing to do with counterintelligence. It had everything to do with Hoover's narrow view of internal security, a myopia that occupied what was probably the world's finest counterintelligence organization with such tasks as pawing through the garbage of old Communist Party faithful to determine what plots they might be hatching. Agents with advanced college degrees and the best counterintelligence training money could buy were spending their time with such duties as harassing a New Jersey scoutmaster because his wife was a socialist. Others were wasting their time keeping tabs on another Hoover obsession, the tiny Socialist Workers Party, the American Trotskyist faction. For thirty-one years, the FBI recruited informants, carried out break-ins, and generally made life miserable for the Trotskyists (who in 1966 amounted to a grand total of five hundred adherents).

But to Hoover, the Trotskyists were Communists in sheep's clothing, and therefore worthy of the extensive FBI resources deployed against them, including, at one point, one hundred agents. The fact that the Socialist Workers Party was a fringe group far out of the American political mainstream and posed no internal security threat made no difference.

Hoover's offensive virtually destroyed what was left of both the Communist and Socialist Workers parties, and although he considered Cointelpro a success, the FBI Director seemed not to have realized that he had taken a very dangerous step. He had moved from being the head of a federal law enforcement and counterespionage organization to secret police chief, deciding which political organizations had a right to exist.

Hoover did realize that Cointelpro, if ever discovered, could have severe legal complications—break-ins, warrantless wiretaps, criminal provocations—so he imposed the most rigid secrecy, even within the Bureau. Documents relating to the program were marked "do not file," meaning they were withheld from the FBI filing system. The documents also were prepared without the filing system's sequential serial numbers, removing any clues that any such documents even existed.* Cointelpro material was hidden away in an entirely separate filing system; most of the documents were burned after a certain period of time.

Hoover believed that Cointelpro's secrets were secure, and he was ready for the next step, a program called Cominfil, Bureau argot for "Communist Infiltration." Still another Hoover obsession lay behind this new program, the conviction that despite their small numbers, the cunning and devious Communists—having been destroyed as a political organization by Cointelpro—would now seek to infiltrate and take over mass political organizations. Under Cominfil, the FBI would be able to investigate *any* political organization on the pretext of checking to see if it had been infiltrated by Communists. And any such organization infiltrated would be subjected to an intensive FBI smear campaign accusing them of being "dominated by Communists."

Cominfil provided Hoover with an unparalleled power, and he soon took full advantage of it, conducting large-scale investigations of groups that ranged across the entire American spectrum, from the NAACP to women's rights organizations. (One branch of Cominfil, known by its code name of Homex, investigated homosexual organizations; Hoover believed that homosexuals were subject to Communist blackmail and therefore most vulnerable to Communist penetration and takeover.)

How much President Eisenhower—and, later, presidents Kennedy, Johnson, and Nixon—knew of Cointelpro and Cominfil remains an open question. Hoover, as he had since the time of President Roosevelt, bombarded the White House with an endless stream of memos on the dangers of the domestic Communists, and provided strong hints that he was moving very aggressively against this stark threat. There is no record that anyone at the

---

* That would allow FBI officials, if ever called to testify, to say that a "review of the files" had turned up no Cointelpro documents. Anyone looking at the files would find documents perfectly sequenced with no missing numbers, the usually certain clue that sensitive documents had been removed.

White House asked any searching questions about what exactly Hoover was doing. Likewise, Congress adopted a laissez-faire attitude toward Hoover and the FBI, its lack of oversight perhaps spurred by persistent rumors that Hoover had been collecting dirt on House and Senate members—material that might find its way into the columns of such close Hoover friends as Walter Winchell and Westbrook Pegler.

As a result, only Hoover and a small circle of FBI officials knew that the Bureau had recruited an army of 5,000 informants to infiltrate and disrupt nearly 400 political, civil rights, and other organizations; that selected FBI agents were being given lessons in illegal break-ins at the FBI Academy; that the FBI was compiling a "Security Index" of Americans to be detained in event of war—including 200,000 "dangerous" persons; and that the FBI had begun a "Student Agitation Report" system to spy on college and university student groups throughout the country.

In short, Hoover was busy creating a federal political police force. Free of presidential and congressional oversight, he could turn the FBI's capabilities loose against the obsessions that dominated his life. His control of the FBI was total, and he set the Bureau's agenda, decided on its methods, and preordained the results. Every scrap of paper dealing with Cointelpro or any matter involving communism was seen by Hoover; even the smallest administrative matters were decided by him. He operated in virtually total isolation, arriving at conclusions about the larger world around him without ever spending any time in that world. For that reason, Hoover rejected the advice of agents who had the temerity to tell him that any of his convictions might be wrong. (The head of the Chicago FBI office once told Hoover there was no point in tying up precious manpower investigating the city's women's liberation movement. He was sharply rebuked by Hoover, who told him that the movement was supported by the Socialist Workers Party and that the movement must be investigated to determine its "subversive ramifications.")

Hoover had even less patience with any FBI agent who questioned another of his obsessions, black civil rights groups. Hoover for many years resisted the hiring of blacks as FBI agents, and the entire FBI force of more than five thousand men and women by 1960 only had five blacks—who happened to be chauffeurs and personal servants at Hoover's home. Hoover called them "honorary special agents," for he had previously ruled that no black person could ever be given the title "Special Agent," the designation for all graduates of the FBI Academy who worked as field agents.

A man very much of his Southern, segregated upbringing, Hoover reserved special suspicion for the civil rights movement, an animus that began to focus on one man, the Reverend Martin Luther King, Jr.

The reason for Hoover's specific dislike for King remains unknown. The prevailing speculation is that Hoover was convinced that the civil rights leader was a tool of the Communists, whose leadership would lead to eventual Communist domination of the civil rights movement.

Hoover first became interested in King in 1958, when he saw an FBI report noting that King had met with Benjamin Davis, a black American Communist Party leader. Three years later, following the Freedom Rider campaign, Hoover ordered the Bureau to begin a full-scale investigation of King under the Cominfil program; Hoover insisted that King was a Communist "dupe." Illegal wiretaps on King's home telephone revealed that King often sought advice from Stanley Levison, a New York lawyer and civil rights activist. An FBI informant in the Communist Party then reported that Levison was a secret member of the party. The evidence, all circumstantial, was final proof, in Hoover's mind, that his original supposition about King as Communist stalking horse was correct.

The allegation against Levison spurred Hoover to order an all-out investigative effort to prove King's Communist leanings, further spurred when King angered Hoover by criticizing FBI agents in Albany, Georgia, for doing nothing while blacks demonstrating for civil rights were savagely beaten.

Despite Hoover's urging, his agents could find no connection between Communists and the civil rights movement. Five years after the Cominfil investigation began, William C. Sullivan, head of the Bureau's Domestic Intelligence Division, told Hoover that the Communists were ineffectual in influencing the movement. Sullivan, a Hoover acolyte and one of the few Bureau officials Hoover called by his first name, made the bureaucratic mistake of his life, for his boss was furious: how could he possibly reach such a conclusion? Didn't he know—as Hoover did—that the Communists were running the civil rights movement?

Sullivan frantically tried to make amends, and only seven days after telling Hoover on August 23, 1963, that the Communists were not involved in the civil rights movement, prepared a new memo confessing that Hoover was right. This fawning reversal was followed by a further effort of Sullivan to atone: he recommended a full-scale Cointelpro operation be launched to destroy Martin Luther King, Jr. Hoover needed little prompting, and for the next five years, in an operation that did not end until King's assassination in 1968, the FBI did everything in its power to destroy him. The effort included tapes made of King's alleged sexual liaisons with assorted women in motel rooms (these were sent to Mrs. King), and a plan to get King to commit suicide; he would be replaced with another black leader who had already been selected by Sullivan as the official, FBI-approved civil rights leader.

At the same time, Hoover ordered a Cointelpro operation against black nationalist groups on the grounds that the "rise of black revolution" in the United States represented a serious threat to American internal security. Other targeted groups included anti-war organizations. The stated purpose of such operations was to prevent violence at a time in the 1960s when civil unrest was extensive throughout the nation. But in doing so, the Bureau took the law into its own hands.

Cointelpro and Cominfil were pure and simple attempts to stifle political dissent—and it was dissent that most exercised J. Edgar Hoover. In the nearly 330,000 so-called "investigations" carried out under these two programs, not a single instance of any criminal activity was ever prosecuted, nor was there one single instance of Communist success in being able to take advantage of American internal dissent. Indeed, the only success that Cointelpro and Cominfil achieved was to sully the reputation of the FBI, a stain it is still trying to remove, long after the death of Hoover.

But the significance of those two assaults on civil liberties extended further, for they established the pattern for even more widespread attacks, this time from the rest of the American intelligence community. The new assault was, strikingly enough, a reprise of a phenomenon that had happened before in American history: a foreign war, a perceived threat, and a turning inward by American intelligence, against domestic dissent. And, as had happened before, secrecy and presidential power were the essential ingredients to set the process in motion.

In this case, the trigger was the war in Vietnam. By 1965, it was beginning to cause deep divisions in the United States, and a flourishing anti-war movement was determined to end American involvement in the war. In April of that year, McGeorge Bundy, adviser to President Johnson, asked Hoover if he had any information on "Communist infiltration" of anti-war groups. Hoover interpreted Bundy's request as really asking for information that Johnson could use to smear his critics.

The FBI set to work, and emerged with reams of reports on Communist involvement with various anti-war groups, but as Hoover admitted, the Bureau could not find what Johnson was really looking for, intelligence that the Communists were *controlling* the movement. Hoover urged his men on to greater effort, for Johnson was exerting more pressure for results, adding another mission: spy on members of Congress, especially opponents of the President's policies, to determine if they had any "contacts with foreign officials."

Irrespective of presidential sanction, that put the FBI in the highly illegal business of spying on Congress, an ominous step hardly noticed, for events began to move with even greater force. The next step, under White House pressure, was to unleash Cointelpro against the anti-war movement, an action that had no pretense of internal security functions; it was a flat-out attempt to cripple the President's opposition, an opposition Johnson had convinced himself was the chief reason for American failure to achieve victory in Vietnam.

If that weren't enough, Johnson enlisted the rest of the American intelligence apparatus in the drive to stifle dissent against his policies. Beginning in the summer of 1965—shortly after the FBI had been ordered to investigate the anti-war movement—U.S. Army intelligence agents began to infiltrate and spy on a wide range of political groups, including the Ku Klux Klan and a Harvard University anti-war group. In the Army spying effort, which used one thousand investigators and three hundred officers, most of their time was spent assiduously collecting every political utterance considered even remotely "treasonable." The Army attempted to justify the spying on the thin pretense that it was a necessary intelligence-collection effort for a series of secret contingency plans known as Garden Plot, to be used in the event that federal troops were called in to put down urban riots.

Not even that kind of justification existed for the domestic spying of another federal agency, the CIA. In that case, the CIA was in clear violation of the National Security Act of 1947, which flatly prohibited the agency from conducting any "internal security functions."

The 1967 order to begin domestic spying operations, code-named Chaos, was the result of White House pressure on Richard Helms to discover the "foreign connections" that Johnson and his staff were certain lay behind a wave of student unrest in the United States. As Helms understood, the White House believed that Communist agents undoubtedly were financing and leading the unrest.†

The CIA established a partnership with the FBI for Chaos, and half of the forty informants used in the CIA operation were FBI assets Hoover agreed to donate to the agency. Surely there were better things for the CIA to do than spy on anti-war groups and other political dissidents. None of the CIA agents involved could have failed to understand that their activities had not even the remotest connection with foreign intelligence. No such connection existed in Project Merrimac, an offshoot of Chaos that infiltrated and spied upon ten major peace and civil rights organizations in Washington, D.C.: from the beginning, agents involved in Merrimac were told that the spying was related to obtaining advance warning of planned demonstrations outside CIA headquarters that the agency might find embarrassing. And there was even less connection in one of Chaos's more elaborate enterprises, known as Operation Mudhen, which tied up seventeen CIA agents to spy on columnist Jack Anderson and his associates in hopes of discovering his sources within the agency.

Nevertheless, Helms and other CIA officials accepted the White House order for illegal spying without a murmur of protest, one of the reasons being that the agency was already in-

† No such connections were ever found, and Helms ran afoul of the Nixon White House in 1969 by presenting a CIA report saying that youth unrest around the world, the United States included, was the result of "internal policies" (a polite reference to Nixon's controversial Vietnam war policy). Nixon and Kissinger were displeased.

volved in illegal domestic operations. One of them, known as HT/Lingual, had started in 1955. Until finally ended in 1973, HT/Lingual read all mail addressed to the Soviet Union dispatched through the New York Post Office; more than 2 million pieces of mail were photographed, and 215,000 pieces opened and read.

Another clear violation of the Internal Security Act, HT/Lingual was run by one of the CIA's most intriguing characters, the agency's chief of counterintelligence, James Jesus Angleton. He had been deeply involved in that arcane field since joining the CIA in 1947; characteristically stubborn and tenacious, he had immersed himself so deeply in the world of moles, double agents, and double-cross, there were those in the CIA who thought he had become consumed by his mission of preventing Soviet KGB penetration of the CIA.

HT/Lingual seemed to summarize the problem. Angleton paid not the slightest attention to the legal aspects of the operation, and in the face of all evidence, insisted that KGB agents would use the U.S. mails to convey orders and intelligence. (Considering the delays in mail deliveries, it could not have been a very efficient system for sending intelligence information.) Angleton stubbornly insisted later that the operation had been "useful," but when asked to cite examples, refused on the grounds that the CIA was probably infiltrated by the KGB.

There was no question of Angleton's deep patriotism, but like many others in the American intelligence community, that devotion to his country often blinded him to the realities of the American democratic system. He could speak eloquently, for example, on the American ideals and freedom that made the American democracy so cherished—and then, almost in the same breath, justify the illegal imprisonment of a KGB defector to the United States for *three years* on the operational grounds that since the man was a suspected KGB infiltrator, such measures were justified.

Angleton lived in a world of triangulated suspicion and shifting loyalties— "a wilderness of mirrors," in his elegant phrase— but his supreme error was in elevating the operational requirements of counterintelligence above the law. How far Angleton seemed to have strayed was exemplified in 1975, when, during a private session with investigators from the Church Committee questioning him about CIA domestic spying, he said, "It is inconceivable that a secret intelligence arm of the government has to comply with all the overt orders of the government."

Angleton claimed later that this disturbing assertion was misunderstood, but it was Angleton who did not understand. Like Hoover—another man whose deep patriotism was unquestioned —he did not understand that whatever the dimensions of the external threat facing the United States at any given moment, no perceived threat was worth scrapping the Constitution in the name of preserving its principles.

By the time President Nixon took office in 1969, there was a massive domestic spying operation underway, with just about every component of the American intelligence community involved. The operation involved wholesale violations of the law, and it would appear, at first glance, that in terms of sheer size and freedom of unsupervised operations, American intelligence had reached an apex of sorts. With presidential sanction to commit those violations, and a Congress that either did not know or chose not to know what was going on, there did not appear to be much in the way of restraints at work. But there would be worse, much worse, to come.

Richard Nixon scowled, regarding the ground below as his plane flew over the Potomac River. His attention was fixed on the large building in the Virginia suburbs, with thousands of cars parked in the lots around it. "All these people working out there," he said to his Budget Director, James Schlesinger. "They're probably not accomplishing too much."

Schlesinger, later briefly DCI, would remember that remark, for it indicated Nixon's deep-seated antipathy to the federal agency sprawled out below him, the Central Intelligence Agency. Nixon's attitude stemmed from several complicated motives, among them the conviction that the agency was staffed with "Ivy League liberals" who were opposed to him. At the same time, however, Nixon had uses for the CIA—and the rest of the intelligence community.

Essentially, Nixon believed that the intelligence agencies had not yet done enough to combat the enemies of the United States, both foreign and domestic. The more opposition Nixon encountered, the more he was convinced that these "enemies" had grown ever stronger and more powerful. Like his predecessor, he believed firmly that domestic opposition was largely controlled and funded from the outside. He was determined to bring this opposition to an end, lest it wreck his grand design for a new world, especially his "secret plan" for ending the war in Vietnam, detente with the Soviet Union, and opening relations with China.

To that end, Nixon assigned one of his White House assistants, Tom C. Huston, as the czar of domestic security, with a sweeping mandate to "improve" the intelligence agencies' role in this area. Nixon wanted the CIA, the Defense Intelligence Agency (the Pentagon's chief intelligence organization), the FBI, and the National Security Agency to do much more than they had ever done in uncovering what he knew to be foreign intelligence agencies' role in fomenting unrest in the United States.

Huston, a Nixon loyalist, immediately went to work. He convened a meeting of the heads of the intelligence agencies to come up with a plan. It was remarkable that either J. Edgar Hoover or Richard Helms was able to keep a straight face while Huston told them of the President's desire for a more "forceful" domestic intelligence operation. What was needed, Huston said, was for the FBI and the CIA, especially, to carry out warrantless wiretapping and other such techniques.

Huston did not know that both the CIA and FBI were already busy breaking the law. He also did not realize that there was no way his overall plan for virtually unlimited domestic spying would ever survive in the jungle of the intelligence community's bureaucratic politics; Hoover, who was becoming increasingly cautious about illegal FBI activities, balked. Sure enough, no sooner had Nixon approved Huston's recommendations, when Hoover talked him out of it, arguing that the Huston plan, which gave the intelligence community unprecedented and sweeping powers for domestic spying, would probably leak out.

Nixon didn't need the Huston plan to carry out the kind of domestic intelligence he wanted. He put continuous pressure on the CIA for such operations, enlisted the Internal Revenue Service as another weapon in the battle, and compiled an "enemies list" of Americans considered to be his leading opponents. Those who made the list, in addition to whatever troubles they may have experienced at the hands of the FBI, CIA, and other intelligence agencies, could now expect tax troubles, too.

Convinced that a host of enemies were conspiring against him,

Nixon lashed out, removing virtually all legal restraints. He had no concern that his attorney general would question such tactics. John Mitchell possessed an astonishingly lax attitude toward the law; in one incident, he admitted to a shocked federal judge that he was too busy to sign some federal wiretap warrants, so he had one of his assistants forge his name to them.

Nixon was angered over what he believed was an unnecessary fastidiousness within the intelligence community over risky operations, particularly domestic spying. Hoover, increasingly worried that the FBI break-ins would be exposed, ordered an end to all "black bag jobs," while Helms, it appeared, was now dragging his feet over Nixon's demands for increased domestic spying. To Nixon's annoyance, everybody in the intelligence community suddenly seemed to be nervous about illegal activities, even with full presidential authorization.

Impatient for results, Nixon finally decided that the intelligence agencies and the FBI offered no real hope of destroying the enemies. He made a fateful decision to create, in effect, his own intelligence apparatus, a secret group composed of men—mostly ex-FBI or ex-CIA agents—who were much more attuned to his way of thinking and much more willing to plunge full steam ahead in domestic security investigations without much thought devoted to how legal any of them might be. Men like G. Gordon Liddy, formerly of the FBI, and E. Howard Hunt, formerly of the CIA, happily signed up for the new unit, known informally as "the plumbers."

As J. Edgar Hoover understood, the "plumbers" were intended to be replacements for his FBI agents. To his shock, despite his long and friendly relationship with Nixon dating back to the days of the Alger Hiss case, Hoover suddenly found that Nixon really had little further use for him. Hoover felt the chill when he made his first contact with Nixon aide John Ehrlichman, who made it clear that the Nixon White House wanted much more than Hoover and his FBI, for all their illegal operations, could offer. For his part, Ehrlichman considered Hoover a cautious old fossil. Attending a dinner one night in September 1969, at Hoover's home, Ehrlichman distastefully regarded the walls jammed with the plaques, mementos, and photographs testifying to Hoover's career. It was not a house; Hoover was living in a museum.

When it all came crashing down around Nixon's head at Watergate, Hoover was not around, having died in 1972. His last months in office were preoccupied with worry about exposure of illegal operations. Hoover was retrenching, as were other elements of the intelligence community. The CIA was in the process of closing down HT/Lingual, the Army's domestic spying operations were ended in 1971, and the FBI was scaling back Cointelpro operations. Further, with Hoover gone and Helms eased out of his job (he was given the post of ambassador to Iran, after quietly noting the inappropriateness of Nixon's first offer, ambassador to the Soviet Union), everybody seemed to be getting cautious. New men, with different attitudes, were moving in—men like James Schlesinger, the new DCI in 1973, who not only announced his intention to pare one thousand people from the CIA bureaucracy, but also demanded that agency officials provide him with written reports on any "illegal activities" in which the CIA had been involved.

It was no time for anyone to take chances. The intelligence community seemed to sense, as Nixon did not, that the heyday of domestic spying operations was about to end. Things were changing in the country; there seemed to be a new, skeptical attitude about the long tradition of executive power. Vietnam was the main contributor to that skepticism, but there were also several events which caused the first serious public concern about what the intelligence community had been doing all those years.

It began one night in March 1971, when someone (or several people) broke into the FBI field office in Media, Pennsylvania, and stole all the files. Subsequently, the burglar(s), whoever that was (the burglary was never solved), began releasing some of the documents found in the FBI office, a number of which bore the mysterious heading "Cointelpro." Nobody at that point knew what Cointelpro meant, but the documents were very disturbing, for they clearly outlined FBI-sponsored disruptions of domestic political groups.

Then came the "family jewels" episode, the name given to the written reports of malfeasance, ordered by Schlesinger. He was shocked to find so many illegal operations in which the CIA participated —including assassinations—and wound up with nearly seven hundred pages, a virtual catalogue of criminality. Suddenly shifted to another job in the government, Schlesinger left the so-called "family jewels" report to his successor, William Colby, to deal with. But before Colby could decide how to proceed, some of the report's revelations wound up on the front page of the New York *Times*.

Now the proverbial cat was out of the bag. In an effort to defuse the growing public controversy, President Gerald Ford, Nixon's successor, hurriedly appointed a special commission (named after its chairman, the new Vice President, Nelson Rockefeller). Ford followed that by issuing the first Executive Order setting guidelines for American intelligence agencies.

But too many revelations were leaking out; there was the sense that the Rockefeller Commission was a Band-Aid, and that a much more in-depth investigation was necessary. What was happening was not only a profound shift in public opinion, but an equally profound shift in the outlook of Congress, as well. The congressional elections of 1974, which brought into Congress the so-called "Watergate class," resulted in a significant movement in congressional power, from the small circle of men who exercised a casual (at best) oversight of the American intelligence community to new members who were determined to reassert Congress's constitutional role as watchdogs over the Executive Branch of government.

What would end was the "ostrich era" of congressional oversight, a time when, in the words of Senator John C. Stennis—a key Southern conservative power in that body—he and other members of Congress supposedly charged with the duty of overseeing the intelligence agencies felt compelled to "shut your eyes some" when dealing with intelligence matters. Clearly, the time when intelligence matters were handled almost as an afterthought would no longer work.

As events had proven, that casualness had led to disaster. What system would replace it was still an open question, but first priority was to find out just what the American intelligence community had been doing. The result was the appointment of two select committees in the House and Senate, with sweeping investigative mandates. They were ready to turn the American intelligence apparatus inside out.

Which was precisely what worried William Colby, who as DCI would face the burden of confronting the committees' unprecedented charge into a world Congress had long avoided. In the end, it was Colby who was to play the key role in how those investigations were conducted.

First, Colby decided that, judged overall, it was probably a healthy development for American democracy to take a long look at what his agency and others had been doing. Second, in a private meeting with Senator Frank Church, chairman of the Senate investigating committee, Colby made it clear that the investigation would not divulge names of agents or American intelligence assets still operating. However salutary the democratic process, he was not about to get people killed in its name. Church agreed. Third, Colby tried to eliminate some of the more troublesome flashpoints certain to create difficulties. To Colby, the chief irritant was the man most directly associated with illegal domestic spying activities, James Angleton; Colby eased him into retirement.‡

Colby's greatest fear was that the two congressional inquiries would turn into circuses. Initially, they did not, but when the House committee—under the chairmanship of Representative Otis Pike of New York—began garnering bigger headlines than its Senate counterpart, Colby sensed that Church and the senators were about to make a grandstand play to recapture the front page. Church began speculating aloud about the possibility of a CIA "rogue elephant" on the loose.

Church's description infuriated CIA officials, but there was worse to come. Colby was ordered to bring with him for the next hearing a poison dart gun the CIA had developed (but never used). Colby dutifully brought it along to the Senate hearing room, and found the place packed with television cameras and reporters, tipped ahead of time that they were in for a great show. Colby wanted no part of the poison gun, but as it was handed up to the committee, and the television cameras focused in, senators virtually elbowed each other in an effort to hold the gun. Handling the exotic-looking gun was a certain guarantee of television time, and a probable front-page picture in the next day's newspapers.

Overall, though, the Senate committee investigation was thor-

‡ Thus ending many years of tension between the two men. An extreme conservative, Angleton considered Colby a mushy-headed liberal, and after his forced retirement from the CIA began privately hinting that Colby was probably a KGB mole.

ough and fair. The House committee's performance was much less impressive. Afflicted by staff problems and Pike's confrontational style, that committee's final report was rejected by the full House and ordered kept secret (it was later leaked).

However, the Senate committee's final report, which took up six volumes, represented the most extensive examination in American history of its intelligence agencies. The report concentrated almost exclusively on the agencies' illegal operations, and was scathing in its examination of how far so many operations had strayed from the principles and laws of American democracy. There was a tragic irony: the crimes of the American intelligence agencies were carried out against a threat that did not exist. There was no Ulster in the United States, no hostile states on American borders, and no totalitarian political movement within the United States that ever came close to destabilizing or even threatening American democracy. The real enemy, clearly, was ourselves and our own fears.

Nobody summed it up better than a man who was not a member of Congress, nor did he have anything to do with intelligence. His name was John W. Nields, Jr., the federal prosecutor for the case involving the only members of the American intelligence community ever prosecuted for officially sanctioned, but illegal, activities.* Nields had listened with some distaste as the defense for Mark W. Felt and Edward S. Miller, former FBI officials charged with ordering illegal break-ins during the Bureau's hunt for members of the Weathermen, defended their actions on the grounds of "national security." Felt and Miller, the defense attorneys argued, had the right to commit illegal acts for the "higher purpose" of apprehending the dangerous Weathermen, who were setting off bombs.

Nields disposed of that tired old argument during his summation to the jury, telling its members they would hear the sounds of Weathermen bombs, but they should also "listen for the sound of the Constitution of the United States. It doesn't quite make as much noise as the Weathermen bombs. It doesn't shriek at you. It doesn't even whisper. It just sits there silent, as it's done for 200 years."

* Nields was also Majority Chief counsel for the House of Representatives during the Iran-Contra hearings.

PART FOUR

Time of the Spy
1974–1988

TEN

The Crown Jewel

NO ONE who knew anything about Lieutenant General William E. Odom, a thin, bespectacled man of owlish and academic looks, doubted the depth of his hawkish outlook. That view was honed during a career in the intelligence wars—Army intelligence, Defense Intelligence Agency, military attaché in Moscow, and National Security Council—and he had publicly articulated it in many forums.

So when Odom strode to a podium before the annual meeting of the Association of Former Intelligence Officers in Washington, D.C., on October 10, 1987, it could be safely anticipated the audience was in for another talk on the Soviet menace, cloaked in the characteristic Odom stridency.

And yet, the mere fact that Odom was even appearing in public that day was extraordinary. Two and a half years before, he had been appointed director of America's National Security Agency, and since then had been working hard to keep both himself and the agency as far out of public sight as possible. It was very much in the tradition of NSA, sometimes jokingly referred to as "Never Say Anything" and "No Such Agency." America's largest intelligence organization is deliberately designed to be the least understood. Its basic function is simple, yet its job is immense: to eavesdrop on the entire world, picking up all electronic transmissions, no matter how faint or what the point of origin, then to plow through this pile of chaff to find the kernels of intelligence—the telephone conversation between a Soviet general and a subordinate in the field; the enciphered radio messages vulnerable to attack by NSA cryptanalysts; the teletyped orders conveying troop movements.

Odom presided over an agency that was something like a black hole capturing light. Around the clock, NSA vacuums up electronic signals; operating in deepest secrecy, it emits little evidence of its existence, despite its massive size and multibillion-dollar budget. Odom, like his predecessor, kept an extremely low profile, thus it was not surprising that prior to the beginning of his speech, he demanded that a television crew vacate the room. Then, hardly glancing at a few print journalists with writing pads in hand, Odom launched into a tirade against the American media. His audience of ex-spooks nodded their heads in agreement. What gave the media the right, Odom demanded, under the First Amendment to reveal the government's most precious secrets?

"They [the media] are deceiving themselves and the public about their role," Odom complained. "Quite simply, there is no comprehensive 'right to know' included, either explicitly or implicitly, within the First Amendment. If we do not save our intelligence capabilities, if we fritter them away through leaks and publicity, we may pay a very large price in blood to save not only the First Amendment, but also the Constitution."

This was Odom's message for over thirty minutes, but his most caustic line came after the speech. After finishing, Odom was approached by one of the men he regarded as a prime sinner, James Bamford. A lawyer-turned-journalist, Bamford was the author of *The Puzzle Palace*, a highly praised examination of the National Security Agency—a work that was not only very revealing of secret NSA operations, but also shed much light on the agency's forays into domestic spying.

Introducing himself and offering his outstretched hand, Bamford was coldly regarded by Odom. "You, sir," the general snapped, refusing to shake his hand, "I regard as an unconvicted felon."

No more revelatory moment could be imagined to illustrate the long struggle, unique to the American democratic process, between those who try to keep secrets and those involved in the "people's right to know." The struggle lies at the very heart of modern democracy. On one side are men like Odom who have spent a lifetime in the secret world, and understand that in a world where Armageddon is only fifteen minutes away, the intelligence they collect may mean the difference between the life and death of a nation and its people. Reduced to its essentials, their argument is that for the intelligence process to work, it must operate in secrecy. On the other side are men like Bamford, who believe that not *all* secrets deserve to be kept, and that no democracy can long function without even its most secret agencies' activities being held publicly accountable.

There is merit in both sides of the argument, and the debate is at its sharpest at the apex of American intelligence, the National Security Agency. Indeed, it is the very heart of modern American intelligence, for in a culture dominated by a technological ethos— the conviction that there is a technological fix for virtually every problem—the U.S. intelligence apparatus is dominated by technology. And it is technology that provides the real strength of American intelligence and at the same time represents a grave threat to democracy.

On the morning of October 29, 1975, Senator Frank Church, Democrat from Idaho, struck his gavel in a Senate hearing room, and with that act shattered twenty-three years of tradition. For the first time, the National Security Agency and its activities would be seriously discussed in an open hearing as part of the overall intelligence review by Congress.

There was much to discuss. Following newspaper disclosures that the NSA had been enlisted during the Vietnam war as part of the government's large-scale domestic spying program, the committee staff spent five months investigating the agency. What they found disturbed Church: there appeared to be a real rogue elephant on the loose, and a very big one at that—a mammoth technological intelligence machine that had been spying on American citizens.

As Church noted in his opening remarks, the NSA spying underscored a larger problem: NSA was an agency without a federal statute to define its responsibilities and limitations; it operated (then and now) under executive directives that authorized NSA to collect "technical and intelligence information" without ever specifying just what that meant.

These remarks displeased conservative senators on the committee, who did their best to have the open hearing canceled entirely. John Tower of Texas complained that NSA officials were being paraded before the committee to "explain the awesome technology and the potential abuses of a huge vacuum cleaner." Tower and the rest of the minority conservatives lost when the question was put to a vote, but Church promised to move cautiously, so as "not to impair the excellent contributions made by the NSA to the defense of our country." In other words, the committee would not delve into the highly secret specifics of how NSA collected its intelligence, but would take a hard look at the agency's involvement in domestic spying.

So Church and the committee majority were going to open the door just a crack, but it was enough to reveal that on the other side there were disturbing problems.

In 1940 President Roosevelt issued a presidential directive declaring that electronic surveillance was permissible where "grave matters involving defense of the nation" were at issue. That gave the FBI a mandate for warrantless wiretapping, and similar directives from Roosevelt authorized military intelligence to review all international cable, radio, and telegraph messages.

With the stroke of the pen, Roosevelt gave military intelligence —most notably its code-breaking establishment—an awesome tool. The military went to work inside three major international communications companies—RCA Communications, ITT Communications, and Western Union Telegraph Company. It was an enormous source of intelligence: unlimited access to the cable traffic of private citizens, companies, and governments.

The wartime censorship laws sanctioned the peering into private communications only as long as the country was at war, but the code-breaking apparatus saw this intelligence bonanza as an asset it did not want to lose. Not surprisingly, within days of the surrender of Japan, officers of the Signal Security Agency could be found in the waiting rooms of the three cable companies, seeking permission to continue the arrangement.

The first response, from ITT, was no. Next, Western Union decided that it would participate "unless the Attorney General rules that such intercepts were illegal." Agency officials used that tentative agreement to exert pressure against ITT, whose officials gave in; RCA fell into line shortly thereafter. It had taken some serious arm twisting, but the operation was back in place.

To keep logistics simple, RCA agreed to allow Army cryptanalysts to set up shop inside RCA facilities, provided that the Army men wore only civilian clothes. ITT and Western Union were even more cautious, keeping a discreet distance by copying their cable traffic onto microfilm, which was then handed over to the Army.

This arrangement continued for two years, but in 1947 the companies had become increasingly nervous and began demanding more solid assurances that what they were doing was not illegal (which indeed it was). Secretary of Defense James Forrestal met with representatives of the companies and made a strong case that it was all a matter of patriotism. Admittedly, there was no financial reward in the arrangement, but, Forrestal argued, wasn't it their patriotic duty to help their country? Forrestal conceded the legal riskiness as well, but added that the request came straight from the Oval Office. To reassure the businessmen, Forrestal vowed that the Administration would introduce legislation that would make the intercept activity permissible under the law. (Forrestal kept his word, yet was unsuccessful in getting Congress to pass an amendment to the Federal Communications Act of 1934.)

The company executives left the meeting certain that they were doing the country's patriotic, if illegal, bidding. Operation Shamrock, as it came to be called, was now permanently in place, an operation so secret that no other President would know of its existence for the next thirty years.

Shamrock was the responsibility of the U.S. Army Security Agency first, and later of the U.S. Armed Forces Security Agency. The operation was inherited by the National Security

Agency at the time of the NSA's creation in 1952. No one knows just how many private messages were intercepted during the operation's lifetime, but they undoubtedly number in the millions (in the early 1970s, NSA analysts were examining some 150,000 telegrams a month).

Only three NSA staff members—the director, deputy director, and a lower-level manager—were privy to the magnitude of the operation. To further preserve secrecy, direct meetings between cable company officials and NSA were avoided; contacts were made via delivery boys who shuttled the messages back and forth.

The sheer volume kept a staff of NSA analysts very busy: sorting by hand through an endless stream of paper and microfilm for intelligence gems was an enormous task. The job was considerably eased in 1963, when RCA Global pioneered the use of computerized magnetic tape, a development that not only helped revolutionize communication, but intelligence-gathering as well. Instead of poring through messages for days, searching for specific references to a particular subject, the analysts could now program computers to seek out certain key words and phrases. So programmed, the computers could search through memory banks, stored on round spools of magnetic tape, and pluck out those key words or phrases in seconds.

All of this amounted to a capability almost irresistible to the rest of the intelligence establishment, and NSA soon had other customers. The FBI, the Secret Service, the CIA, and other agencies submitted "watch lists," compilations of names or organizations in which the agencies had a particular interest. The lists became highly popular. They were also quite illegal, a clear violation of the Fourth Amendment, which guarantees citizens the right to be "secure in their papers . . . against unreasonable searches and seizures." To be reasonable, searches and seizures require warrants issued on "probable cause."

No warrants existed for Shamrock, which began to stray from its original intelligence-collection justification into much broader areas. Robert Kennedy, appointed in 1961 by his brother as U.S. Attorney General—and thus versed in constitutional law—saw Shamrock as an opportunity to aid his crusade against organized crime. Later, Kennedy broadened his Shamrock requests even further, assigning the FBI the task of tracking the names of citizens and business firms transacting business with Cuba. The FBI provided a "watch list" of such American citizens to the NSA; they had committed no crime, save having been in contact with a country the current Administration disliked.

Shamrock was taken one last, fateful step: using it against domestic dissidents. In 1967 President Johnson, convinced of the foreign inspiration behind the protest movement against his Vietnam war policies, turned to the intelligence community to provide the proof. NSA was duly provided with watch lists that read like a Who's Who of the American protest movement.

By 1969, the operation had become large enough to earn its own code name, Project Minaret. It also took on a new mission; the target was now not the foreign influences, but U.S. protesters themselves. Nearly twelve hundred perceived dissenters, from ordinary citizens to such better-known activists as Dr. Benjamin Spock and Jane Fonda, had all their communications read. (NSA also maintained a large file on about seventy-five thousand American citizens, including members of Congress and prominent businessmen.)

NSA officials were perfectly aware that Project Minaret was illegal, so access to the secret was severely restricted. Any intercepted communications between two Americans was tagged "Top Secret," and stripped of anything that would reveal NSA as the source. Ironically, the deep security was not to protect the content of the intercepted communications—most concerned personal or other innocuous matters—but the very fact of Minaret. There was also increasing worry in NSA about the large staffs of analysts involved in the project, many of them young military draftees with short tours of duty: how many of them could be reasonably expected to keep the secret? One remedy, which lasted only three months, was to use career CIA technicians to run the program; the CIA's general counsel ordered them out on the grounds that the legal risk was just not worth the take.

Intelligence officials conducting Minaret had little to show for their efforts. No evidence of foreign financial support for the anti-Vietnam war movement was ever found. As one FBI agent put it, the extremists were "credit card revolutionaries," sons and daughters of middle- and upper-class America. The enemy had been uncovered, and it was the next generation of Americans.

Minaret ended in 1973, when four members of the militant Weathermen went on trial on charges of terrorism and bombing.

Their attorneys did not know that the Weathermen were prime targets of the NSA snooping project, but they had suspicions that the government might have used some form of illegal surveillance against their clients. There were suggestive hints everywhere: the Watergate break-in, revelations in the New York *Times* about the ill-fated "Huston plan" to remove legal constraints against domestic spying, and suggestions of illegal government spying in the Pentagon Papers.

Hoping to get lucky, the lawyers filed a motion requesting the disclosure of all potential illegal federal surveillance against their clients. They hit the jackpot when the federal judge approved the motion, on the grounds that the defendants had the right to be confronted with *all* the evidence against them. Now NSA was in big trouble.

NSA Director Lieutenant General Lew Allen, Jr., informed the Justice Department that "communications involving the defendants had been intercepted," an admission that was followed by NSA's destruction of all evidence of that surveillance. The case against the Weathermen was severely jeopardized; unable to press forward without revealing the illegalities of Minaret, the U.S. Government decided it was more prudent to protect the NSA. The case against the Weathermen was dropped. The Justice Department immediately informed the FBI, Secret Service, and other agencies that the entire practice of watch lists was to end forthwith. Minaret expired, and in 1975, Secretary of Defense James Schlesinger ordered Shamrock terminated, too.

By then, times had changed, and one unit of the Justice Department had begun preparation of a criminal case against NSA officials involved with Shamrock. No prosecution ever took place, for despite revelations about NSA's illegal activities, there was a pronounced reluctance throughout the government to do anything that might injure the one great, glittering crown jewel of American intelligence. As the intelligence community was aware, the single most important inner secret of their world was technology; indeed, without it, there was no American intelligence— especially on the subject of the Soviet Union.

To the U.S. Air Force officers peering into the mysterious void of the Soviet Union in 1949, there was danger lurking in the darkness. They knew about the Soviet development of an intercontinental bomber, and the military airfields that had been constructed all over the Russian land mass. But what they did not know was how many bombers existed, and worse, they had no method of early warning of a possible launch against the United States.

The Air Force arrived at a terrible conclusion: unless there was some way of detecting the onset of a Soviet surprise attack, the American air defenses would have no chance. It would be worse than Pearl Harbor, as the fleet of Russian bombers, carrying the Soviet Union's new nuclear weapons would devastate the United States. There had to be a way of getting advance warning.

Traditional intelligence seemed to offer the answer. As in World War II, "watchers" would be infiltrated near the military air bases; when the bases suddenly went to war footing and planes began taking off, the "watchers" would alert the United States by radio. Armed with the advance warning, the Air Force could launch its own bombers and at the same time organize air defenses against the Russian attack.

To accomplish this, the Air Force went to the CIA: we need agents to operate inside the Soviet Union, and we need them *fast*. And how many agents would be needed? Well, the Air Force people replied, there are hundreds of Soviet military airfields, so . . .

Impossible, replied the CIA; the idea of infiltrating hundreds of agents into the Soviet Union all at once, and setting them up near air bases with radio communications, was far beyond the capabilities of American intelligence. The Air Force would have to figure out an alternative.

There seemed no alternative. The greatest military threat the United States had ever confronted was a total mystery. Neither the military nor the CIA had any real idea of how many Soviet bombers there were (or their precise locations), the status of Soviet defense industries, the real size of the Red Army, the scope of the Soviet nuclear weapons program, the arrangement of the Soviet transportation system, the progress of the Soviet ballistic missile program—in short, nearly everything worth knowing. Above all, nobody had any idea of Soviet intentions.

The CIA tried parachuting agents into the Soviet heartland, but those operations were failing. Recruitments of Soviet nationals as assets were also unproductive; in a police state like the Soviet Union, where citizens were required to possess "internal passports" simply to travel from one city to another, and where even the Moscow telephone directory was a state secret, penetrations of the vast internal security apparatus looked increasingly hopeless.*

One possibility was aerial reconnaissance. The Air Force had made great strides in that area since the war, and was fond of showing off its capabilities. (Once, when a delegation of Norwegian Defense Ministry officials was visiting the Strategic Air Command headquarters in Nebraska, the unit's commander, General Curtis LeMay, presented the officials with very sharp aerial reconnaissance pictures of Oslo. "Gentlemen," LeMay boasted, "one of our RB-47s took those pictures this morning."

Very impressive, but Oslo did not have bristling air defenses, MIG fighters on constant alert, and new radar systems to track incoming planes. The Russians did, and that made any conventional air reconnaissance impossible. RB-47s (a souped-up reconnaissance version of the B-47 bomber) were capable of skirting the edges of Soviet borders and with special cameras, looking a short distance inside the Soviet Union, but they dared not fly into the teeth of fighters and radar-directed anti-aircraft gun defenses.

Reconnaissance of the Soviet Union could only be done provided there was the right kind of technology to keep ahead of Soviet countermeasures. What was needed was a stable platform that could fly very high and use advanced cameras that could take pictures of wide swaths of territory.†

The National Security Agency also needed an effective platform. It wanted to capture Soviet communications traffic, but most of that traffic was deep inside the Soviet Union, far out of reach of the listening posts and "ferret" flights. The Air Force

---

* In 1954, following the Khrushchev "thaw," when American tourists were allowed entry visas to the Soviet Union, the CIA recruited from their ranks for spying. Instructed to memorize serial numbers on military vehicles, take snapshots of strategic installations, and note the color of smoke from factories, some of the tourists, fancying themselves James Bonds, exceeded their instructions, and ran afoul of the KGB. The KGB actually tolerated the amateurs for a short while, then got serious: dozens of Americans were arrested and jailed. That led to tightened surveillance of American tourists, and the whole spying operation was dropped as too risky.

† In 1953 the British tried at least one mission in a B-57 bomber, but gave up after it returned riddled with bullet holes. A high-altitude intercontinental American bomber, RB-36, also flew reconnaissance missions during this period.

pilots who ran these flights (they liked to call themselves "crows") were involved in the front-line combat of the intelligence war, zooming across Soviet borders for short distances, collecting the signals of alerted radar stations and other communications facilities, then zooming back out again, pursued by MIG fighters.

The cost was high: by 1947, thirty such "ferret" flights had been shot down, with heavy losses (The worst such loss came in 1958, when an Air Force C-130 transport crammed with NSA interception gear strayed too far across the border of Soviet Armenia and was jumped by a flight of MIGs. Monitors at an NSA listening post in Turkey listened in horror as they eavesdropped on Soviet fighter cockpit transmissions and heard the pilots describe the plane breaking up as they riddled it with cannon fire. Seventeen U.S. servicemen were lost.)

Despite the pilots' bravery, their reach was limited, even under the best of circumstances. Radar signals and radio transmissions travel in straight lines, so an aircraft at, say, 35,000 feet could pick up only those signals within its horizon—about 228 miles. And in a nation as vast as the Soviet Union, 228 miles meant little.

Advances in technology, especially lightweight materials and special fuels, began to overcome the barriers of high altitudes. The CIA, under the direction of Richard Bissell, was given the go-ahead in 1954 to oversee construction of a new fleet of airplanes, part jet and part glider, that could soar high above Soviet territory. The design for the plane was already on the drawing boards at Lockheed Aircraft in Burbank, California. Lockheed's famous designer, Clarence L. ("Kelly") Johnson went to work under tight security building the aircraft. The result was an odd-looking jet featuring extra-long wings with the then extraordinary range of over 2,500 nautical miles.

In short, a perfect spy plane. It first overflew the Soviet Union on July 4, 1956, and until its final flight over Soviet territory in 1960—when Francis Gary Powers was shot down and captured—there were a total of some fifty missions. The flights revolutionized American espionage, for the clear photographs from over the Soviet Union (and China) at last shed light into a dark room. By 1959, the U-2 photographs and signals collected for NSA by detection gear inside the spy planes provided nearly 90 percent of all intelligence on the Soviet Union.

The U-2 success began the technological overhaul of American intelligence, accelerated by the first successful spy satellites: on August 18, 1960, the aptly named *Discoverer*, launched into space, crisscrossed the Soviet Union, and later ejected a pod of undeveloped film that was snared in mid-air by a special recovery plane that hooked the package's parachute. On January 31 of the following year, a special NSA electronics intelligence package was piggybacked aboard a Samos 2 spy satellite.

And with that launch, a deep veil of secrecy was drawn over the American technological-espionage empire. Few people are aware of the National Reconnaissance Office (NRO), a Pentagon-CIA-NSA central clearinghouse that decides the priorities of targets. First set up in 1960, its very existence was not revealed publicly until thirteen years later, when a congressional report inadvertently mentioned it.

Suggestive hints have leaked out over the years, however, to give some outline of a vast electronic web: phased array radars beamed deep into the Soviet Union to detect airborne objects as small as the size of a basketball; NSA listening satellites with onboard computers that instantly analyze detected signals and compare them with a memory bank of previously recorded signals; monitoring stations in Turkey and China that read every electronic emission from a Soviet missile test; highly advanced infrared photo satellites that can see in the dark; overhead detection satellites that "read" and track the distinctive electronic signal of every Soviet nuclear submarine.

Despite strict secrecy, the very size and sophistication of America's electronic eyes and ears mean that bits and pieces of them pop into public view. One such case involved the secrets of *Rhyolite*, an advanced electronic listening spy satellite, which were sold to the Russians by Christopher Boyce and Andrew Daulton Lee over a twenty-one-month period. The two were eventually caught (Boyce was sentenced to forty years in prison while Lee got life), but not before severely damaging the *Rhyolite* program.

Of course, the Soviets were delighted with the walk-in information, until they realized just how badly they had underestimated the *Rhyolite*'s capabilities. Assuming that the satellite's high space orbit precluded it from intercepting the relatively weak telemetry signals of their missile tests, the Russians did not bother to encrypt those signals. Thus, for two years, every Soviet missile test was an open book to NSA and the CIA. In 1975, when the Soviets got their first look at the satellite's technical data that Boyce and Lee had sold them, they immediately began encrypting all missile telemetry.

Missile telemetry is a highly sought-after intelligence prize; it is the stuff of which nuclear missile treaties are made. Besides listening satellites such as *Rhyolite*, America utilizes sophisticated picture-taking satellites in space for monitoring Soviet missile tests. One such satellite is the Key Hole-II, which was first launched in December 1976. Unlike earlier pictorial satellites such as *Discoverer*, the KH-II, which is the size of a small house, has eliminated the need to have film returned to earth. Its images are digitized and transmitted electronically to land-based receivers, which means they can be viewed almost instantaneously. The possibilities of digital photography are enormous, not only for treaty makers, but for military strategists as well.

No one was more excited over the development of the KH-II than Jimmy Carter, who was sworn in as President only weeks after the first KH-II went into orbit. One of the major goals of his Administration was a new Strategic Arms Limitation Treaty (SALT II) with the Soviet Union, an ambition that would require the capabilities of the KH-II and the rest of the intelligence empire. Carter and his new DCI, Admiral Stansfield Turner, dove into the esoterica of espionage high tech. This, it was clear to the new President and his CIA Director, was the future of intelligence. Compared with the frailties of human spies, satellites were reliable and safe.

An ex-Navy nuclear engineer fascinated with technology, Carter was aware that Senate ratification of any SALT agreement would hinge on what was known as "verification," the ability of American intelligence's technical apparatus to monitor Soviet compliance with a treaty's provisions. Could it be done with confidence?

Carter decided yes, one of the reasons for that conviction being the ingenious KH-II, whose digital imaging system had completely fooled the Russians. Because the previous generation of American photographic satellites all used a film cartridge ejection system, the Russians assumed the KH-II was not taking pictures. Therefore, they made no effort to cover up their missile silos as the satellite passed overhead.

But while Carter was mastering the details of KH-II, so was a disgruntled CIA clerk. William Kampiles joined the CIA in March 1977 and was assigned to a round-the-clock technical monitoring center that also contained satellite reference materials. Kampiles quickly realized that watch-duty was not the glamorous life of espionage he had hoped to join. Failing in his request for a transfer, he quit after eight months on the job, walking out the door with a KH-11 manual in hand. American intelligence first knew something was very wrong when the Soviets suddenly began covering up their missiles and silos whenever the KH-11 passed overhead. An investigation eventually led back to Kampiles, who had certainly gotten the intrigue he was after. The KGB gave him three thousand dollars for his trouble. He also got forty years in an American jail.

Turner understood the implications of the Kampiles theft, but he remained convinced that verification was still possible, given the range and capabilities of the rest of the technical intelligence systems. To prove it, he convened a team of experts, told them to pretend they were the most devious Russians imaginable, and devise ways to cheat on a SALT agreement. The experts arrived at a few ingenious ideas—such as constructing ICBM silos inside large buildings and then firing the missiles through the roof—but Turner concluded that even if the Russians tried to cheat any "undetectable compliance" would not make any strategic difference.

The argument might have worked, except that in 1979, the Iranian revolution closed American intelligence's most valuable electronic snooping post, code-named Tracksman 2. Located in northern Iran in a perfect site to monitor launchings at the main Soviet missile center at Tyuratam, Tracksman 2 was invaluable. The American technicians who ran the operation were taken hostage in March of 1979, eight months prior to the assault on the U.S. embassy in Teheran. A $200,000 ransom bought them their freedom, but the listening post was lost.

The closing of Tracksman 2 in Iran, combined with the compromise of *Rhyolite* and KH-11, caused doubts in the Senate that any SALT agreement could be effectively monitored. The final blow came in December 1979, when the Soviets invaded Afghanistan, thereby ending any possibility of ratification (although both sides have generally respected the provisions of the unratified agreement).

The wary senators had good reason to be concerned: American verification capabilities were questionable at the time, and no one knew it better than the Russians. Turner himself had a good sense of those limitations. Early on, he was asked by Carter to provide some KH-11 pictures of a low-scale battle between two factions in a Third World country. Turner recognized the President's request as a test, and he ordered his staff to get results immediately. When days and then weeks went by with no pictures, Turner discovered that the technicians had focused the KH-11 cameras on every place but the actual battlefield. In frustration, Turner ordered a light plane to overfly the areas, with the pilot taking pictures with a hand-held camera. That didn't work either: the plane crashed, with no pictures taken. It was a rude awakening for Carter and his DCI. "Here I was," Turner later recalled, "the head of the whole intelligence community of the United States, and I couldn't even produce a few pictures of a Mickey Mouse war."

Some of the veterans at CIA could only shake their heads. They had warned of the consequences of relying on engineers, and now, they believed, America was beginning to pay the price. Turner dismissed their complaints: "Human espionage people used to be the center, the end all, the be all, of intelligence collection." Times had changed, and the old-timers now being phased out "did not understand." Billions of dollars were being spent on hardware, not human agents, and as Turner saw it, the sheer amount of money demanded the DCI's primary attention.

Although embarrassed by his inability to respond quickly to Carter's request for pictures of a Third World battlefield, Turner was certain that the future for intelligence was technology-laden. He had "retired" seven hundred CIA officers, mostly in the Operations Directorate—home of human spies—on the grounds that increasingly expensive intelligence systems made such cuts mandatory: the CIA could either have large staffs of human spies or it could have highly complex and costly technical systems, but not both.

But as the fired spies noted, a human spy can be replaced relatively cheaply; when a technical system failed or was compromised, hundreds of millions of dollars went down the drain. America learned this lesson the hard way when the space shuttle *Challenger* blew apart on January 28, 1986. By then the National

Reconnaissance Office had put "all its eggs in one basket," as one former U.S. Secretary of the Air Force had predicted. The eggs were spy satellites; the basket was the cargo bay of the shuttle, the sole means at that time for launching the next generation of large satellites. The grounding of the shuttle also grounded these large satellites for over two years.

But in Turner's tenure, the impact of the *Challenger* disaster on the intelligence community was still years away—although ominous warnings of overreliance on machines were already emerging. There seemed to be critics of high-tech intelligence everywhere, even in the White House. "You haven't got a single asset in the Soviet Union," Carter's National Security Adviser, Zbigniew Brzezinski, snapped at Turner during one meeting, and he might just as well have added: and hardly anyplace else, either. Brzezinski had a point, although he too was unaware that the real failure of American intelligence was occurring not in the Soviet Union, but in the mosques and back alleys of Iran's cities.

ELEVEN

Desert One

THERE WAS NO QUESTION, the Iranian noted politely, choosing his words carefully: the Americans had planned meticulously. It had all the genius of a fine Swiss watch, with all the movements precisely coordinated.

He was effusive in his praise. Amazing, how everything was figured to the minute, with helicopters swooping in at the precise second, trucks hidden in warehouses to move at just the right moment, agents dressed as policemen, and prereconnoitered escape routes. All in all, a monument of contingency planning, taking into account every possible eventuality.

To be sure, such detailed planning was necessary; the Americans were about to attempt what would surely be one of the most audacious commando operations in history, rescuing U.S. hostages from their imprisonment at the U.S. embassy, plucking them right from the middle of Teheran.

The Iranian, a longtime asset of the CIA, had been called into a meeting of American intelligence officials involved in planning the operation. They had worked for months putting an intricate plan together. Now, they wanted to know from one of their best Iranian assets: can it work?

A former diplomat, the Iranian was an invariably polite man. He lavished praise on the planners before getting to what was really on his mind. A marvelous plan, he repeated, yet there was a question in his mind of whether it was *too* complicated. Perhaps, he suggested, the Americans had made the whole thing overly complex; if even one tiny component of the plan went wrong, then the rest of the operation would collapse. CIA officials at the meeting frowned: didn't he understand that rescuing American hostages in the capital of revolutionary Iran, all of them guarded around the clock by fanatical guards, required a detailed plan, with absolutely nothing left to chance? The Iranian agreed, but insisted that the plan was overcomplicated.

The Americans planned to fly eight helicopters and eight C-130 aircraft under darkness at low altitudes a distance of six hundred miles to a site called Desert One, a barren, arid stretch outside Teheran. There, the helicopters would be refueled by the large C-130s for the daring Delta commando force raid on the American embassy. Once near Teheran, the commandos would transfer to local vehicles for the ride through the city. With the hostages recovered, the helicopters would quickly swoop in and fly them back to Desert One for loading onto the awaiting C-130s.

On April 24, 1980, the operation commenced as eight helicopters departed from the carrier USS *Nimitz*. Only two hours into the flight, one helicopter was abandoned after an instrument indicator lit up warning of a possible rotor blade failure. Like the stray thread that ultimately unravels a sweater, the mission began to come apart. Only five usable helicopters made it to Desert One. Then a busload of startled Iranians stumbled upon the mission and had to be taken prisoner. Next a helicopter collided with a C-130, setting off a fireball explosion killing eight American servicemen and wounding five others.

The rescue was abandoned, as the complex mission was unable to accomplish even the first step of securing its airstrip in the Iranian desert. The Iranian CIA asset had been right. The plan was too complicated.

The impact of the Delta Team disaster was felt in many directions, not the least of them the presidency of Jimmy Carter. The man who had taken office and immediately immersed himself in the wonders of the American technical intelligence empire had in the end become fascinated by it. As much as Carter wanted to believe that espionage technology would tell him all that he really needed to know, in fact even the wondrous American technology could never hope to achieve such a goal.

The sin was not in the technology itself, but in a tendency toward overreliance on technology as some sort of magic wand that settled all intelligence questions. The overreliance represented a sharp shift in how the government sought to use its intelligence apparatus, and that, in turn, determined the shape of American intelligence. In previous administrations when the CIA was used by presidents to help covertly contain the Soviet Union, the agency was dominated by men of action who made things happen. By the time Carter took office the new emphasis was on technology, and the covert-action operators and secret agents watched the men they derisively called "the guys in the white coats"—the technicians and engineers—dominate intelligence.

Although Carter was best known within the intelligence community for his fixation on technology, in fact he wrought, quite unnoticed, something of a revolution in the entire intelligence structure. He began to reorient it away from its traditional and abiding concern with the Soviet Union and direct more resources to a world now composed of 177 different nations. The world had changed, Carter argued; what Moscow did or didn't do was no longer the most important concern of the United States. What would probably have much more impact on the United States was a sudden glitch in the new global economy, or some sort of political unrest that would threaten vital natural resources—resources no longer controlled by the West or Moscow.

Actually, something along Carter's line of thinking was already underway in the CIA. The man responsible for it was William Colby, who several years earlier, as DCI, had ordered some fresh thinking in an institution whose very existence had been born in the U.S.–Soviet struggle, a circumstance that had dominated the outlook of the agency's leadership for nearly two decades.

The shock of the OPEC oil boycott in 1973 demonstrated just

how much new thinking was needed. While the CIA continued to devote the bulk of its resources to the Soviet Union, China, and the rest of the so-called "Soviet bloc," on the theory that Moscow represented the single great danger to the United States, a coalition of oil producers caused grave shocks to the American economy. The shocks were all the greater because the United States had not prepared for them; the CIA, especially, had paid very little attention to the potential clout of the oil-producing cartel.

The hard lesson driven home by the oil boycott galvanized American intelligence's upper echelons. A 1974 memorandum from the CIA's senior leadership to the lower ranks summarized the change in outlook. The agency's concerns, the memo said, should henceforth be ". . . the pricing debates of OPEC . . . and the size of this year's Soviet [wheat] crop . . . the intricacies of Chinese politics, with the water supply in the Middle East, with the quality of Soviet computers and its impact on our own export controls, with the narcotics trade in Southeast Asia, even with the struggle for East Timor."

This sort of outlook was all to the good, as far as Carter was concerned, and he further applauded the CIA's new emphasis on "topics": debt financing in the Third World, North-South economic issues, natural resources, immigration trends, human rights, "international energy matters" (especially oil), science and technology, terrorism, illegal narcotics, arms sales, and agriculture.

Precisely the emphasis Carter wanted, and as he was to say some time later in 1978, he was determined to change an intelligence system in which "the intelligence community itself set its own priorities as a supplier of intelligence information. I felt that the customers . . . ought to be the ones to say this is what we consider to be the most important."

By the end of Carter's term, the Soviet Union and associated matters accounted for only about half of U.S. intelligence resources, a far cry from the days when that subject took up the overwhelming majority of such resources. The remainder of the intelligence community was retargeted against what the CIA called "National Intelligence Topics" (NIT), a list of 185 "issues of importance." (These replaced a system, instituted by Colby, called "Key Intelligence Questions"—KIQs, known more familiarly around the agency as "kicks." Like a supermarket checkout list, the KIQ system listed seventy subjects, any number of which policymakers could check off as of interest, or even add some of their own.)

Carter, as his 1978 remarks indicated, was quite confident that he had achieved the proper intelligence structure for the United States. It had been reoriented toward areas that represented the real threats to American national security: rapidly shifting trends in global economics, vital natural resources controlled by coalitions of producers, political unrest in the Third World, and a worldwide quest for improvement of human rights.

Intelligence agency abuses appeared to have been curbed, and there was formalized congressional oversight, along with plans to write the nation's first intelligence agency charters. The Soviet problem would be handled primarily by technology, which would also provide the verification basis for strategic arms control. Carter envisaged a new dawn for American intelligence, a new role in a world where everything seemed to have changed. A man who often spoke of "limits," Carter made it clear that the days were over when American governments, using the intelligence arm as a covert weapon, could shape any part of the world in its own image.

Certainly, it appeared that Congress would no longer tolerate the Executive Branch's abuse of the covert action weapon. In 1974, Congress had passed the Hughes-Ryan Amendment, a significant effort to bring covert intelligence operations under some form of control and accountability. Basically, it required the President to report "in a timely fashion" to Congress any covert intelligence operations used for anything other than "obtaining necessary intelligence." Further, the President would have to certify to Congress that the covert political operation was "important to the national security of the United States." (These presidential certifications, which were to be addressed to congressional intelligence committees, came to be known as "findings.")

The Hughes-Ryan Amendment amounted to a classic demonstration of Congress's strategy of setting controls on Executive Branch actions not by second-guessing the actual decisions, but by altering the decision-making process. The significance of the act was that it removed the notion of "plausible deniability," the habit of presidents claiming they knew nothing of assassinations and overthrows of governments. Now, the President would have to sign a document proving that he was aware of the operation and its dimensions from the very beginning.

It would also end the kind of dilemma in which Richard Helms found himself in 1973. Called to testify before the Senate Foreign Relations Committee on his nomination as U.S. ambassador to Iran, Helms was confronted with a battery of questions, not about Iran, but Chile. It was a subject Helms preferred to avoid.

As Helms was aware by 1973, the CIA's covert operation in Chile three years before had become perhaps the most widely publicized such operation in the agency's history. Thanks to extensive press revelations, almost everybody knew that President Nixon was nearly beside himself with rage at the thought that Marxist Salvador Allende might win the 1970 presidential election in Chile. Nixon ordered the CIA to prevent Allende's election at all costs; when that failed, the CIA was instructed to destabilize his government.

Called to the White House on September 15, 1970, for a meeting with President Nixon and his National Security Adviser, Henry Kissinger, Helms discovered just how passionate the issue had become. "I don't see why," Kissinger fumed, "we need to stand by and watch a country go Communist due to the irresponsibility of its own people." Nixon then ordered Helms to mount a full-scale operation against Allende's new government, including, as Helm's notes of the meeting reflect, to "make the economy scream." Eventually a U.S.-encouraged coup overthrew Allende, who was killed. The other victim was Chilean democracy, for White House policy and CIA activities resulted in a repressive dictatorship. The American "cure" for Chile's ills was worse than the disease.

Three years after this episode, Helms found himself before the Senate committee, being peppered with questions about the CIA's Chilean operation. A loyalist, Helms believed that the injunction from his boss, President Nixon, applied in full force: he had been ordered not to tell Congress, the State Department, nor anyone else not directly involved in the operation. Additionally, the conversations between himself and the President were secret; no DCI could reveal such secrets. On the other hand, he was hardly in a position to keep silent under Senate questioning.

Asked by Senator Stuart Symington, "Did you try in the Central Intelligence Agency to overthrow the government of Chile?"

Helms responded, "No, sir." Several weeks later, in another session of the Foreign Relations Committee, Helms faced a similar question, this time from Senator Frank Church. Asked if the CIA had attempted in any way to influence the outcome of the 1970 presidential election in Chile, Helms again responded, "No, sir."

These untruths led to Helms's conviction four years later on a charge of testifying falsely, for which he received a suspended sentence. Helms's defense was that he had become caught between two branches of government. The mere fact that Helms had even been charged showed how times had really changed; the unmistakable message was that a DCI and his organization were not above the law, no matter the orders from higher authority.

But that raised a question: what about the President, the American intelligence community's commander in chief? Was he, too, above the law? The answer, ultimately, would come in the form of new laws passed by Congress holding the President accountable for his direction of that community. But first, there was a nasty confrontation between Congress and the White House on just how accountable the President was, a tug of war finally swung in Congress's favor by a man perhaps least expected to play that role: William Colby.

The stage for the confrontation was set in 1975, when the House Select Committee on Intelligence Activities—popularly called the Pike Committee, it was the House equivalent of the Senate's Church Committee—prepared to publish its final report. Colby, the DCI, objected to some portions of the report, because CIA documents were quoted. President Ford entered the fray, declaring he was ordering Colby not to furnish any further material to the committee on the grounds of executive privilege. The committee warned it would cite Colby for contempt, and a major constitutional confrontation was underway.

The House finally rendered the issue moot by voting to keep the Pike Committee's final report classified, but not before Colby made it plain he thought that whatever the merits of the White House-Pike Committee argument on either side he felt a broader principle was at stake: Congress had a constitutional right to investigate the intelligence community. Further, Colby believed that as DCI he had a constitutional obligation to cooperate with Congress.

Such talk was heresy to the Ford administration, which came to believe that it was Colby's attitude, so in contrast with that of Helms, that was responsible for the embarrassing revelations pouring out of the congressional investigating committees. The prevailing belief was that if only Colby had stonewalled from the beginning, none of those revelations would have happened. The growing animus toward Colby within the White House was underscored in November 1975, when he was called to a meeting at the White House and unceremoniously fired.

But Colby's attitude, an astonishing change from his predecessors, contributed greatly to the general consensus that the time had come to rein in the intelligence agencies and establish Congress's long-disused oversight functions. In no small measure, it helped convince Congress that the time had arrived, at long last, to assert its authority.

The chance to exercise it came almost immediately, in the former Portuguese African colony of Angola.

Like so many other similar perceptions, it is difficult to determine just when the Ford administration's perception of Angola as a critical battleground in the Cold War was first shaped. It is known that beginning in the 1960s, the CIA began funneling money to several of the guerrilla factions fighting the Portuguese regime. The idea was that the colonial regime would eventually fall, and it was necessary for a newly independent Angola to be pro-American.

The operation simmered quietly on one of the CIA's back burners until 1974, when the sudden coming to power in Portugal of a socialist government led quickly to that country's decision to abandon the Angolan colony. It also ignited a civil war in Angola among the various factions battling for control of the country, one of them a Marxist group known as MPLA, a group supported by Cuban forces. The MPLA was pro-Moscow, and that was enough to convince the Ford administration that the Communists were about to take control of one of the most mineral-rich countries in Africa.

The CIA, ordered to mount a covert operation to prevent the MPLA from taking power, joined forces with Communists—the ones from China who were operating in Angola as a means of twisting the hated Russian bear's tail. Things got even more confusing when the CIA began to support two factions considered "pro-Western," one called the FNLA, the other UNITA. The head of UNITA, Jonas Savimbi, was intermittently supported by the Chinese and North Koreans (he also worked with the South Africans), and the head of FNLA, Holden Roberto, had not lived in Angola for many years—preferring instead to live in bordering Zaire, a country run by his brother-in-law, Joseph Mobutu.

It was a mess, made even messier when two important events occurred. One was the MPLA's decision to ask the Soviet Union for arms. The second stemmed from the first: the deduction by the Ford administration that the arms deal signaled a major attempt by Moscow to take over Angola, a perception sharpened when the MPLA emerged victorious in the early struggle with two other factions and took control of the government.

The result was a secret decision, in July of 1975, that would lead to providing almost $32 million for a CIA task force in Angola to ensure that the MPLA would be overthrown. The Portuguese pulled out in November 1975, and soon there was a full-scale war. The South Africans were encouraged to invade Angola and militarily support the UNITA faction; the MPLA in response brought in Cuban troops (eventually 30,000 of them); the Russians shipped in more arms; Holden Roberto and the FNLA were bloodied in battle, then went back to Zaire; the CIA hired mercenary soldiers, while the Chinese went home, having decided all the madness was not worthwhile.

It was like some crazy poker game, with the players pushing stacks of chips into the middle of the table without bothering to look at their cards. What made the whole thing truly bizarre was that while Kissinger and the Ford administration were pronouncing Angola a vital battleground in the Cold War, the United States was also happily signing agreements to buy oil from the very same MPLA government it was trying to destroy. (Later, the American Import-Export Bank lent that government $85 million for a natural gas development project.)

Congress put an end to America's secret involvement in this African war in December 1975, by refusing the Ford administration's request for $25 million to become further involved. To ensure that there would be no attempted end run, Congress attached a rider to an appropriations measure barring the CIA from spending any money to carry out military operations in Angola.

The swiftness and decisiveness with which Congress acted in

shutting down the Angola operation were nothing short of remarkable, considering that body's long record of hardly paying any attention to what the U.S. intelligence agencies were doing. The principle of congressional oversight of intelligence operations was firmly established by the time Jimmy Carter took office in 1977, and while he was fully in favor of the new rules of the game, he would have cause to wonder if somebody might have forgotten an essential ingredient. It was called politics.

During his first month in office, as he began to fathom the depths of American intelligence operations around the world, Carter was most struck by the in-depth coverage of an abiding American concern, the island of Cuba. Indeed, the coverage was total: overflights by SR-71 reconnaissance planes, extensive NSA interception operations (including a large balloon floating over the Florida keys that snatched every telephone conversation in Cuba), U.S. Navy intelligence operations using ships and submarines, and an active on-ground collection of Cuban assets run by the CIA.

In this last category were Cubans who had been recruited by the CIA to spy on their country, with particular reference to the movements of Fidel Castro. All these people, the CIA assured Carter, were Cuban patriots in a variety of sensitive government jobs or other important positions; they were fed up with Castro, and willing to provide whatever information they encountered to the CIA and help speed the day when Castro and his government were overthrown.

They included a man code-named Julio by the CIA—actually, an official of the Cuban State Planning Board named Ignacio Rodríguez-Mena Castrillon. Rodríguez-Mena had been first recruited in 1966, and by 1976, was a fully trusted source, the longest-operating asset in Cuba. Like the other assets, Rodríguez-Mena was forever telling the CIA pretty much what the agency wanted to hear: there was widespread dissatisfaction with Castro among the Cuban people, Castro was a puppet of the Russians, and some sort of popular uprising was inevitable.*

* Unfortunately, Rodríguez-Mena—and every other CIA Cuban asset—was a double agent working for the DGI, Castro's intelligence service. The game was blown in June 1987, when a DGI major, Florentino Aspillaga Lombard, defected to the CIA in Vienna and revealed how his agency actually controlled all the

Despite the reports from Julio and others that Castro was virtually on the ropes, Carter had no interest in beginning any operation to topple him. Carter was thinking the other way: Cuba had long been a festering sore, swallowing up a disproportionate share of American attention, intelligence, and otherwise. Perhaps it was time to turn down the volume a little and see if Castro and the Russians responded.

Carter canceled the SR-71 flights over Cuba, a gesture that went unrecognized by either Cuba or the Soviet Union. There were some positive signs—such as the opening of the U.S. Interests Section in Havana, a *de facto* American diplomatic presence—but overall there was still a distinct chill in Washington-Havana relations. Obviously, any warming would take quite some time, and such topics as the Cuban military presence in Angola were still too sensitive to discuss.

Things limped along on a low flame until early 1979, when DCI Stansfield Turner read an astonishing intelligence report. It was prepared by NSA, which claimed, via radio interceptions, to have discovered a Soviet "combat brigade" operating in Cuba. Turner was puzzled: there had been no previous indication at all of such a unit in Cuba; had it suddenly appeared overnight? More to the point, why would the Russians put a combat brigade—anywhere up to seventeen thousand troops—in Cuba, without airlift or sea lift capability? What would be the point—unless Moscow intended them to invade Key West by swimming across the Florida Straits?

The adjective "combat" attached to the brigade report precipitated disquiet throughout the intelligence community, and Turner was pressed to find out what was really going on in Cuba. He submitted the island to the intelligence version of a CAT scan. While that process was underway, the military intelligence agencies fretted that the Soviet combat brigade perhaps signaled the beginning of a large-scale Soviet effort to move militarily in the Caribbean or Central America.

CIA's Cuban assets. Following the revelation, the Cuban government presented all twenty-seven of those assets in a government television show, during which they detailed their lives as double agents. Also shown were videotapes and photographs made of CIA agents who worked under cover as diplomats attached to the U.S. Interests Section in Havana, delivering spy equipment to their Cuban "assets." The CIA operation in Havana collapsed.

The brigade episode might have remained just another in the many squabbles that often preoccupy the American intelligence community, except that it became embroiled in politics. Senator Richard Stone of Florida, facing a tough reelection battle against conservative opposition, heard rumors of the intelligence dispute. He mentioned them during a public hearing of the Senate Foreign Relations Committee, and the brigade issue became a full-fledged political controversy—even as far as Idaho, where Senator Frank Church, also facing a tough reelection battle, demanded that removal of the combat brigade be made a precondition for Senate ratification of the SALT II treaty.

Turner was able to defuse the political controversy when he discovered that the "combat brigade" was in fact a Soviet unit for training the Cuban Army. Not only that, it turned out that the brigade had been in Cuba for sixteen years. But how had it gotten there? The answer was that the entire American intelligence community had somehow suffered a massive memory lapse. As Turner discovered, in 1963, following the Cuban missile crisis, the Kennedy administration had agreed that a Soviet Army unit of approximately 17,500 men (later reduced to 12,500) could remain on the island. Then everybody promptly forgot about it, until the NSA many years later detected the Russian brigade's communications, dusted off an old report noting the presence of the brigade, unaccountably added the word "combat," and managed to create a mess. New intelligence finally dampened the controversy, and it disappeared from the front pages.†

In the aggregate, however, the combat brigade fiasco demonstrated the problem of mixing politics with intelligence. It also demonstrated a more serious problem: overreliance on intelligence technology. The entire controversy had been touched off when the NSA made what turned out to be a colossally incorrect assumption about some intercepted military radio signals. The billions of dollars' worth of technology that monitored Cuba, despite the wizardry of its components, still lacked that most efficient of all intelligence detectors, the human eye and brain. One

† Some years later, a similar incident took place when an argument broke out within the intelligence community about the significance of large crates that were spotted being offloaded from a Russian ship in Nicaragua. The debate, centering on esoteric analyses of Soviet crate-packing procedures, could have been settled by a low-scale agent among the port's stevedores.

good on-ground agent near the Soviet brigade's operating area
could have easily told American intelligence all it wanted to
know—especially the fact that the brigade had been there for sixteen years.

In the case of the Soviet combat brigade, the eventual consequences were not serious, although it should have alerted Turner
that his and Jimmy Carter's romance with technology had its
flaws. Just how dangerous those flaws could be was demonstrated
by a significant intelligence failure that took place in the one
place nobody expected it: Iran.

In late August of 1978, William H. Sullivan, the American ambassador to Iran, returned to Teheran from a three-month vaca-
tion. Whatever relief his body and mind had received during that
break from his difficult job was immediately dispelled upon meeting Mohammad Reza Pahlavi, the Shah of Iran.

The Shah, as Sullivan later reported to Washington, was "re-
mote, nervous and suspicious." As usual, he was complaining: the
Americans weren't doing enough to help him, he was besieged on
all sides by intense opposition, things were very difficult. Sullivan
did his best to soothe the man known to his followers as "Shah of
Shahs" and "Shadow of God," among other modest titles, but the
Shah clearly was agitated about the opposition he was encounter-
ing from the Islamic religious leaders (mullahs), most notably
their leader, an exiled fundamentalist cleric, the Ayatollah
Khomeini.

The Shah's increased edginess did not impress Washington, accustomed to the fretting of that very insecure man. Iran, the bulwark of American foreign policy in the Persian Gulf, was a firm
American ally—and had been since 1953, when the CIA gave back
the Shah his Peacock Throne. The throne seemed secure:
equipped with a large military machine purchased from the
United States with billions of dollars in oil money, the Shah also
presided over a vast internal security network run by his infamous secret police force, the SAVAK. The Communist Party was
outlawed in Iran, and all internal dissent was ruthlessly stifled.

To American intelligence, Iran appeared secure. The Soviet
threat to the north was checkmated by the Iranian military; to the
south, the Soviet ally Iraq, ancient enemy of Iran, was similarly

deterred by the Iranian military machine and its lavish stock of advanced American military technology, including F-14 jet fighters. The Iranian Navy kept peace in the Persian Gulf. There seemed little doubt, as the Shah's court often proclaimed, that the Peacock Throne would last a thousand years.

Even the restiveness of the Islamic fundamentalists failed to mar this vision. The Shah was dealing with this problem, the American intelligence officials in Teheran were assured; he had total power in Iran, and no Islamic cleric was going to tell him how to run his country. Among the tight circle of Iranian Government ministers and SAVAK officials who served as American intelligence's only human sources in Iran, there were confident assurances that all was well.

No wonder, then, that in the summer of 1978 a report landed on DCI Stansfield Turner's desk from the CIA station in Iran informing him that "Iran is not in a revolutionary or even a prerevolutionary situation." It seemed to make sense: the same conclusion could also be deduced from the great American technical intelligence web that concentrated much of its attention on the critical Persian Gulf area. There were no mass armies, revolutionary or otherwise, on the march; no battles were being fought; no transmissions from clandestine radio networks; no sign of any unusual activity along the Iranian-Russian or Iraqi borders.

But there *was* a revolution occurring. It was taking place where the Americans had no eyes, in the back alleys and mosques in towns and cities all over Iran. There were no guns, tanks, or bombs; the weapons were cassette tapes of Ayatollah Khomeini's speeches, smuggled into Iran by his followers, who made the tapes at Khomeini's Paris exile headquarters. The taped sermons, a mixture of politics and religion, inveighed against the corruption of the Shah's regime, the pervasive American influence, the cultural "pollution" by Western ideas, the internal repression, and the ostentatious life style of the Shah's court while so many Iranian peasants lived in utter poverty. Khomeini urged his people to rise up against the Shah.

The flame had been smoldering for nearly ten years among Iran's Islamic devout, and now Khomeini fanned it into a bonfire of revolution. By late 1978, Khomeini's movement had accomplished the impossible, overcoming the Shah's vast military and internal security apparatus. Like a tidal wave, the masses of pro-Khomeini demonstrators marched into the teeth of machine guns; mowed down by the hundreds, they just kept coming. Within two months, they engulfed the Peacock Throne. On a chilly morning in January 1979, the world's most powerful despot hurriedly left Teheran aboard a jetliner. Shah Mohammad Reza Pahlavi was never to return to his native land; the man on whom so many American geostrategic hopes rested flew off into exile. Not too long afterward, he was dead of cancer.

The performance of American intelligence could hardly have been worse. Everything of importance had been missed: the Shah's growing unpopularity among his own people, the rise to power of the mullahs, the importance of Islam among the Iranians, the influence of Khomeini, and the range of anti-American feeling among wide sections of the Iranian population.‡

The consequences were momentous, for the United States was suddenly confronted with a bitterly anti-American revolutionary regime astride the Persian Gulf. The more immediate consequences, which were to destroy Carter's presidency, included the seizure of American hostages at the U.S. embassy and the failure of an American rescue mission in getting them back.

Before then, however, there was an attempt by the CIA to create the kind of good human sources of intelligence it failed to develop before the Khomeini revolution. The idea was to recruit assets among the Revolutionary Council running Iran, some of them former students who had studied in the United States.

The key target was a revolutionary leader considered close to Khomeini, a man named Abolhassan Bani-Sadr. In early 1979, a CIA agent under cover as a European businessman slipped into Teheran and recruited Bani-Sadr. For a CIA largesse of $1,000 a month, he agreed to keep the CIA informed of important decisions taken inside the Revolutionary Council. He was given the code name of SD/Lure-1, and seemed an enormous intelligence

‡ The disaster included a disaster-within-a-disaster. When Islamic fundamentalists seized the U.S. embassy in 1979, they found CIA agents had shredded secret documents into strips one-sixteenth of an inch wide. But the CIA forgot that Iran has a long tradition of rug-making. The descendants of the famed Persian rug weavers painstakingly wove all those paper strips together and reconstructed the CIA's secret documents.

asset, especially after Bani-Sadr was installed as President in January 1980.*

The CIA's hope in these hastily recruited assets was dashed when the seizure of the U.S. embassy occurred; Bani-Sadr had somehow neglected to mention that the council had heard and approved the seizure plan. And with the seizure of the embassy, all hope for any kind of American role in Iran collapsed.

The important question was not *how* it happened; it did not require much sophistication to spell out the specific failings of American intelligence that had led, inevitably, to the kind of failure Iran represented. The real question was *why* it happened, for that addressed the broader aspects of the American intelligence setup as it had evolved to this point.

Looked at one way, the failure in Iran really had nothing to do with the basic structure of American intelligence as crafted by Carter, DCI Turner, and Congress. The assumption that formed the foundation of that structure—an assumption which Carter and Turner both shared—was that American intelligence was able to function in a democratic society of media attention and congressional review. Further, the "right to know" was paramount over the requirements of secrecy, the necessity of protecting American citizens against intelligence agency abuses was more important than shielding intelligence agencies against adversaries, and it was morally wrong to defend American values by using the questionable means sometimes adopted by America's adversaries.

But there was another view, and it began to coalesce among a group of men whose political power grew as the Carter administration began to pass from the scene. In their perception, the congressional investigations of the intelligence community and the Carter administration's willingness to abide by new rules signified that Nixon's warning of the United States one day becoming a "pitiful, helpless giant" was coming true. And what better example existed of that syndrome than the embassy seizure in Iran—a group of Iranian students holding hostage the diplomats

---

* Another recruit was Mehdi Bazargan, former Iranian prime minister. CIA documents recovered at the seized U.S. embassy proved Bazargan's CIA role; he was later arrested and executed. Bani-Sadr fled for his life to France, where today he heads an anti-Khomeini exile organization.

of the mightiest nation on earth, virtually sneering at a super-power that had become a joke?

In this view of American inferiority and drift, the American intelligence community was regarded as a victim of softheaded thinking. What some in Congress had once referred to as a "rogue elephant" had now, in the assessment of a White House official, turned "chicken."

The emasculation, so the argument ran, was the fault of Congress, whose investigations and new laws on accountability had immobilized American intelligence. No one in the intelligence community wanted to take chances for fear of running afoul of the new regulations; the classic bureaucratic response—inertia—had settled over American intelligence.

The people who held these views most strongly had coalesced around a striking political figure in the conservative wing of the Republican Party, California governor Ronald Reagan. Their arguments were shared by Reagan, who believed, as they did, that American intelligence had been turned upside down during the Carter administration. Unlike Carter, he had no intention of failing to use American intelligence aggressively to support and justify American foreign policy.

Above all, such thinking was dominated by a concern that the United States had not reacted aggressively enough against Soviet threats and Soviet-supported regimes around the world. One particular area of concern was Central America.

And there, the new Reagan administration decided, was where a newly aggressive American intelligence would make its stand and achieve a long-overdue victory over what Reagan would call "the evil empire."

But to fight that battle would require a severe rattling of the American constitutional system.

TWELVE

Ends and Means

ONE AFTERNOON in September 1985, Robert C. McFarlane, President Reagan's National Security Adviser, went to the Capitol's fourth floor and walked through a soundproof door into the inner sanctum of the House Permanent Select Committee on Intelligence. There, he shook hands with a man he knew quite well, Representative Lee Hamilton, the committee chairman.

The encounter was a summit meeting of sorts between the executive and legislative branches of government, and concerned a recurring flashpoint between those two branches: covert intelligence operations. "Bud" McFarlane represented an administration that from the moment it took office in 1981 made clear a general distaste for the whole idea of congressional oversight. The congressionally imposed oversight system was tying the President's hands, so it was argued, preventing the intelligence agencies from fully exercising their options. The whole system made people too timid; intelligence agents had the sense they were being continually second-guessed by Congress.

On the other side, Hamilton, a veteran legislator and Indiana lawyer, was equally insistent that the system was working, that the congressional oversight function was critical to preventing the kind of abuses that were revealed in the 1970s. No longer would the Executive Branch, without regard to Congress, be able to make foreign policy covertly by unleashing the power of intelligence agencies.

Which was why Hamilton had invited McFarlane to his committee's sealed-off hearing room for a private conversation. A quiet-spoken man, Hamilton preferred to resolve problems privately, if possible. And he certainly had a big problem on his mind: the New York *Times* had published a disturbing story some time before, to the effect that a National Security Council aide, Marine Lieutenant Colonel Oliver North, was running an operation to raise money for the Nicaraguan resistance, and was providing military advice.

If true, Hamilton reminded McFarlane, that action was clearly illegal, in violation of the Boland Amendment, a congressional amendment to the military spending bill which prohibited any "entity of the United States involved in intelligence activities" from giving military support to the Nicaraguan resistance movement. Was it true that North was doing such a thing?

"Not true," McFarlane replied.

Hamilton asked the same question in several different forms; as a lawyer, he knew that a truthful answer often depended on the precise framing of the question. But no matter from which direction Hamilton addressed the question, McFarlane's answer was the same: no one on the National Security Council, North included, was involved in any way with efforts to evade the Boland Amendment. As McFarlane understood, the National Security Council was obviously "involved in intelligence activities."

After a while, Hamilton ended the conversation. He shook McFarlane's hand and said, "I, for one, am willing to take you at your word."

Thus ended the committee's informal inquiry into the first revelation that the White House knowingly was breaking the law. McFarlane had issued his denials with earnest sincerity; a former

Marine colonel, he conveyed the spirit of the Corps' officer honor code that an officer's word is his bond.

Nearly two years later, he found himself in the witness chair before Hamilton and a combined Senate and House committee, attempting to explain why the White House felt compelled to break the law.*

In between these two events was an extraordinary series of happenings now known as "the Iran-Contra affair," or variety thereof. All in all, as a congressional investigating committee said later, it was an affair of "confusion, secrecy and deception." Even in summary form, Iran-Contra sounds bizarre: the Reagan administration tried to dramatically affect the future of Iran-U.S. relations by beginning a covert program to provide advanced American weapons to so-called "moderate factions" in Iran. The idea was to encourage those "moderates" to alter the radicalism of the ruling Khomeini regime—and at the same time, provide "good faith" evidence of U.S. support that would compel the "moderates" to obtain the release of American hostages held by an Iranian-backed political faction in Lebanon. As an extra twist to an already-complicated scenario, the Reagan administration then used the profits of the sales of arms to the Iranians to covertly aid the Nicaraguan rebels and evade congressional restrictions on such aid.

The Iran-Contra affair left much wreckage in its wake. The Reagan administration was irretrievably damaged, and the President himself, who claimed not to have known of the covert operation to aid the Nicaraguan resistance, was not widely believed. More important, the whole process of congressional oversight of intelligence operations—and the larger issue of the roles of the Executive and Legislative branches—suffered severe damage. The consensus of the 1970s that had built the structure was left in tatters, and it is bitterly ironic today to read Senator Barry Goldwater's 1983 optimistic conclusion that the White House-congressional partnership in intelligence had become one of "trust and confidence."

The congressional investigation of Iran-Contra laid the respon-

---

* In early 1988, McFarlane pleaded guilty to charges of lying to Congress, having resigned his NSC post some months before. Lieutenant Colonel North, among others, was charged at the same time with assorted offenses in connection with the Iran-Contra operation.

sibility for the destruction of that partnership directly at the feet
of President Reagan. A fair indictment, to a certain extent, although the man really responsible for it was no longer alive when
the Iran-Contra operation became a full-fledged scandal.

His name was William J. Casey, Director of Central Intelligence, the first DCI to hold cabinet rank. He died of a brain
tumor in May 1987, as the congressional investigation of Iran-
Contra began, so he was not available to answer questions. But
there were plenty of his footprints, enough of them to make clear
that to understand the Iran-Contra affair—indeed, to understand
anything at all about the functioning of American intelligence
during the Reagan administration—it is necessary to understand
William J. Casey.

Casey, known as "Cyclone" for his blustery style, was a man
forged by his World War II experience. He was recruited into the
OSS by the man who would come to have the most influence on
his life, William Donovan. It was Donovan who set up Casey in
the tiny OSS secretariat at the beginning of American involvement in World War II, carefully grooming him for a bigger assignment in Europe where Donovan planned to run large-scale
guerrilla and resistance operations behind German lines.

Casey became close to Donovan, and often accompanied him on
his assorted whirlwind tours to the OSS outstations (Casey later
repeated this habit when he became DCI and was known derisively around some sections of the CIA as "The Wanderer" for
the practice). Casey was very much taken with the OSS director's
style. Donovan was a man who understood the "big picture." As
Casey summarized him, "He loved ideas and he'd make very fast
decisions."

Blunt and forceful, Donovan was pure action, and was sometimes accused of loving action for action's sake. Perhaps so, but
what most impressed Casey about Donovan was his ability to get
things done. Donovan loved to cut red tape; to him, all bureaucra-
cies were impediments to be bulldozed, evaded, or leaped over in
the name of operations.

Donovan sanctified operations; they were the primary reason
for OSS's existence. And the more operations, the better: any
scheme, however wild, was certain to get at least a hearing from
Donovan, who more often than not would give sanction to begin

the operation on the spot. He could see no reason for such delays, for it was a war unto death against the evil of Adolf Hitler, and delay only meant that the war would last that much longer.

Above all, in Casey's view, Donovan had *guts*. A Congressional Medal of Honor winner from World War I, Donovan gave the appearance of total fearlessness. He expected boldness in his subordinates: when they were out in the field, they were expected to let no obstacle stand in the way of the higher operational imperative.

Based in London in 1944 to run OSS penetrations of Nazi-occupied Europe, Casey was a virtual Donovan clone. Whether it was arranging for the dropping of propaganda leaflets over Germany showing Hitler with half his face rotted away, or dispatching anti-Hitler exiles on dangerous missions far behind German lines, Casey demonstrated the Donovan flair for the imaginative and daring in operations. It was a heady time: in the name of winning the war, OSS operatives, despite Army ranks and uniforms, operated outside normal Army channels, had wide decision-making latitude, had virtually no limits set on the scope of operations, and had only limited accountability.

Casey had little contact with the intelligence community after the war. A businessman, he served a stint in government as head of the Securities and Exchange Commission, and in 1980 worked as Reagan's campaign manager. His ambition was to become Secretary of State, but Reagan offered Casey a job he thought much better suited to the former OSS officer's background: Director of Central Intelligence.

Why did Casey, a millionaire in his sixties, want to join the new Administration? The answer lay in his political outlook: a conservative Republican, Casey, like many other conservatives, fervently believed that the United States was on the road to disaster. The disaster had begun in Vietnam, when the United States had demonstrated its first hesitation in combating the evils of international communism; it had continued in Angola, in Ethiopia, and, most recently, in Nicaragua.

The Reagan administration, in Casey's view, represented a real attempt to stop the drift toward national suicide. Reagan, a visceral anti-Communist, would tolerate no further Soviet expansionism, by proxy (as in Nicaragua), or otherwise. There would be a new aggressiveness in American foreign policy; the Soviet threat would be forcefully rolled back.

Casey believed that the CIA could play the lead role in this strategy. Direct military confrontation with the Soviets was out of the question, but the Soviet proxies—especially in Latin America and Africa—could be defeated by means of covert action. In other words, the CIA would return to the old days, running operations and supporting exiles to destabilize or destroy regimes perceived to be part of the Soviet master plan for world conquest. No holds would be barred in these operations; as with Hitler, Casey saw little sense in playing by the rules against an opponent who did not recognize any rules.

Such operations, as Casey was the first to admit, would have to be carried out in the deepest secrecy, a belief that put him at odds with some of the hawks in the Administration. One of them, Jeane Kirkpatrick, U.S. Ambassador to the United Nations, warned Casey that times had changed: no longer could the United States run covert political operations without popular consensus and congressional support.

But Casey had no time for such impediments. The danger was immediate, growing every hour. Congress could debate, the people would argue, and by the time they figured out what to do, the Communists would be paddling their assault boats across the Rio Grande. Delay and consensus-building were anathema to Casey; things had to be done the Donovan way—do it now, and consider the consequences later.

As events later proved, there would be serious consequences from this mind-set, for Casey decided there was one place in the world where the new American activism had to be immediately implemented: Nicaragua.

Making Nicaragua a test case for the new activism had certain advantages. Unlike places like Yemen or Ethiopia, Nicaragua was in America's Central American backyard.† It was free of the complexities of Angola, where the Americans were still supporting the cause of anti-Communist rebels—while at the same time making friendly overtures to the ruling Marxist regime to involve the

† The most fierce and effective proxy fighters are in the Soviet Union's backyard: the Mujahedeen of Afghanistan. The CIA simply supplies them with weapons via Pakistan; the Mujahedeen accomplishes the rest. It is a rare CIA activity that enjoys White House, congressional, and public support.

Angolans in a complex American diplomatic initiative for a peace plan covering the entire southwestern area of Africa.

Nicaragua did have the Sandinistas, whose Cuban-style approach to revolution and increasing repression since taking power in 1979 had made them unsympathetic figures to most Americans: promised elections were postponed, freedom of the press was suspended, and political opponents were jailed. Further, they were building up their military forces with Cuban and Soviet arms, and were suspected of serving as arms brokers for leftist guerrillas in El Salvador.

One of the central convictions of Casey—along with Reagan and many other conservatives—was that the Carter administration had made a hideous mistake in allowing the Sandinistas to come to power. This view did not accept Carter's central rationale that the Sandinistas would inevitably win their guerrilla war in Nicaragua against the corrupt and brutal regime of dictator Anastasio Somoza; therefore, it was in the United States best interest to ease out Somoza and attempt to develop some sort of understanding with his successors. Carter had been confronted with the dilemma created by decades of American policy in Latin America: American support for dictators, who usually murdered or imprisoned their moderate opposition. That left (as in Cuba and Nicaragua) only the radical—and often Communist—opposition.

Somoza was a classic example of the problem. Propped up by a succession of American administrations for over forty years, the Somoza family ruled Nicaragua with an iron fist, at the same time stealing everything they could get their hands on. The moderate opposition was murdered or driven into exile, and the leftists, encouraged by the example of Cuba, began a guerrilla war that slowly weakened Somoza's grip. The Sandinistas, as they called themselves, had a distinct anti-American tinge, blaming the overt American support for Somoza as an important reason for his continued existence.

To Casey, all these facts amounted to unimportant distinctions. The important fact was that Somoza was a virulent anti-Communist, and the Sandinistas included many Castroites and Communists; that was all that mattered. Further, as in the case of Fidel Castro, the Sandinistas were merely instruments in a larger scheme: they were to serve as the proxies for Soviet penetration of Central America, the first important step in Moscow's scheme to isolate, then destroy, United States dominance in the Western Hemisphere.

Casey was determined to keep such a scenario from occurring. But the DCI was in very dangerous waters, for he had elevated himself above the democratic process, deciding that process was too slow to accomplish what he was convinced was some sort of sacred mission. Was that mission directly ordered by Casey's boss, Ronald Reagan? Did he order Casey to destroy the Sandinista regime by any means, fair or foul? Or, having made his deep-seated hostility toward the Sandinistas well known, did he simply leave it to others like Casey to guess that they were to observe no limits in getting rid of the Sandinistas?

There is no question that Reagan approved the CIA's marching orders to carry out a covert operation against the Nicaraguan regime, but things get obscure after that. He has denied having anything to do with the funding portion of the Iran-Contra scheme, and has also disavowed any knowledge of some of the worst excesses of the CIA operation in Nicaragua. Casey himself, right to the end, claimed that the President "didn't know," presumably meaning the things he wasn't supposed to know about.

So "plausible deniability" had entered the presidential lexicon again, and that wasn't the only echo from the past in Casey's operation.

Edén Pastora was dumbfounded. They acted as if this were Yugoslavia or France in World War II; hadn't they looked at a map?

Pastora, the famed "Commandante Zero" of the Sandinista revolution, was amazed, once again, by how little the CIA people seemed to know about the realities of guerrilla warfare in the Latin American jungles. Now they were proposing that he take his meager force of several hundred guerrillas across the Nicaraguan border, attack a port on Nicaragua's Atlantic coast, then somehow make their way back to their base in Costa Rica.

Pastora knew a great deal about guerrilla warfare in the jungles. One of the Sandinista guerrilla army's most dashing leaders and later a member of the ruling council, he had left Nicaragua in disgust when he perceived that the pro-Cuban Marxists in the government were trying to set up a dictatorship. That was not why Pastora had been fighting the *Somocistas* for twenty years, and he moved himself and several hundred like-minded men to Costa Rica. There, he formed an organization called ARDE and began a guerrilla war against the Sandinistas.

Coincidental with the advent of the Reagan administration, Pastora was approached by the CIA. He was promised money, arms, and lavish American support if he enlisted in a large-scale operation sponsored by the CIA to destroy the Sandinista regime. Pastora agreed, but would come to have some doubts about the decision.

The problem was that the CIA was in a hurry, and the CIA men who arrived at his base camp, dressed in new jungle fatigues, wanted results—now. To no avail, Pastora pointed out that it had taken twenty years of guerrilla warfare to get rid of Somoza. Further, the grand CIA plans, with arrows drawn on maps showing bold guerrilla thrusts against Sandinista troops and bases, made no sense on the ground. The terrain on the other side of the Costa Rican-Nicaraguan border was largely wild jungle. Troop movements of any size were very difficult, and it would be a long time before ARDE forces were strong enough to challenge Sandinista troops in open combat.

But the CIA had its own ideas, and began talking in terms of a "southern front" that would coordinate with the "northern front" then being formed in Honduras. Southern front? Northern front? Pastora thought such talk absurd, and he held an equal amount of disdain for the CIA's insistence on delivering new uniforms and boots to his men along with arms, part of a CIA conviction that Pastora's men would fight better if properly outfitted.

Despite his steadily growing disenchantment with the CIA, Pastora agreed to the plan under which his men would attack a port facility in Nicaragua known to have plenty of Sandinista troops and men from a new military force in Nicaragua, recently armed local militia forces. The attack, as Pastora feared, was premature; his men were soundly defeated. The defeat marked the beginning of Pastora's eventual estrangement from the CIA, and he later quit the business of guerrilla warfare against Nicaragua altogether, believing that no success was possible in the struggle so long as the CIA was running it. (Pastora now operates a fishing business in Costa Rica.)

Pastora was always puzzled about the mind-set of the CIA men who arrived in Costa Rica to tell him how to run a guerrilla campaign. He would have understood a great deal more if he had ever met William Casey, for the entire agency effort was very much a reflection of its director.

Casey's plan echoed the standard OSS operations against the Nazis: brave anti-Sandinistas would be collected into a guerrilla force, and some black cork put on their faces; they would then go blow up power lines, plant dynamite on railroad tracks, ambush isolated enemy units, and generally make life miserable for the enemy. But occupied Europe had a complex communications and transportation system vulnerable to sabotage; Nicaragua, one of the poorest countries in Latin America, had nothing like it. Occupied Europe had an alien and despised foreign occupation force spread thinly all over the countryside; Nicaragua had a home-grown army and militia that were distinctly Nicaraguan. Occupied Europe had whole populations seething with hatred for the Nazis; Nicaragua had a regime that while not supported by all Nicaraguans, nevertheless enjoyed considerable popularity in the countryside. Occupied Europe had large groups of resistance fighters united by a common goal of getting rid of the Nazis; the Nicaraguan resistance to the Sandinistas was badly split among many different political factions, including remnants of Somoza's hated National Guard.

Casey shaped the anti-Sandinista resistance (usually called Contras) in the image of World War II OSS resistance movements. They were paid, armed, trained, and then sent into Nicaragua with the mission of attacking what passed for the Nicaraguan government infrastructure. Not surprisingly, they wound up conducting a war of random shooting, where targets were as likely to be civilian as military.

Nor did the Contras have a political program with which Nicaraguans could sympathize and rally around. As one of Casey's predecessors, William Colby, observed, the CIA had put the cart before the horse, trying to win a guerrilla war without bothering to tell anybody what they were fighting for, except the immediate objective of getting rid of Sandinistas.

Still, Casey persisted. He performed a minor miracle of finance by managing to build a Contra army out of funding that was barely adequate for the purpose, aware at every moment that to seek much larger funding might create too many questions in

Congress. There was already uneasiness in Congress, for as the months went by, the Contras did not seem to be making much of a dent in the Sandinista regime; the Nicaraguan economy was in shambles, but the Sandinistas were firmly in power.

When things did not go quite the way Casey had anticipated, he decided to step up the pressure by mining Nicaraguan harbors. It caused an outcry, followed by an attempt to claim that the Contras did it on their own. (No one could imagine the Contras manufacturing sophisticated anti-ship mines in jungle workshops.) Judged operationally, the mining made little sense; it very much reflected the OSS heritage of bold sabotage operations, but again, Nicaragua was not occupied Europe. Besides which, what nation —especially the Soviet Union—would believe, in the event any of their ships were sunk, that the Contras had done it on their own?

Congress was already in a dither about the mining when Casey put them in an uproar with another operation: a Cessna light plane, piloted by a Contra and armed with two five-hundred-pound bombs strapped to its wings, was dispatched to Managua to bomb the airport. It crashed into the airport terminal, killed an airport worker—and thoroughly unsettled Senators Gary Hart and William Cohen, who arrived in Managua only hours later on a fact-finding trip. Both men immediately deduced that the bombing was a CIA operation, and furiously protested to Casey: what exactly was the bombing supposed to prove?

Casey did not understand, because to him, such an operation, irrespective of the consequences, was sufficient justification by its very definition; it was an *operation*, part of the effort to destroy evil. There was nothing else to discuss. By the same token, Casey apparently did not understand the outcry that greeted the CIA's publication of a guerrilla warfare manual which among other things recommended assassination of Nicaraguan government officials. However evil he thought the government officials of Nicaragua, the United States some years before had firmly renounced assassinations. Yet, here was a document produced by a government agency advocating just that, along with instructions on whom to kill.

It is likely, then, that Casey had no understanding that he had gone too far. By 1984 Congress was fed up, and passed the Boland Amendment to prohibit support for the Contras by the CIA—or any other component of the American intelligence community.

But the Reagan administration had firmly committed itself to the Contra cause, and it hardly could be expected simply to give up. Given the administration's outlook, and the presence of Casey as DCI, there should have been little doubt that an attempt would be made to circumvent the Boland Amendment in some way. Further, there were already plenty of clues testifying to the Administration's view of the place of American intelligence operations in the democratic system.

One important clue came early in Reagan's presidency, when he issued full pardons for former FBI officials Edward S. Miller and Mark W. Felt, who had been convicted for their role in illegal break-ins during the Bureau's hunt for Weathermen fugitives in the 1960s. The break-ins had occurred at the homes of persons suspected of providing aid to the fugitives; none of these people was ever charged with a crime.

Were the pardons meant as a signal that the Administration was shifting the FBI back into the political spying business? The question has not yet been resolved, although it was discovered in 1988 that the FBI had been conducting, beginning in 1983, investigations of a dozen American political groups on the grounds that they might have been involved in aiding "terror organizations" in El Salvador. Perhaps not so coincidentally, all the groups happened to be opponents of President Reagan's Central American policy.

There was also the matter of a disturbing development inside military intelligence. In late 1981, the Administration created an organization called the Special Operations Division, a secret U.S. Army unit initially designed to perform anti-terrorist operations. Gradually, however, the unit began to drift into intelligence operations, and by 1983 had become a miniature CIA, operating under commercial cover. The unit began working with the CIA in Central American operations, a partnership that made the few senior Army officers who were aware of the unit's existence very nervous—Special Operations Division had no real mandate, no charter, no limits, no control, and was now working closely with the CIA.‡

The Army officers were quite right to be concerned about an

‡ The Special Operations Division was closed down in 1985 after Army investigators discovered it was riddled with corruption; officers of the unit used their commercial cover and virtually unlimited funds to underwrite lavish life styles.

intelligence unit operating without any oversight or controls, but it turned out that they didn't know the real dimension of the problem. In 1983, the unit's commanders were approached by the CIA with a plan: in the event aid for the Contras was cut off by Congress, the CIA would set up a "back channel" to evade the cutoff and provide weapons to the Contras. The Army unit personnel would be needed to build and operate covert airstrips in Costa Rica, to be used for secret flights of arms to Contra units.

The Army unit commanders raised no objection to what was clearly an illegal operation. They had taken the first step in the curious affair known as Iran-Contra.

Throughout 1984, CIA general counsel Stanley Sporkin took pains, as often as possible, to remind Casey and the rest of the CIA that the Boland Amendment had to be complied with. Sporkin took the action largely because of his awareness of Casey's predilection for activism, no matter what the law said.

But Casey was a lawyer too, and subscribed to the old legal aphorism that where there's a will, there's a loophole. He believed there were two in the Boland Amendment: (1) the amendment did not apply to the National Security Council,* and (2) there was nothing in the amendment to prevent private groups from donating money to the Contras, nor was there anything specific barring the officials of the government from "encouraging" such contributions.

Casey conveyed this legal analysis not to Sporkin, but to Oliver North of the National Security Council. And with good reason: if ever there was a perfect patsy, North was it. Fanatically loyal to his commander in chief—he once said that if Reagan told him to go in a corner and sit on his own head, he would do it—he was clearly willing to do just about anything to help the Contras, a Reagan obsession. And he was willing to do it even without the protection lower-ranking government officials usually seek in

---

A joint Army-Justice Department prosecution convicted two officers connected with the unit on fraud and other charges.

* Casey should have known better. Reagan's Executive Order 1233 of December 1981 specifically assigned the National Security Council to coordinate and direct American intelligence operations—clearly within the Boland Amendment's parameters covering "intelligence entity." As DCI, Casey was well acquainted with this document, since it told him to whom he should report.

memos, unmistakable lines of authority, and the willingness of higher-ups to take responsibility for controversial (or illegal) actions.

Casey in effect became North's case officer for what was now an effort to evade the Boland Amendment. As it turned out, North was already involved in an even more sensitive operation, known as Staunch. The operation sought to impose a total arms embargo on Iran by pressuring arms-producing nations to join in the American ban on arms sales to Teheran. It was enjoying modest success when a discredited Iranian arms broker and former CIA asset floated a tantalizing idea: there was a "moderate" faction in Iran determined to take over the country after Khomeini's death. They wanted to restore Iran's close relations with America, but needed an expression of American sincerity—namely, the sale of several hundred anti-tank and anti-aircraft missiles. There was an extra bonus: if the Americans made the sales, the moderates would then arrange for the release of American hostages held in Lebanon.

What happened next represented a very dark chapter in the history of American covert foreign operations. In the face of all evidence that the entire offer was a swindle, and over the strong objections of Secretary of State George Shultz and Secretary of Defense Caspar Weinberger, the Reagan administration began selling arms to Iran. Justified under the grand-sounding title of "Iran Initiative," it soon degenerated into a straight arms-for-hostages deal—the kind of tribute to terrorists the Administration publicly vowed it would never make.

Congress knew nothing of this astonishing foreign policy initiative and reversal of official American policy against terrorism until November 1986, when a Lebanese newspaper revealed it. That was disquieting enough, but there was another Administration secret yet to be revealed: an odd convergence had been forged between the Iran operation and another one to aid the Contras in violation of the congressional prohibition.

Again, the guiding force was Casey. Convinced (on very thin evidence) that the President himself had ordered the Contra assistance operation, North was willing to be the point man, taking guidance from Casey. North represented plausible deniability; if the evasion of the Boland Amendment became known, the CIA would not have any direct involvement.

Whatever else may be said about North, he proved to be a veritable dynamo in the business of getting things done. In only a short period of time, he set up a network of private donors to the Contra cause, formed a covert group to handle the purchase and delivery of arms, and created a propaganda operation to discredit the Sandinistas. With covert aid from the CIA, North had an efficient enterprise that siphoned off money from high profits on the sales of arms to the Iranians and converted it to an arms and money pipeline for the Contras.

It was all supposed to occur in conditions of the deepest secrecy, but the sheer scope of the operation already was setting off whispers that there was some sort of covert deal underway to keep the Contras in business. It began to unravel in October 1986, when a civilian transport was shot down over Nicaragua. The American pilot and co-pilot were killed, but another American crewman, Eugene Hasenfus, survived and was captured.

Hasenfus denied being a CIA agent—true enough—but the Nicaraguans found a treasure trove of documents aboard the plane that gave the broad outlines of an ostensibly private aid operation for the Contras that had CIA fingerprints everywhere. (Hasenfus didn't know all the details, but said that the "private" operation was in fact an elaborate cover to hide CIA involvement.) A month later, the Iranian operation was revealed, along with its connection to the Contra operation.

Unlike the Watergate hearings or the 1975 congressional investigations of intelligence agency abuses, the congressional hearings on Iran-Contra had some difficulty in finding a clear focus. The converging Iran and Contra operations were hard to follow, there were many loose ends, officials had strange lapses of memory on important points, and the key personnel involved said the President didn't know anything about diversion of money to the Contras. (So did the President.)

But the real reason for much of the mystery was because the final secrets of what really happened reposed in the head of the man most responsible for it all, William Casey. And William Casey was dead.

His death was a tragic irony, for Casey, hooked as a young man by the adventure of espionage, was for the remainder of his life a man who could never quite shake the lure of the secret world, a world that finally consumed him. Most of all, Casey was a man

indelibly stamped with his World War II OSS experience, those
heady days when young Americans wielded a secret weapon that
could decide the destiny of nations. And they could wield it free
of the distractions of legality, congressional oversight, and accountability.

But the world had changed, and what had worked in World
War II would not, as it turned out, work so easily afterward.
Some, like Casey, would insist that the world hadn't really
changed that much: evil was evil, and America was foolish to
equivocate in deciding what methods would be suitable in combating it.

For many years, Casey wanted to control the wellsprings of
American intelligence, in order to demonstrate just what could be
accomplished by the proper, forceful leadership. He was finally to
achieve that goal, but despite his singleminded efforts to change
the course of history, he was finally done in by the very forces he
tried to shape. Largely, that was because Casey made the same
mistakes that had been made so often before, mistakes that have
everything to do with the place of secret intelligence operations
in American democracy.

The most prominent example was Nicaragua. Casey, like his
President, was determined to covertly destroy a government both
men believed represented a grave danger to the United States. It
is possible history will record that Nicaragua did in fact represent
a threat of such magnitude, but the contemporary problem was
that no real public and congressional consensus existed on Nicaragua. Impatient, Reagan and Casey tried to force the issue—and
learned, as Woodrow Wilson did in Russia during 1919, John Kennedy in Cuba in 1961, and Lyndon Johnson in Vietnam in 1968,
that a policy pursued covertly which could not be accomplished
overtly without consensus was doomed from the start.

Similarly, Casey was part of an overall effort within American
intelligence to tighten up internal security. Unlike several previous efforts in this area, it did not take the form of a turning
inward by U.S. intelligence agencies, and instead concentrated on
restricting access to secrets. A much-publicized campaign, including a plan for mandatory polygraph tests for all employees with
access to classified information and talk of prosecuting newspapers that published classified information, finally collapsed. As
had happened before, a general American consensus emerged that

no matter how grave the threat from outside enemies, the cost of sacrificing or amending certain freedoms was simply not worth it.

This consensus remained firm despite a sudden spate of spy cases that broke out during Casey's term in office. First, it was discovered that a former U.S. Navy noncommissioned officer, John Walker, his brother, and his son sold the Navy's cryptographic communications secrets to the Russians. Then, even more shockingly, it was learned that a former CIA official, Edward Lee Howard, had betrayed agency secrets, including the identity of CIA assets in the Soviet Union. That was followed by the revelation that a National Security Agency employee, Ronald Pelton, had sold important NSA information to the Russians. (And, for good measure, a U.S. Navy intelligence employee, Jonathan Pollard, was caught passing secrets to the Israelis.)

Although the Reagan administration attempted to use these cases as evidence for the need to "tighten up" internal security, there was, perhaps surprisingly, no groundswell of support. The problem was that the cases had nothing to do with ideology, and very little to do with active operations by the Soviet KGB. Each one of the spies betrayed his country strictly for money; in every case, they simply contacted the Russians and offered to sell their country's secrets.†

Nevertheless, Casey was upset by plans of the Senate intelligence committee to investigate the betrayals and prepare a highly sanitized report generally summarizing their counterintelligence implications. Casey's protests were turned aside by senators who told him that the American people had a right know, with deletions, what had happened and its impact on American national security.

The real importance of that argument was that it encapsulated, in very clear form, how secret intelligence has divided the two great power centers of American government that lie on opposite ends of Pennsylvania Avenue.

What had happened was an old story, one whose real beginning

† The existence of three of these spies was provided the CIA by Vitaly Yurchenko, a KGB colonel who defected in 1985. A major catch, Yurchenko spent a short while in Washington, including an intimate dinner with Casey. A few days later, to the mortification of Casey and the CIA, Yurchenko redefected back to the Soviet Union.

was in the hot summer of 1787. At the Constitutional Convention, there was a fierce debate among the delegates about the powers of the office of the presidency in the new Constitution. The debate was focused on that most contentious issue, how much power should the President have in the matter of war and foreign policy.

"The Executive magistracy," as Roger Sherman of Connecticut put it, was nothing more than an institution for carrying out the will of Congress, where the "depositary of the supreme will of society" resided. James Madison of Virginia agreed, arguing that Executive Branch powers did not include "the rights of war and peace."

These arguments, which took the position that the powers of war and the conduct of foreign policy properly belonged in Congress, the voice of the people, went to the very heart of the constitutional system. The power to make war was even greater than the power to tax, and the question was: who in the government would have such power?

Alexander Hamilton of New York and James Madison, in their famous debates in *The Federalist*, had tried to settle the question, but did not succeed in changing each other's minds. Hamilton advocated a strong presidency—especially in the area of war-making powers—while Madison argued, "War is in fact the true nurse of executive aggrandizement."

In the end, the final draft of the Constitution compromised by splitting the war-making and conduct of foreign policy between the Executive and Legislative branches of government. In fact, the Constitution is notably terse on these subjects. Article I, Section 8, says that Congress has the power to "provide for the common defense" and to declare war. Article II, Section 2, empowers the President to make treaties (with the "advice and consent" of a two-thirds majority of the Senate), to appoint ambassadors (with the same advice and consent), and to be the commander in chief of the armed forces.

The very terseness of these provisions has amounted to an invitation for the Executive and Legislative branches to battle over which branch is responsible for directing foreign policy. Some constitutional scholars argue that the Constitution implicitly charges Congress with making foreign policy, and the President with carrying it out. This view is not universally accepted, and presidents since Theodore Roosevelt have insisted that they are responsible for the conduct of foreign policy.

Modern presidents have extended the argument by claiming the power to conduct foreign policy includes, by implication, the power to direct American intelligence. That argument is still controversial, and it is further complicated by another one: that the direction of American intelligence includes the implicit right of presidents to use it in the conduct of foreign policy when more open means are inconvenient.

Here is where the real dilemmas in the relationship between intelligence and the American democratic system arise, for intelligence operations are supposed to be secret. And if they are secret, and also part of the foreign policy process, then how is Congress supposed to perform its constitutional "advice and consent" function?

There is no easy answer to this problem. On one hand, few Americans would want to give the President and his intelligence agencies carte blanche to conduct foreign policy; as history has shown, presidents and their intelligence agencies tend to run out of control quickly when exempted from the system of checks and balances. President Reagan's covert intelligence operation in Nicaragua is instructive in this regard: what began as a relatively simple effort to arm anti-Sandinista forces mushroomed into one of the largest undertakings since the Vietnam war. Clearly, the President sought to conduct war against Nicaragua without having to go to Congress and seek a declaration of war.

But it is also true to say that the United States lives in a dangerous world of uncertainty and rapid change, a world poised on the edge of nuclear Armageddon. No one has yet been able to figure out a system where the Legislative and Executive branches can share responsibility for the conduct of foreign policy—and at the same time act with great speed in the event of sudden crisis. It is one of democracy's central flaws.

Still, democracy is a flawed process, and it may well be that this central question will remain a permanent source of tension, so long as there is a constitutional system. The flaw, indeed, seems to serve as an effective reminder that the Constitution is a remarkably flexible document, but not so flexible that it can tolerate such potentially troublesome institutions as the American intelligence community operating outside its democratic context. Above all, it may be helpful to remember just what the Constitution is: it is protection against ourselves.

Notes and Sources

INTRODUCTION: "An Enemy to the Liberties"

p. xiii "THE NECESSITY": Quoted in George S. Bryan, *The Spy in America*, Philadelphia, 1943.

p. xiii AMERICAN ESPIONAGE EMPIRE: Jeffrey T. Richelson, *The U.S. Intelligence Community*, Cambridge, 1985.

p. xiv CONSTITUTION AND INTELLIGENCE OPERATIONS: Henry Steele Commager, "Intelligence: the Constitution Betrayed," *New York Review of Books*, September 30, 1976.

p. xiv PRESIDENTIAL PERCEPTIONS: Remarks, F. A. O. Schwarz, Jr., chief counsel Select Senate Committee to Study Governmental Operations with Respect to Intelligence Activities [hereafter Church Committee], New York City Bar Association, November 16, 1976.

p. xiv PRESIDENTS AND INTELLIGENCE OPERATIONS: Walter Laqueur, "Spying and Democracy," *Society*, November–December 1985.

p. xiv "IT IS NOW CLEAR": *Report of the President's Commission on the Organization of the Executive Branch of the Government*, September 30, 1954 (see especially Appendix, *Report of the Special Study Group on the Covert Activities of the Central Intelligence Agency*. Former President Herbert Hoover was chairman of the commission.

p. xv   DILEMMA OF INTELLIGENCE OPERATIONS: Edward F. Sayle, "The Historical Underpinnings of the U.S. Intelligence Community," *International Journal of Intelligence and Counterintelligence* (vol. 1, no. 1) 1986.

p. xv   WASHINGTON AND INTELLIGENCE: Bryan, *Spy in America.*

p. xvi   CONTINENTAL CONGRESS AND SECRECY: Sayle, "Historical Underpinnings."

p. xvii   NEW OUTLOOK: Glenn Hastedt, "The Constitutional Control of Intelligence," *Intelligence and National Security* (no. 1), 1986.

p. xvii   ALIEN AND SEDITION ACTS: John C. Miller, *Crisis in Freedom: the Alien and Sedition Acts*, Boston, 1951.

p. xvii   "IT IS SEDITION": James Morton Smith, *Freedom's Fetters: The Alien and Sedition Laws and American Liberties*, Ithaca, New York, 1956.

p. xvii   QUEBEC OPERATION: Sayle, "Historical Underpinnings."

p. xviii   ISRAELI MURDER OPERATION: Elihu Avraham interview.

p. xviii   FRANCE: Roger Faligot and Pascal Krop, *La Picine: Les Services secrets Français 1944–1984*, Paris, 1985.

p. xviii   GREAT BRITAIN: Peter Wright, *Spycatcher*, New York, 1987; "Who Polices Britain's Secret Policemen?" editorial, Manchester *Guardian*, March 3, 1985.

p. xviii   EARLY AMERICAN OPERATIONS: William R. Corson, *The Armies of Ignorance*, New York, 1977.

ONE: On the Road to Shevogarsk

p. 3–4   RUSSIAN-AMERICAN BATTLE: E. M. Halliday, *The Ignorant Armies*, New York, 1958.

p. 4   AMERICAN DEFEAT: Bruce Bidwell, *History of the Military Intelligence Department of the Army General Staff: 1775–1941*, Washington, D.C., 1954.

p. 4   "NEVER HAVE ANY": Remarks, Nikita Khrushchev, Los Angeles, quoted in New York *Times*, September 20, 1959.

p. 5   RUSSIA 1917: George F. Kennan, *Russia Leaves the War*, Princeton, 1956.

p. 5   WILSON'S OUTLOOK: Lloyd C. Gardner, *Safe for Democracy*, Oxford, 1984.

p. 6   "WE SAW A STATE": Winston Churchill, *The World Crisis*, London, 1929.

p. 6   BOLSHEVIK REVOLUTION, "PEACE DECREE": E. H. Carr, *The Bolshevik Revolution, 1917–1923*, London, 1953.

p. 6   WISEMAN: Wilton B. Fowler, *British-American Relations, 1917–1918: the Role of Sir William Wiseman*, Princeton, 1969.

p. 6–7   MAUGHAM'S SPY MISSION: Robert L. Calder, *W. Somerset Maugham and the Quest for Freedom*, London, 1972.

p. 7   ROOT MISSION: Peter G. Filene, *Americans and the Soviet Experiment, 1917–1933*, Cambridge, 1967.

p. 7   AMBASSADOR FRANCIS: David Francis, *Russia from the American Embassy*, New York, 1931.

p. 7   AMERICAN INTELLIGENCE IN RUSSIA: Christopher Dobson and John Miller, *The Day They Almost Bombed Moscow*, New York, 1986; George Hill, *Go Spy the Land*, London, 1932; Major David B. Morgan, *American Intervention in Russia, 1917–1918*, Master's degree thesis, United States Army Command and General Staff College, Fort Leavenworth, Kansas, 1987.

p. 7   FRANCIS' ATTITUDES: Kennan, *Russia Leaves the War.*

p. 7   KALAMATIANO: William R. Corson, *The Armies of Ignorance*, New York, 1977.

p. 7   U.S. ARMY INTELLIGENCE: Bidwell, *History of the Military Intelligence Department.*

p. 7   RUSSIA AS INTELLIGENCE MAELSTROM: Samuel Hoare, *The Fourth Seal,* London, 1930.

p. 8   THOMPSON: Herman Hagedorn, *The Magnate,* New York, 1935; Kennan, *Russia Leaves the War.*

p. 8   ROBINS: Testimony, Raymond Robins, hearings, subcommittee Senate Judiciary Committee, *German and Bolshevik Propaganda,* Washington, 1919; William Hard, *Raymond Robins' Own Story,* New York, 1920.

p. 8   YMCA: Associated Press, *Service With Fighting Men,* New York, 1922.

p. 8   ACTIVITIES OF THOMPSON, ROBINS: Kennan, *Russia Leaves the War.*

p. 8   "NEITHER WAR, NOR PEACE": Ibid.

p. 8   MCCULLY: C. J. Weeks and J. O. Baylen, "Admiral Newton A. McCully's Missions in Russia, 1904–1921," *Russian Review,* January 1974.

p. 9   GERMAN OFFENSIVE: C. N. Barclay, *Armistice 1918,* London, 1968.

p. 9   SISSON DOCUMENTS: George F. Kennan, "The Sisson Documents," *Journal of Modern History,* June 1956.

p. 9   GENERAL GRAVES IN SIBERIA: William S. Graves, *American Siberian Adventure,* New York, 1931.

p. 10   ARCHANGEL: Halliday, *Ignorant Armies.*

p. 10   FBI AND GRAVES: Betty M. Unterberger, *America's Siberian Adventure, 1918–1920,* Durham, North Carolina, 1956.

p. 10   SOLDIERS IN ARCHANGEL: Halliday, *Ignorant Armies.*

p. 10   MILITARY DISASTER: Bidwell, *History of the Military Intelligence Department.*

p. 11   "ADVANTAGE IS OURS": *The American Sentinel,* Archangel, April 12, 1919 (authors' collection).

p. 11   MUTINIES: Ibid.

p. 11   "IT IS HARDER": Gardner, *Safe for Democracy.*

p. 11   "WE ARE NOT AT WAR": Graves, *American Siberian Adventure.*

p. 12   FINAL TOLL: Bidwell, *History of the Military Intelligence Department.*

p. 12   MCCULLY AT ARCHANGEL: Weeks and Baylen, "Admiral Newton A. McCully."

p. 12   BIRTH OF CHEKA: John Dziak, *Chekisty,* Lexington, Massachusetts, 1987.

p. 12–13   DZERZHINSKY: Roland Gaucher, *Opposition dans l'U.R.S.S. 1917–1967,* Paris, 1967.

p. 13   "WE REPRESENT": Dziak, *Chekisty.*

p. 13   CHEKA TERROR: George Leggett, *The CHEKA,* Oxford, 1981.

p. 13   RUSSIANS INFORMED IN 1922: Dziak, *Chekisty.*

p. 13   KEDROV: Alexander Orlov, *The Secret History of Stalin's Crimes,* London, 1974.

p. 13   EIDUK: Gustav Hilger and Alfred G. Meyer, *The Incompatible Allies,* New York, 1953.

p. 14   AMERICAN RELIEF ADMINISTRATION: E. M. Halliday, "Bread Upon the Waters," in *America and Russia,* edited by Oliver Jensen, New York, 1962.

p. 14   END OF EIDUK, KEDROV: Orlov, *Secret History.*

p. 14   CHEKA'S PROBLEMS: Leggett, *Cheka.* For the Soviet version of these events, see especially *Iz Istorii Vserossiyskoy Chrezvychaynoy Komissii 1917–1921*, Moscow, 1958.

p. 14 BRITISH-FRENCH PLOT: Yakov Peters, "Vospominaniya o rabote v VChk v pervyi god revolyutsii," *Proletarskaya Revolyutsiya*, October 1924. Peters, one of Dzerzhinsky's most important aides, was head of the Moscow Cheka. He disappeared during the Stalin purges. See also R. H. Bruce Lockhart, *British Agent*, Garden City, New York, 1933.

p. 14 OPERATIONS AGAINST FOREIGN FORCES: S. I. Tsybov and N. F. Chistyakov, *Front Taynoy Voyny*, Moscow, 1965. [English translation *The Secret War Front*, United States Air Force Foreign Technology Division FTD-H C-23-151-70, Dayton, Ohio, 1970.]

p. 14 DECEPTION OPERATION: Natalie Grant, "Deception on a Grand Scale," *International Journal of Intelligence and Counterintelligence* (vol. 1, no. 4), 1987. For the Soviet version, see Lev Nikulin, *Mertvaya Zyb'*, Moscow, 1967 [English translation *The Swell of the Sea*, National Technical Information Service, JPRS 55686, Washington, D.C. 1972].

p. 14–15 "SOON WE SHALL SEE": Vladimir Lenin, speech to Third International, Moscow, March 14, 1919 (in Lenin, *Collected Works* (vol. 29), Moscow, 1965.

p. 15 CHEKA FOREIGN INTELLIGENCE: Jeffrey T. Richelson, *Sword and Shield*, Cambridge, 1986.

p. 15 AMERICAN PANIC, THEODORE ROOSEVELT: Paul L. Murphy, *World War I and the Origins of Civil Liberties in the United States*, New York, 1979.

p. 15 WILSON SPEECH: Quoted in New York *Times*, June 15, 1917.

p. 15–16 DOMESTIC CRACKDOWN: Paul L. Murphy, *World War I and the Origins of Civil Liberties*.

p. 16 WAR AGAINST DISSENT: William Preston, Jr., *Aliens and Dissenters: Federal Suppression of Radicals, 1903–1933*, Cambridge, 1963.

p. 16 IWW ARRESTS: Melvyn Dubofsky, *We Shall Be All: A History of the Industrial Workers of the World*, New York, 1969.

p. 16 SCOPE OF CRACKDOWN: Paul L. Murphy, *World War I and the Origins of Civil Liberties*.

p. 16 ANTI-SEMITISM: Ernest Volkman, *Legacy of Hate: Anti-Semitism in America*, New York, 1982.

p. 17 SENATE HEARINGS: Hearings, Overman subcommittee, Senate Judiciary Committee, *Bolshevik Propaganda*, Washington, D.C., March 1919.

p. 17 YARNELL: Jeffrey M. Dorwart, *Conflict of Duty*, Annapolis, 1983.

p. 18 STATE DEPARTMENT: Rhodri Jeffreys-Jones, *American Espionage*, New York, 1977.

p. 18 ARMY MID: Corson, *Armies of Ignorance*.

p. 18 OREGON: Bidwell, *History of the Military Intelligence Department*.

p. 18 BURNS AND BI: Andrew Sinclair, *The Available Man*, New York, 1965.

p. 19 PALMER AND ROUNDUP: Robert K. Murray, *Red Scare*, Minneapolis, 1955.

p. 19 SUPREME COURT: See especially *Fiske v. Kansas* (274 U.S. 380 1927), overturning Kansas's syndicalist law.

p. 20 NAVY ONI AND CONGRESS: Dorwart, *Conflict of Duty*.

p. 20 REPUBLICAN CHANGE: John Lewis Gaddis, *The Long Peace*, Oxford, 1987.

TWO: Papa's Crook Factory

p. 22   HEMINGWAY AND THOMASON: Roger Willock, *Lone Star Marine*, Princeton, 1961.

p. 22–23   HEMINGWAY AS SPY: Carlos Baker, *Hemingway*, New York, 1969.

p. 23   PREWAR ERA: Raymond J. Sontag, *A Broken World, 1919–1939*, New York, 1971.

p. 23   CUTS IN INTELLIGENCE: U.S. Army Intelligence Center, *The Evolution of American Military Intelligence*, Fort Huachua, Arizona, 1973.

p. 24   ATTACHÉS: Bruce Bidwell, *History of the Military Intelligence Department of the Army General Staff: 1775–1941*, Washington, D.C., 1954.

p. 24–25   MOE BERG: Louis Kaufman, Barbara Fitzgerald, and Tom Sewell, *Moe Berg*, Boston, 1974.

p. 26   BERG IN JAPAN: Ibid.

p. 26   ELLIS: P. N. Pierce, "The Unsolved Mystery of Pete Ellis," *Marine Corps Gazette*, February 1962.

p. 26–27   ELLIS' MISSION: Ibid.

p. 27   EARHART: Don Wade, "What Really Happened to Amelia Earhart," *Nautical Brass*, January–February 1985. The authors are grateful to Wade for sharing the result of his researches into the Earhart matter.

p. 27   STORIES BY ISLANDERS: Vincent V. Loomis with Jeffrey Ethell, *Amelia Earhart*, New York, 1985.

p. 27   FDR AND EARHART: Wade, "Amelia Earhart."

p. 28   NOONAN: Confidential interview.

p. 28   ARMY INTELLIGENCE INVESTIGATION: U.S. Army G-2 HQ Memorandum, Subject: Amelia Earhart, Tokyo, August 4, 1949.

p. 28–29   LINDBERGH: Report, Major Truman Smith, *Air Intelligence Activities: Office of the American Military Attaché, American Embassy Berlin Germany, August 1935–April 1939 With Special Reference to the Services of Colonel Charles A. Lindbergh, Air Corps (Res.)*, 1946 (now in Sterling Library, Yale University).

p. 28   JAPANESE FORTIFICATIONS: Maria Wilhelm, *The Man Who Watched the Rising Sun*, New York, 1967.

p. 29   FDR AND "THE ROOM": Jeffrey M. Dorwart, "The Roosevelt-Astor Espionage Ring," *New York History*, July 1981.

p. 29   "JAPAN WOULD DO NOTHING": Bradley F. Smith, *The Shadow Warriors*, New York, 1983.

p. 29   CARTER: Dorwart, *Confict of Duty*.

p. 30   "APPEARS TO BE SUCCEEDING": Quoted in Charles Callan Tansill, *Back Door to War*, Chicago, 1952.

p. 30   JEWS "SERIOUS MENACE": Report 245-71-1, Major T. Worthington Halliday, U.S. Army Military Intelligence Division, Riga, Latvia, November 27, 1920.

p. 30   JAPANESE ZERO FIGHTER: Martin Caidin, introduction to Masatake Okumiya and Jiro Horikoshi, *Eagles of Mitsubishi: The Story of the Zero Fighter*, Seattle, 1981.

p. 30   TUNGSTEN: Letter, John P. Conlon, *Armed Forces Journal*, January 1981.

p. 30   ARMY CAVALRY: Major General John K. Herr testimony, reprinted in *Journal of the U.S. Cavalry Association*, May–June 1940. Herr had tried to block development of U.S. armored forces for years, and had a special dislike for two pro-mechanization officers, Dwight Eisenhower and George Patton.

p. 30–31 GODFREY VISIT: Bradley F. Smith, "Admiral Godfrey's Mission to America, June/July 1941," *Intelligence and National Security*, September 1986.

p. 31 J. EDGAR HOOVER: Richard Gid Powers, *Secrecy and Power: The Life of J. Edgar Hoover*, New York, 1987.

p. 31 BONUS MARCH: Donald J. Lisio, *The President and Protest*, Columbia, Missouri, 1974.

p. 32 J. EDGAR HOOVER AND FDR: Richard Gid Powers, *Secrecy and Power*.

p. 33 HERBERT HOOVER BREAK-IN: Dorwart, *Conflict of Duty*.

p. 33 J. EDGAR HOOVER'S CONCERN: Richard Gid Powers, *Secrecy and Power*.

p. 34 INVESTIGATION OF WRITERS: Natalie Robins, "The Defiling of Writers," *The Nation*, October 10, 1987.

p. 34 HEMINGWAY'S "CRIMES": Ibid.

p. 34 HEMINGWAY AS SPY: Jeffrey Meyers, "Wanted by the FBI!" *New York Review of Books*, March 31, 1983.

p. 34 "PAPA'S CROOK FACTORY": Ibid; Baker, *Hemingway*.

p. 36 PEARL HARBOR: Roberta Wohlsetter, "Cuba and Pearl Harbor: Hindsight and Foresight," *Foreign Affairs*, July 1965; see also her "The Pleasures of Self-Deception," *Washington Quarterly*, Autumn 1979.

p. 36 GENERAL FAILURE OF AMERICAN INTELLIGENCE: Ernest Volkman, "God and Ice Water," *Defense Science and Technology*, Spring 1982.

p. 37 OP-20-G: E. B. Potter, "The Crypt of the Cryptanalysts," *United States Naval Institute Proceedings*, August 1983.

p. 37 BREAKING OF JAPANESE DIPLOMATIC CODES: David Kahn, "Codebreaking in World Wars I and II: The Major Successes and Failures, Their Causes and Their Effects," *The Historical Journal*, September 1980; see also his *The Codebreakers*, New York, 1967.

p. 37–38 BICKERING: Patrick Beesly, review of E. T. Layton, *And I Was There: Pearl Harbor and Midway*, in *Intelligence and National Security*, September 1980.

p. 38 LACK OF MILITARY PREPARATION: Claude R. Sasso, "Scapegoats and Culprits: Kimmel and Short at Pearl Harbor," *Military Review*, December 1983.

p. 38 STATE DEPARTMENT: Homer N. Wallin, *Pearl Harbor*, Washington, 1968.

p. 38 LACK OF INSIGHT: Irving L. Janis, *Victims of Group-think*, Boston, 1972. Admiral Husband Kimmel, commander in chief of the Pacific Fleet, was sacked, as was General Walter C. Short, commanding general of the U.S. Army Hawaiian Department, but General Douglas MacArthur, whose obstinate blindness in the Philippines led to an equal disaster, was not. Congressional investigations into the disaster were aimed at deflecting as much blame as possible away from President Roosevelt and other high-level officials who bore equal responsibility. See Martin V. Melosi, "National Security Misused: The Aftermath of Pearl Harbor," *Prologue* (National Archives), Summer 1977.

THREE: "We Cannot Afford to Be Sissies"

p. 40–41 HEISENBERG KIDNAP PLOT: Ibid.

p. 41 MISSION SCRUBBED: Ibid.

p. 42   NATURE OF OSS: Thomas Powers, "The Underground Entrepreneur," *New York Review of Books*, May 12, 1983.

p. 42   DEMOCRACY AND OSS/CIA: On this point, see especially E. Drexel Godfrey, "Ethics and Intelligence," *Foreign Affairs*, April 1978; Michael J. Barrett, "Honorable Espionage," *Defense and Diplomacy*, February, March, and April 1984; William J. Barnds, "Intelligence and Foreign Policy: Dilemmas of a Democracy," *Foreign Affairs*, September 1970.

p. 43   "ONE HALF COPS AND ROBBERS": Bradley F. Smith, *The Shadow Warriors*, New York, 1983.

p. 43   OSS MODEL: Charles Whiting, *The Spymasters*, New York, 1972.

p. 43   BRITISH SIS: Bruce Page, David Leitch, and Phillip Knightley, *The Philby Conspiracy*, London, 1968.

p. 43   "WE CANNOT AFFORD": Anthony Cave Brown, *Wild Bill Donovan, the Last American Hero*, New York, 1982.

p. 43   OSS BUDGET: Harry H. Ransom, *The Intelligence Establishment*, Cambridge, 1970.

p. 43   OSS GUERRILLA OPERATIONS: Kenneth Macksey, *The Partisans of Europe in the Second World War*, New York, 1975.

p. 43   INDOCHINA: Report, HQ OSS China Theater, Subject: Deer Mission, September 17, 1945.

p. 44   OPERATION BANANA: Donald Downes, *The Scarlet Thread*, New York, 1953.

p. 44   OPERATION SPARROW: Cave Brown, *Wild Bill Donovan*.

p. 44   HITLER ASSASSINATION PLOTS: Robin Winks, *Cloak and Gown*, New York, 1987.

p. 44   BSC: H. Montgomery Hyde, *Secret Agent*, London, 1982.

p. 44   1940 PAMPHLET: Recollection of John McAleer (author of *Rex Stout: A Biography*), in *Foreign Intelligence and Literary Scene*, December 1982.

p. 45   OSS PORNOGRAPHY: Bradley F. Smith, *The Shadow Warriors*.

p. 45   HITLER PSYCHOANALYZED: The study was prepared by Walter Langer, brother of William, head of the OSS Research and Analysis Branch, and published commercially long after the war: *The Mind of Adolf Hitler: The Secret Wartime Report*, New York, 1973.

p. 45–46   OSS AND ATOMIC BOMB: David Irving, *The German Atomic Bomb*, London, 1967.

p. 47   JAPANESE ATOMIC BOMB: Report, Office of the Chief Ordnance Officer (Occupation), Japan, *Technical Intelligence Report Number 20*, subject: National Resources Council of Japan, 1946.

p. 46–47   ATOMIC "SECRET": Gregg F. Herken, "A Most Dangerous Illusion: The Atomic Secret and American Nuclear Weapons," *Pacific Historical Review*, February 1980.

p. 47   GENERAL SCIENTIFIC KNOWLEDGE: R. H. Strewer, editor, *Nuclear Physics in Retrospect*, Minneapolis, 1979.

p. 47   BRITISH INTELLIGENCE ON ATOMIC BOMB: Arnold Kramesh, *The Griffin*, New York, 1986.

p. 47   ARMY INTELLIGENCE TEAMS: Samuel A. Goudsmit, *Alsos*, New York, 1947.

p. 47–48   GERMAN ATOMIC BOMB: Alan D. Bergerchen, *Scientists Under Hitler*, New Haven, 1977; Irving, *The German Atomic Bomb*.

p. 48   "Look here": Robert Jungk, *Heller als Tausend Sonnen*, Bern, 1956.

p. 48   OSS struggle for life: William R. Corson, *The Armies of Ignorance*, New York, 1977.

p. 48   Donovan memo: Thomas F. Troy, *Donovan and the CIA*, Frederick, Md., 1984.

p. 49   Luning: Leslie B. Rout, Jr., and John F. Bratzel, *The Shadow War*, Frederick, Maryland, 1986.

p. 49   Abwehr operations in South America: Stanley E. Hilton, *Hitler's Secret War*, Baton Rouge, 1981.

p. 50   FBI operation: Rout, Jr., and Bratzel, *Shadow War*.

p. 50   Enemy agents: Joseph Gollomb, *Armies of Spies*, New York, 1939.

p. 50   "Dillinger mentality": Peter Wright, *Spycatcher*, New York, 1987.

p. 51   Germans and Norden Bombsight: Ladislas Farago, *The Game of Foxes*, New York, 1971.

p. 51   Japanese obtain bombsight: Robert C. Mikesh, "Japan's Little Fleet of Big American Bombers," *Air Force/Space Digest*, August 1969.

p. 51   "Fifth column": Francis Selwyn, *Hitler's Englishman*, London, 1986.

p. 51   Hysteria: Beatrice B. Berle and Travis Beal, editors, *Navigating the Rapids, 1918–1971: From the Papers of Adolf A. Berle*, New York, 1973.

p. 51   "Crawling with fifth columnists": Dorwart, *Conflict of Duty*.

p. 52   Relocation of Japanese: Jacobus tenBroek, Edward N. Baihart, and Floyd W. Matson, *Prejudice, War and the Constitution*, Berkeley, 1954.

p. 52   Hoover and Communists: Richard Gid Powers, *Secrecy and Power: The Life of J. Edgar Hoover*, New York, 1987.

p. 53   Brazen Russians: William H. Standley, *Admiral Ambassador to Russia*, New York, 1955.

p. 53   Abraham Lincoln Brigade: Richard Gid Powers, *Secrecy and Power*.

p. 53–54   Anti-OSS leak: Thomas F. Troy, "Knifing of the OSS," *International Journal of Intelligence and Counterintelligence* (vol. 1, no. 3), 1986.

FOUR: Black Jumbo in the Ether

p. 57–58   Life at Coonawarra: Confidential interview.

p. 58   Coonawarra's role: Nigel West, *GCHQ*, London, 1986.

p. 59   Interceptions of Soviet traffic: Ibid.

p. 59   Espionage and radio: Dan Tyler Moore and Martha Waller, *Cloak and Cipher*, Indianapolis, 1962.

p. 59   "One-time pads": David Kahn, *The Codebreakers*, New York, 1967.

p. 60   Russian errors: Peter Wright, *Spycatcher*, New York, 1987.

p. 60   Stanley, Hicks, Johnson: Nigel West, *The Circus*, London, 1982.

p. 60   Philby, Burgess, Blunt: Wright, *Spycatcher*.

p. 61   Agent 19: Confidential interview.

p. 61   Eight hundred American sources: Ibid.

p. 61   Manhattan Project infiltrated: Robert J. Lamphere, *The FBI-KGB War*, New York, 1986.

p. 61   Black Jumbo, Bride: West, *GCHQ*.

p. 61   Fuchs, Rosenbergs: Lamphere, *FBI-KGB War*. Lamphere experienced considerable difficulty in getting his book published because of its extensive treatment of Venona and Bride; the published version reflects considerable editing in that sensitive area.

p. 62 YARDLEY: Kahn, *The Codebreakers*; James Bamford, *The Puzzle Palace*, New York, 1982.

p. 64 THE BLACK CHAMBER: Herbert O. Yardley, *The American Black Chamber*, New York, 1931.

p. 64 JAPANESE DIPLOMATIC CIPHERS: J. W. Bennet, *Intelligence and Cryptanalytic Activities of the Japanese During World War II*, Laguna Hills, California, 1986.

p. 64 WASHINGTON NAVAL CONFERENCE: Yardley, *American Black Chamber*.

p. 65 YARDLEY'S IDEA: Ibid.

p. 65 ROOM 40: Patrick Beesly, *Room 40*, New York, 1982.

p. 65 ZIMMERMANN TELEGRAM: William F. Friedman and Charles J. Mendelsohn, *The Zimmerman Telegram of January 16, 1917 and its Cryptographic Background*, Laguna Hills, California, 1976. This is the commercial version of a top-secret study prepared by Friedman and one of his cryptanalysts in 1941, and not declassified until thirty-five years later.

p. 66 IMPACT OF ZIMMERMANN TELEGRAM: Barbara W. Tuchman, *The Zimmermann Telegram*, New York, 1958.

p. 66 YARDLEY IN ENGLAND: Bamford, *Puzzle Palace*.

p. 66 POST-WORLD WAR I CRYPTOLOGY: West, *GCHQ*.

p. 66 POLAND: Stefan Korbowski, "The True Story of Enigma—the German Code Machine in World War II," *Eastern European Quarterly*, Summer 1977.

p. 67 ONI OPERATION: Ladislas Farago, *The Broken Seal*, New York, 1967.

p. 67 FRIEDMAN: Ronald Clark, *The Man Who Broke Purple*, New York, 1977.

p. 67 DIFFERENCES WITH YARDLEY: Ronald Lewin, *American Magic*, New York, 1982.

p. 68 SIGNAL INTELLIGENCE SERVICE: Ibid.

p. 68 ROWLETT: Ibid.

p. 69 STIMSON: Testimony, William F. Friedman, hearings, Joint Congressional Committee on the Pearl Harbor Attack, December 1945.

p. 69 "GENTLEMEN DO NOT": Henry L. Stimson with McGeorge Bundy, *On Active Service in Peace and War*, New York, 1947. There is now considerable controversy over whether Stimson in fact said those words. One prevailing theory is that he intended them only for show, as a means of reassuring other nations that the United States would never stoop so low as to intercept their diplomatic communications.

p. 69 BLACK CHAMBER'S PROBLEMS: William F. Friedman, report, *A Brief History of the Signal Intelligence Service*, June 29, 1942. This report, which reflects Friedman's deep-seated antagonism toward Yardley, was not declassified until 1972.

p. 69 YARDLEY OFFER TO JAPANESE?: Lewin, *American Magic*.

p. 69 BLACK CHAMBER BOOK: Bamford, *Puzzle Palace*.

p. 69 YARDLEY'S LATER CAREER: Kahn, *The Codebreakers*.

p. 70 CIPHER MACHINES: Ibid.

p. 70 RED NAVAL ATTACHÉ CODE: U.S. Department of Defense, *The MAGIC Background to Pearl Harbor* (vol. 1), Washington, D.C., 1977.

p. 70 PURPLE MACHINE: Ibid.

p. 71 CRACKING OF PURPLE: Clark, *Man Who Broke Purple.*

p. 71 ENIGMA, ULTRA: Gustave Bertrand, *Enigma,* Paris, 1972. This was the first public revelation of the Ultra secret, followed by the semi-official British version two years later: F. W. Winterbotham, *The ULTRA Secret,* London, 1974.

p. 71 U.S.-BRITISH LIAISON: Thomas Parrish, *The ULTRA Americans,* New York, 1986.

p. 72 "BUT THEY KNEW!": Lewin, *American Magic.*

p. 72 PEARL HARBOR POSTMORTEMS: *Joint Congressional Committee on the Pearl Harbor Attack* (pt. 14), Washington, D.C., 1946.

p. 72 POSTWAR ENIGMA: West, *GCHQ.*

p. 73 SIGNAL SECURITY SERVICE: U.S. Army Security Agency, Historical Section, *A Lecture on the Origin and Development of the Army Security Agency, 1917–1947,* March 1948. This brief, but enlightening, overview was declassified in 1975. The Army Security Agency was the acronymic descendant of the original Signal Intelligence Service, and was later subsumed into the new National Security Agency in 1952.

p. 73 UKUSA AGREEMENT: West, *GCHQ.*

p. 73 LISTENING POSTS: Bamford, *Puzzle Palace.*

p. 73 LESSONS OF WORLD WAR II: West, *GCHQ.*

p. 73 UKUSA NETWORK: Desmond Ball, *A Suitable Piece of Real Estate,* Sydney, 1980, which concentrates on installations in Australia, including Pine Gap, the most important "downlink" station for U.S. spy satellites. For Great Britain, see Duncan Campbell, *The Unsinkable Aircraft Carrier,* London, 1986.

p. 73 OPERATION CANDY: Anthony Cave Brown and Charles B. Macdonald, editors, *The Secret History of the Atomic Bomb,* New York, 1977.

p. 74 CREATION OF NSA: George A. Brownell, *The Origin and Development of the National Security Agency,* Laguna Hills, California, 1981.

p. 74 CIA STAFF D, FBI SECTION: Wright, *Spycatcher.*

p. 75 COMMUNICATIONS LAWS: Lewin, *American Magic.*

p. 75 ASTOR: Dorwart, *Conflict of Duty.*

p. 75 SARNOFF: Lewin, *American Magic.*

p. 75 HOOVER AND WIRETAPS: Select Senate Committee to Study Governmental Operations with Respect to Intelligence Activities [Church Committee], *Final Report* (Book 3).

FIVE: Admiral with a Wooden Sword

p. 76 TRUMAN'S CEREMONY: Trevor Barnes, "The Secret Cold War: The CIA and American Foreign Policy in Europe, 1946–1956" (pt. 1), *Historical Journal,* June 1981.

p. 77 ELEANOR ROOSEVELT AND TRUMAN: Margaret Truman, *Harry Truman,* New York, 1973.

p. 78 TRUMAN'S OUTLOOK: Albert D. Sander, "Truman and the National Security Council: 1945–1947," *The Journal of American History,* September 1972.

p. 78 FORRESTAL: Arnold Rogow, *Victim of Duty,* London, 1966; Walter Millis, editor, *The Forrestal Diaries,* New York, 1951.

p. 78 INFLUENCE OF FORRESTAL: Ellis M. Zacharias, *Behind Closed Doors,* New York, 1950.

p. 79 SMITH'S VIEW: U.S. Bureau of the Budget, *Report on the Intelligence and Security Activities of the Government*, September 20, 1945.

p. 79 TRUMAN'S PROBLEMS: William R. Corson, *The Armies of Ignorance*, New York, 1977.

p. 79 FAULTY ARMY ESTIMATE: Joint Chiefs of Staff, Joint Working Committee, report, *Soviet Strengths and Weaknesses*, September 12, 1946.

p. 80 STRUGGLE OVER INTELLIGENCE: See especially the critical report on military intelligence prepared by the House Military Affairs Committee, *A Report on the System Currently Employed in the Collection, Evaluation, and Dissemination of Intelligence*, December 17, 1946.

p. 80 EVALUATIONS OF OSS: Corson, *Armies of Ignorance*.

p. 81 COLBY, CLINE RESERVATIONS: Colby, Cline interviews.

p. 81 OPERATIONS DIRECTED BY CASEY: Joseph Persico, *Piercing the Reich*, New York, 1983.

p. 81 DONOVAN'S MANAGERIAL STYLE: Select Senate Committee to Study Governmental Operations with Respect to Intelligence Activities [hereafter Church Committee], *Final Report* (Book 1), 1976.

p. 81 DONOVAN FORAYS: Anthony Cave Brown, *The Last American Hero*, New York, 1986.

p. 82 TRUMAN, FORRESTAL PERCEPTIONS: Ernest Volkman, "God and Ice Water," *Defense Science and Technology*, Spring 1982.

p. 82 HOOVER'S PLAN: Corson, *Armies of Ignorance*.

p. 82–83 TRUMAN AND HOOVER: Richard Gid Powers, *Secrecy and Power: The Life of J. Edgar Hoover*, New York, 1987.

p. 83 HILLENKOETTER: Ray S. Cline, *Secrets, Spies and Scholars*, Washington, D.C., 1976; John Prados, *Presidents' Secret Wars*, New York, 1986.

p. 83 BIRTH OF CIA: Tom Braden, "The Birth of the CIA," *American Heritage*, February 1977.

p. 84 BIRTH OF NSA: James Bamford, *The Puzzle Palace*, New York, 1982.

p. 84 SIGINT: Nigel West, *GCHQ*, London, 1986.

p. 85 MERCHANT SHIP OPERATIONS: House Armed Services Committee, Investigating Subcommittee, report, *Review of Department of Defense Worldwide Communications*, May 10, 1971.

p. 85 ATTACK ON *Liberty*: James M. Ennes, Jr., *Assault on the Liberty*, New York, 1979.

p. 85 "CRUNCHERS," "TRAFFIC ANALYSIS": West, *GCHQ*.

p. 86 "FERRETS," "HOLYSTONE": Bamford, *Puzzle Palace*.

p. 86 POSTWAR SOVIET MENACE: Daniel Yergin, *Shattered Peace*, New York, 1982.

p. 86 "THIS WAR IS NOT": Milovan Djilas, *Conversations With Stalin*, London, 1962.

p. 87 DULLES WARNING: Bradley F. Smith, *The Shadow Warriors*, New York, 1983.

p. 87 "NATIONAL COMMITTEES": Remarks, Stephen de Mowbray, *Encounter*, July–August 1984. Mowbray was an SIS officer.

p. 87 POLAND: Anthony Glees, *The Secrets of the Service*, London, 1985.

p. 87 COMINTERN: Anthony Cave Brown and Charles B. Macdonald, *On a Field of Red*, New York, 1980.

p. 87 OSS X-2: Robin Winks, *Cloak and Gown*, New York, 1987.

p. 88   ITALY: Ibid. The most noted X-2 officer in Italy was James Jesus Angleton, later the famed head of counterintelligence for the CIA.

p. 88   GERMAN INEPTITUDE: George C. Constanstinides, "Tradecraft: Follies and Foibles," *International Journal of Intelligence and Counterintelligence* (vol. 1, no. 4), 1987.

p. 88   NKVD: Harry Rositzke, *The CIA's Secret Operations*, New York, 1977.

p. 88   "MAX" OPERATION: David Thomas, "The Legend of Agent Max," *Foreign Intelligence and Literary Scene*, January 1986.

p. 89   NKVD OPERATION IN POLAND: Rositzke, *CIA's Secret Operations*.

p. 89   ROMANIA, FINLAND, HUNGARY: Hanson W. Baldwin, "Error in Collecting Data Held Exceeded by Evolutionary Weaknesses," New York *Times*, July 23, 1948.

p. 89   SOVIET INTERNAL SECURITY: Tom Polgar, "Defection and Re-defection," *International Journal of Intelligence and Counterintelligence* (vol. 1, no. 2), 1986.

p. 89   WORLD IN 1945: Yergin, *Shattered Peace*.

p. 90   HOOVER AND COMMUNISTS: David Caute, *The Great Fear*, New York, 1978.

p. 91   STALIN DEPOSED?: Ibid.

p. 91   CHAMBERS'S REVELATIONS: Earl Latham, *The Communist Controversy in Washington*, Cambridge, 1966; Allen Weinstein, *Perjury*, New York, 1978.

p. 92   HARRY DEXTER WHITE: David Rees, *Harry Dexter White*, New York, 1973.

p. 92   TRUMAN SKEPTICISM: Church Committee, *Final Report* (bk. 3).

p. 92   HOOVER SPLIT WITH TRUMAN: Richard Gid Powers, *Secrecy and Power*.

p. 92   TRUMAN LOYALTY PROGRAM: Carey McWilliams, *Witch Hunt*, Boston, 1947.

p. 92   OPPENHEIMER: Caute, *Great Fear*.

p. 93   CALIFORNIA ARCHERY CLUB: McWilliams, *Witch Hunt*.

p. 93   HOOVER, "WITCH HUNT": Caute, *Great Fear*.

p. 92   CHINA EXPERTS: E. J. Kahn, Jr., *The China Hands*, New York, 1975. For the dimensions of the U.S. military defeat by the Chinese some years later in Korea, see S. L. A. Marshall, *The River and the Gauntlet*, New York, 1954.

p. 93   HOOVER'S TESTIMONY: Richard Gid Powers, *Secrecy and Power*.

p. 93–94   TRUMAN'S POLITICAL PROBLEM: Athan Theoharis, *Seeds of Repression*, New York, 1971.

p. 94   SMITH ACT: Frank J. Donner, *The Age of Surveillance*, New York, 1980.

p. 94   SMITH ACT PROSECUTIONS: Michael R. Belknap, *Cold War Political Justice*, Westport, Connecticut, 1977.

p. 94   McCARTHY: Richard M. Freeland, *The Truman Doctrine and the Origins of McCarthyism*, New York, 1972.

p. 94   HOOVER CLAIM: David M. Oshinsky, *A Conspiracy So Immense*, New York, 1983.

SIX: The Nine Lives of the Yellow Cat

p. 96–97   ASSASSINATION OF TRUJILLO: Bernard Diedrich, *Trujillo: The Death of the Goat*, Boston, 1978.

p. 97   ESPAILLAT: Our researches on the Espaillat matter were considerably aided by the generous aid of Robert Roman, who provided much significant material. Roman is a veteran intelligence operative with extensive experience in Latin America.

p. 97 CIA RECRUITMENTS: Confidential interviews; see also A. J. Langguth, *Hidden Terrors*, New York, 1979.

p. 97 COLONEL CHACON: Information kindly provided the authors by investigative journalist John Cummings. Chacon was assassinated by leftist guerrillas in 1974.

p. 98 "OUR SONOFABITCH": Ibid.

p. 98 U.S. DISENCHANTMENT WITH TRUJILLO: Walter LaFeber, *Inevitable Revolutions*, New York, 1983; Diedrich, *Trujillo*.

p. 98 GALINDEZ: This Cold War spy mystery continues. For recent revelations, see especially *Fitzgibbon v CIA* (79-0956 DDC), a Freedom of Information Act suit filed against the CIA by Alan Fitzgibbon, a historian researching the case. See also Harrison Salisbury, "The Strange Correspondence of Morris Ernst and John Edgar Hoover, 1939–1941," *The Nation*, December 1, 1984.

p. 99 CIA PLOT: Robert Roman, "The CIA Assassination of Trujillo," *Soldier of Fortune*, Summer 1975; Select Senate Committee to Study Governmental Operations with Respect to Intelligence Activities [hereafter Church Committee], *Interim Report, Alleged Assassination Plots Involving Foreign Leaders*, November 20, 1975.

p. 99 CIA TRIES TO DELAY: Ibid.

p. 100 "SUCCESS": Ibid.

p. 100 POST-ASSASSINATION: Diedrich, *Trujillo*.

p. 100 FATE OF ESPAILLAT: Confidential interview.

p. 100 FORRESTAL'S QUESTION: Houston interview; William R. Corson, *The Armies of Ignorance*, New York, 1977.

p. 101 COMMUNIST MENACE IN EUROPE: Trevor Barnes, "The Secret Cold War: The CIA and American Foreign Policy in Europe, 1946–1956" (pt. 1), *Historical Journal*, June 1981. For Czechoslovakia, see Claire Sterling, *The Masaryk Case: The Murder of Democracy in Czechoslovakia*, Boston, 1982.

p. 101 PROBLEM OF ITALY: William Colby, testimony, Senate Government Operations Committee, *Oversight of U.S. Intelligence Functions*, January 23, 1976.

p. 102 CIA ITALY OPERATION: William Colby, *Honorable Men*, New York, 1978; Barnes, "Secret Cold War."

p. 102 CREATION OF OPC: Church Committee, *Final Report* (Books 1, 2), 1976.

p. 102 TRUMAN CLAIM: Letter, Allen Dulles to Harry Truman, January 7, 1964 (in Allen W. Dulles Papers, Princeton University).

p. 103 "POLITICAL WARFARE": Church Committee, *Final Report* Book III.

p. 103 "REDUCE AND EVENTUALLY ELIMINATE": National Security Council 58/2, *United States Policy Toward the Soviet Satellite States in Eastern Europe*, December 8, 1949.

p. 103 WISNER: Corson, *Armies of Ignorance*.

p. 103 WISNER'S "MIGHTY WURLITZER": Barnes, "Secret Cold War" (pt. 2), September 1982.

p. 103 OPC BUDGET, GROWTH: Church Committee, *Final Report* (Book 4), 1976.

p. 104 OPC BURMA OPERATION: Corson, *Armies of Ignorance*.

p. 104 RECRUITMENT OF NAZIS: Thomas M. Bower, *Blind Eye to Murder*, London, 1981.

p. 104 SIX, OTHER NAZI WAR CRIMINALS: Beate Klarsfeld, *Wherever They May Be*, New York, 1975; Thomas O'Toole, "Nazi Cold Warriors Went Unpunished," Washington *Post*, November 4, 1982.

p. 104 VON BOLSCHWING: Ernest Volkman, *Warriors of the Night*, New York, 1985.

p. 105 KLAUS BARBIE: Serge Klarsfeld, "L'Affaire Barbie," *Le Monde*, February 16, 1983.

p. 105 OPC's DUBIOUS ASSETS: Harry Rositzke, *The CIA's Secret Operations*, New York, 1977; H. W. Brando, Jr., "A Cold War Foreign Legion?" *Military Affairs*, January 1988.

p. 106 RED CAP OPERATION: Corson, *Armies of Ignorance*; Barnes, "Secret Cold War" (pt. 2).

p. 106 DEATH OF WISNER: Thomas Powers, *The Man Who Kept the Secrets*, New York, 1979.

p. 106 DEATH OF FORRESTAL: Arnold Rogow, *Victim of Duty*, London, 1966.

p. 106 HILLENKOETTER REMOVED: John Ranelagh, *The Agency*, New York, 1986.

p. 106–107 "BEETLE" SMITH: William Leary, editor, *The Central Intelligence Agency*, Tuscaloosa, 1984.

p. 107 DULLES REVIEW: Allen Dulles et al., *The Central Intelligence Agency and the Organization for Intelligence: A Report to the National Security Council*, January 1, 1949 (commonly known as the Dulles-Jackson-Correa Report).

p. 107 ALLEN DULLES: David Atlee Phillips, "The Great White Case Officer," *International Journal of Intelligence and Counterintelligence* (vol. 1, no. 1), 1986.

p. 107–108 DULLES WORLDVIEW: Leonard Mosley, *Dulles*, New York, 1978.

p. 108 KGB DISBELIEVES: Confidential interview, from former KGB officer.

p. 109 TEHERAN CROWDS: Mansur Rafizadeh, *Witness*, New York, 1987.

p. 109 IRANIAN SITUATION 1950s: Gary Sick, *All Fall Down*, New York, 1985.

p. 109 PERCEPTION OF MOSSADEGH: Stephen A. Ambrose, *Ike's Spies*, New York, 1980.

p. 110 AJAX: Kermit Roosevelt, *Countercoup*, New York, 1979. Roosevelt was CIA chief of station in Teheran during this period, and was the originator of the Ajax operation.

p. 110 RESULTS OF IRAN OPERATION: Ambrose, *Ike's Spies*.

p. 110 PROBLEMS OF COVERT OPERATIONS: Jay Peterzell, "Legal and Constitutional Authority for Covert Operations," *First Principles* (Center for National Security Studies, Washington, D.C.), Spring 1985.

p. 111 ARBENZ: Richard H. Immerman, *The CIA in Guatemala*, Austin, Texas, 1982.

p. 111 "ONE NATION": Ambrose, *Ike's Spies*.

p. 112 OPERATION PB/SUCCESS: Stephen Schlesinger and Stephen Kinzer, *Bitter Fruit*, New York, 1982.

p. 111 E. HOWARD HUNT: Tad Szulc, *The Compulsive Spy*, New York, 1974.

p. 112 BOMBING OF BRITISH SHIP: Confidential interview.

p. 112 MEETING WITH EISENHOWER: Phillips interview.

p. 113 CIA IN THE CONGO: Stephen R. Weissman, "The CIA Covert Action in Zaire and Angola," *Political Science Quarterly*, Summer 1979.

p. 113 LUMUMBA ASSASSINATION PLOT: Madeleine G. Kalb, *The Congo Cables*, New York, 1982; Church Committee, *Interim Report*.

p. 114 DOMINATION OF CLANDESTINE SERVICES: Anne Karalekas, "History of the Central Intelligence Agency," in Church Committee, *Final Report* (Book 4).

p. 114 "IF THEY WANT TO KNOW": Ibid.

p. 114 CIA EMPIRE: Ibid; Gregory F. Treverton, *Covert Action*, New York, 1987.

SEVEN: Seeking the Third Force

p. 120 "VICTORY WILL BE OURS": Tad Szulc, *Fidel: A Critical Portrait*, New York, 1986.

p. 120 CASTRO'S 1956 INVASION: Ibid.

p. 120 U.S. INTELLIGENCE CONFUSION: Phillip W. Bonsal, *Cuba, Castro and the United States*, Pittsburgh, 1971.

p. 120 "COMMUNIST LEANINGS": Allen W. Dulles, testimony, executive hearings, Senate Foreign Relations Committee, *The Situation in Cuba*, January 20, 1959.

p. 121 INTELLIGENCE REPORT: Dwight D. Eisenhower, *The White House Years: Waging Peace, 1956–1961*, New York, 1965.

p. 121 "A CHAMPION": Eisenhower, Ibid.

p. 121 NIXON IN LATIN AMERICA: E. W. Kenworthy, New York *Times*, May 14, 1958.

p. 122 "A THIRD FORCE": Eisenhower, *The White House Years*.

p. 122 RADIO SWAN: Tom Kneitel, "Inside the CIA's Secret Radio Paradise" (Part I), *Popular Communications*, November 1985.

p. 122 BISSELL: David Wise and Thomas E. Ross, *The Invisible Government*, New York, 1964; Peter Wyden, *The Bay of Pigs*, New York, 1979.

p. 122 "THEIR MISSION": Interview, Richard Bissell.

p. 123 TECHNICAL SERVICES DIVISION IDEAS: Select Senate Committee to Study Governmental Operations with Respect to Intelligence Activities [hereafter Church Committee], *Interim Report, Alleged Assassination Plots Involving Foreign Leaders*, November 20, 1975.

p. 123 ANTI-CASTRO OPERATIONS: Ibid.

p. 123–24 *Barbudos's* MISSION: Confidential interview.

p. 124 MAFIA-CIA ARRANGEMENT: Memorandum, Howard J. Osborn, Director Security CIA, to DDCI. Subject: Maheu, Robert A., June 24, 1966.

p. 124–25 MAHEU ON ROSELLI: Church Committee, *Interim Report*.

p. 125 GIANCANA'S INVOLVEMENT: Herbert Parmet, *JFK: The Presidency of John F. Kennedy*, New York, 1983.

p. 125 "HEY, WHY DON'T YOU": Confidential interview.

p. 125 HOOVER MEMO: J. Edgar Hoover, Memorandum to DCI. Subject: Anti-Castro Activities, August 18, 1960.

p. 125 EISENHOWER'S KNOWLEDGE: Interview, Richard Bissell.

p. 125–26 "TOLERATING A COMMUNIST REGIME": Sidney Kraus, editor, *The Great Debates*, Bloomington, Indiana, 1962.

p. 126 KENNEDY BRIEFED: Thomas Powers, *The Man Who Kept the Secrets: Richard Helms and the CIA*, New York, 1979.

p. 127 "FLUID SITUATION": Parmet, *JFK*.

p. 127 E. HOWARD HUNT STORY: Interview, E. Howard Hunt.

p. 127   "HE HAD BEEN ASTONISHED": Theodore C. Sorenson, *Kennedy*, New York, 1965.

p. 127   "THERE'S A MAXIM": Interview, David Atlee Phillips.

p. 127   "AN ORPHAN CHILD": Lucian S. Vandenbroucke, "The Confessions of Allen Dulles: New Evidence on the Bay of Pigs," *Diplomatic History*, Fall 1984.

p. 128   "I STOOD AT THIS VERY DESK": Parmet, *JFK*. Attributes source Theodore Sorensen, John F. Kennedy Library—Oral History Collection—Carl Kaysen interview.

p. 128   "SOMEONE WHOSE HEAD": Ibid.

p. 128   "THERE WILL NOT BE": Public Papers of the Presidents, U.S. Government Printing Office, 1961.

p. 128   CHANGE IN LANDING SITE: Cuban Study Group, *Final Report: The Anti-Castro Cuban Operation ZAPATA*, June 13, 1961. Known as the "Taylor Commission" after its chairman, Army General (and Kennedy military adviser) Maxwell Taylor, the Cuban Study Group was appointed by Kennedy to study the planning and conduct of the Bay of Pigs invasion. The commission was highly critical of the CIA.

p. 129   BAY OF PIGS TOLL: Ibid.

p. 129   CIA COMMAND POST: Interview, David Atlee Phillips.

p. 130   "THERE'S AN OLD SAYING": Public Papers of the Presidents.

p. 130   "THERE WAS NO PETTINESS": Interview, Richard Bissell.

p. 130   MOOD OF REVENGE: Chester Bowles, John F. Kennedy Library—Oral History Collection—Robert Brooks Interview.

p. 130   "CHEWED OUT IN THE CABINET ROOM": Church Committee, *Interim Report*. The CIA official is referred to only as "Assistant to the Head of Force W."

p. 130   "THE TOP PRIORITY": Ibid.; George McManus's (Richard Helms's executive assistant) memorandum, January 19, 1962.

p. 130   "WE WERE HYSTERICAL": Church Committee, *Interim Report*.

p. 130–31   "MONGOOSE WAS A PROGRAM": Interview, John McCone.

p. 131   HELMS: Powers, *The Man Who Kept the Secrets*.

p. 131   "WE WANTED TO EARN": Church Committee, *Interim Report*.

p. 131   "BOBBY KENNEDY WAS VERY HANDS-ON": Interview, Richard Helms.

p. 131   "PUT THE AMERICAN GENIUS": Church Committee, *Interim Report*.

p. 131–32   MONGOOSE: Taylor Branch and George Crile, "The Kennedy Vendetta," *Harper's*, October 1976.

p. 131–32   TASK FORCE W: Arthur M. Schlesinger, *Robert Kennedy and His Times*, New York, 1978.

p. 132–33   GIANCANA-MAHEU: David Wise, *The American Police State*, New York, 1971.

p. 133   HOOVER'S BONANZA: Ibid.

p. 133   HOOVER-KENNEDY: Ibid.; confidential interviews.

p. 133   WHITE HOUSE TELEPHONE LOGS: Richard Gid Powers, *Secrecy and Power: The Life of J. Edgar Hoover*, New York, 1987.

p. 133   TECHNICAL SERVICES DIVISION: Church Committee, *Interim Report*.

p. 134   AM/LASH: Ibid.; House Select Committee on Assassination of President John F. Kennedy (vol. 10), March 1979.

p. 134   "I THINK I, FOR ONE": Interview, Richard Bissell.

p. 134 "CRAZY SCHEMES": Interview, Richard Helms.

p. 134 GIANCANA AND ROSELLI FATES: Schlesinger, *Robert Kennedy*.

p. 135 "DAMNED MURDER, INC.": Leo Janis, "The Last Days of the President," *Atlantic Magazine*, July 1973; John Cummings, "Miami Confidential," *Inquiry*, August 24, 1981.

EIGHT: Midnight at Khe Sanh

p. 136–38 TWO OFFICERS' REPORT: Confidential interview; see also Patrick J. Mc-Garvey, "Intelligence to Please," *Washington Monthly*, July 1970.

p. 138 ATTACK AT KHE SANH: Robert Pisor, *End of the Line*, New York, 1982.

p. 138–39 TET OFFENSIVE: Don Oberdorfer, *Tet*, New York, 1971.

p. 139–40 DIEM: Robert Scheer and Warren Hinckle, "The Viet-Nam Lobby," *Ramparts*, July 1965.

p. 140–41 SAIGON MILITARY MISSION: Joseph Burckholder Smith, "Nation-Builders, Old Pros, Paramilitary Boys, and Misplaced Persons," *Washington Monthly*, February 1978.

p. 141 CONEIN: Joseph Burckholder Smith, Ibid.

p. 141–42 LANSDALE: Richard Drinnon, "Who is Edward G. Lansdale?" *Inquiry*, February 5, 1979.

p. 142 DIEM'S REPRESSION: David Halberstam, *The Making of a Quagmire*, New York, 1965.

p. 142 LANSDALE BOOSTS DIEM: Drinnon, "Who Is Edward G. Lansdale?"

p. 142 DIEM 1957 VISIT: Scheer and Hinckle, "Viet-Nam Lobby."

p. 143 REVOLT IN SOUTH VIETNAM: Douglas Pike, *Viet Cong*, Cambridge, 1966.

p. 143–44 DEEPENING U.S. COMMITMENT: George T. McT. Kahin, *Intervention*, New York, 1986.

p. 144 LAOS: Arthur J. Dommen, *Conflict in Laos*, New York, 1964.

p. 144–45 FIRST CIA OPERATION IN LAOS: Shelby M. Stanton, *Green Berets at War*, Novato, Calif., 1985.

p. 145 U.S. COMMITMENT IN LAOS: Hugh Toye, *Laos: Buffer State or Battleground*, London, 1968.

p. 145 AIR AMERICA: Christopher Robbins, *Air America*, New York, 1979.

p. 145 HMONGS AND OPIUM: Alfred McCoy, *The Politics of Heroin in Southeast Asia*, New York, 1972; Christopher Robbins, *Air America*.

p. 145 SCOPE OF U.S. SECRET WAR: John Prados, *Presidents' Secret Wars*, New York, 1986.

p. 145 SECRET BOMBING: Christopher Robbins, *The Ravens*, New York, 1987.

p. 145–46 GREEN BERETS: Aaron Bank, *From OSS to Green Berets*, Novato, California, 1986.

p. 146 COMBINED STUDIES GROUP: Jim Graves, "SOG's Secret War," *Soldier of Fortune*, June 1981.

p. 146 LEAPING LENA: Tony Bliss, Jr., "When They Cared Enough to Send the Very Best . . . Chargin' Charley Got the Call," *Soldier of Fortune*, October 1984.

p. 146–47 MONTAGNARDS: Shelby M. Stanton, *Green Berets at War*.

p. 146–47 FATE OF MONTAGNARDS, MEOS: Thomas Powers, *The Man Who Kept the Secrets*, New York, 1979.

p. 147   SOG: Jim Graves, "SOG's Secret War."

p. 147   TIMBERWORK: Confidential interview.

p. 147–48   DESOTO OPERATION: Eugene G. Windchy, *Tonkin Gulf,* New York, 1971.

p. 148   JULY 30 RAID: Confidential interview.

p. 148   ATTACK ON THE *MADDOX:* Joseph Goulden, *Truth Is the First Casualty,* Chicago, 1969.

p. 148–49   TONKIN GULF RESOLUTION: Ibid.

p. 149–50   SECRET WARS: On this point, see especially John M. Oseth, *Regulating U.S. Intelligence Operations,* Lexington, Kentucky, 1985.

p. 149   COSTS OF VIETNAM WAR: U.S. Commerce Department, *Statistical Abstract of the United States,* 1974.

p. 150   SCOPE OF U.S. INTELLIGENCE IN VIETNAM: Ralph W. McGehee, *Deadly Deceits,* New York, 1983.

p. 150   BIRTH OF PHOENIX: Michael Charles Conly, *The Communist Insurgent Infrastructure in South Vietnam,* Washington, D.C., 1966.

p. 150–51   POLICE APPARATUS: Douglas Blaufarb, *The Counterinsurgency Era,* Glencoe, Illinois, 1977.

p. 151   PHOENIX: Committee for Action/Research on the Intelligence Community, report, *Pacification: the 100-Year Flight of the Phoenix,* Washington, D.C., 1973.

p. 152   NORTH VIETNAMESE GENERAL: Stanley Karnow, *Vietnam: A History,* New York, 1982.

p. 151–52   EXCESSES OF PHOENIX: Ibid.; see also Senate Armed Services Committee, hearings, *Nomination of William Colby,* 1973.

p. 152–53   CHUYEN CASE: Horace Sutton, "The Ghostly War of the Green Berets," *Saturday Review,* October 18, 1969; "The Case of the Green Berets," *Newsweek,* August 25, 1969.

p. 153–54   ARMY ANTIPATHY TO GREEN BERETS: Stanton, *Green Berets at War.*

p. 154   "THE FIGURE": Brigadier General Phillip B. Davidson, Jr., Memorandum, Subject: New Procedures for OB [Order of Battle] HQ MACV, August 15, 1967.

p. 155   INTELLIGENCE CONTROVERSY: Frances Fitzgerald, "The Vietnam Numbers Game," *The Nation,* June 26, 1982.

p. 155   CIA ESTIMATE: House Select Committee on Intelligence [hereafter Pike Committee], hearings, *U.S. Intelligence Agencies and Activities: Risks and Control of Foreign Intelligence* (pt. 5), November–December 1975.

p. 155   "LIKE COUNTING COCKROACHES": Graham interview.

p. 155   MACV INTELLIGENCE GAMBIT: Pike Committee, *Final Report* (sec. 3, "Tet: Failure to Adapt to a New Kind of War"), February 1976.

p. 156   INTELLIGENCE BATTLE: See especially MACV 7849, Memorandum General Creighton Abrams DEPCOMUSMACV to General Earle G. Wheeler, chairman Joint Chiefs of Staff, August 18, 1967. For military intelligence in Vietnam, see Bruce E. Jones, *War Without Windows,* New York, 1987.

p. 156   CIA COMPROMISE: M. A. Farber, "CBS Jury Told of C.I.A. 'Sellout' in '67," New York *Times,* January 24, 1985. The Tet intelligence controversy was refought in 1982 with the broadcast of a "CBS Reports" documentary, "The Uncounted Enemy: A Vietnam Deception." General Westmoreland subsequently sued CBS for libel, but the case was settled in mid-trial.

p. 156 HELMS AND CAMBODIA REPORT: Roberta Wohlsetter, "The Pleasures of Self-Deception," *Washington Quarterly*, Autumn 1979.

NINE: The War at Home

p. 157–59 LIMOUSINE CASE: Confidential interview.

p. 159 DECLINE OF COMMUNIST PARTY: Irving Howe and Lewis Coser, *The American Communist Party*, New York, 1962.

p. 159–60 BIRTH OF COINTELPRO: Select Senate Committee to Study Governmental Operations with Respect to Intelligence Activities [hereafter Church Committee], *Final Report* (Book 3) 1976. Committee investigators found 53,000 pages of Cointelpro documents squirreled away in various corners of the FBI.

p. 160 COMMUNIST GARBAGE: Confidential interview.

p. 160 NEW JERSEY SCOUTMASTER: Nicholas M. Horrock, "The F.B.I.'s Appetite for Very Small Potatoes," New York *Times*, March 23, 1975.

p. 160 SOCIALIST WORKERS PARTY: Ibid.

p. 160–61 COINTELPRO SECRET: Church Committee, *Final Report* (Book 2). The most sensitive FBI secret, break-ins, turned out not to be so secret after all; so many had been carried out, there was no way to conceal them. Hoover, worried about revelations of break-ins, ordered them halted in 1966. Committee investigators found evidence of 238 break-ins that had taken place between 1942 and 1966, believed to be only a small percentage of the actual total. (See William C. Sullivan [head FBI Domestic Intelligence Division], Memorandum to J. Edgar Hoover, Subject: "Black Bag" Jobs, July 19, 1966. The memo is marked "Do Not File.")

p. 161 COMINFIL: Church Committee, *Final Report* (Book 3).

p. 161 HOMEX: Ibid.

p. 161–62 PRESIDENTS' ATTITUDE TOWARD HOOVER: Ovid Demaris, *The Director*, New York, 1975.

p. 162 INFORMATION ON CONGRESS: This material was assiduously collected by Hoover for nearly thirty years and kept in an entirely separate FBI file known as "Secret Hoover Files." Coincidental with Hoover's death in 1972, all but several hundred pages of the files were destroyed. There is ongoing litigation involving the question of public release for the remaining pages.

p. 162 SCOPE OF COINTELPRO: Nelson Blackstock, *COINTELPRO*, New York, 1976.

p. 162 HOOVER'S DICTATORIAL CONTROL OF FBI: Richard Gid Powers, *Secrecy and Power: The Life of J. Edgar Hoover*, New York, 1987. By statute, the FBI is exempt from Civil Service regulations.

p. 162 CHICAGO WOMEN'S LIB: J. Edgar Hoover, Memorandum to SAC [Special Agent in Charge], Chicago, Subject: Women's Liberation Movement (WM), May 11, 1970.

p. 162–63 HOOVER AS RACIST: Richard Gid Powers, *Secrecy and Power*; Max Lowenthal, *The Federal Bureau of Investigation*, New York, 1950; Jay Robert Nash, *Citizen Hoover*, Chicago, 1972; David J. Garrow, *The FBI and Martin Luther King, Jr.*, New York, 1981.

p. 163 HOOVER AND KING: Richard Gid Powers, *Secrecy and Power*; Garrow, *FBI and Martin Luther King, Jr.*

p. 163 LEVISON: Garrow, *The FBI and Martin Luther King, Jr.*

p. 163–64 SULLIVAN: William C. Sullivan, testimony, cited in Church Committee, *Final Report* (Book 2); U.S. Justice Department, *Report of the Department of Justice Task Force to Review the FBI Martin Luther King, Jr., Security and Assassination Investigations*, January 11, 1977.

p. 164 BLACK NATIONALISTS: J. Edgar Hoover, Memorandum, Subject: Counterintelligence Program, Black Nationalist Hate Groups, February 10, 1968.

p. 164 BLACK PANTHERS: Blackstock, *Cointelpro.*

p. 164 SIGNIFICANCE OF COINTELPRO, COMINFIL: Cathy Parkus, editor, *Cointelpro: The FBI's Secret War on Political Freedom*, New York, 1975.

p. 165 ANTI-WAR GROUPS: Church Committee, *Final Report* (Book 3).

p. 165 SPYING ON CONGRESS: Ibid.

p. 165 COINTELPRO UNLEASHED: Parkus, *Cointelpro.*

p. 165–66 ARMY INTELLIGENCE: Christopher Pyle, "CONUS Intelligence: the Army Watches Civilian Politics," *Washington Monthly*, January 1970. (In Army parlance, "CONUS" means "Continental United States," signifying all troops and installations based in the United States.)

p. 166 CHAOS: Richard E. Morgan, *Domestic Intelligence*, Austin, Texas, 1980.

p. 166 HELMS RUNS AFOUL OF NIXON: Richard Helms, Memorandum, Subject: Student Unrest, February 18, 1969.

p. 166 PROJECT MERRIMAC: Central Intelligence Agency, Office of Security, report, *Special Information Project*, July 2, 1970.

p. 166 OPERATION MUDHEN: Central Intelligence Agency, Support Branch, Memorandum for Record, Subject: Operation Mudhen, February 14, 1972.

p. 167 HT/LINGUAL: Richard Helms, Memorandum for Record, Subject: Meeting at DCI's Office Concerning HT/Lingual, June 3, 1971.

p. 167 ANGLETON: Robin Winks, *Cloak and Gown*, New York, 1987.

p. 167 ILLEGAL IMPRISONMENT OF KGB DEFECTOR: David Martin, *Wilderness of Mirrors*, New York, 1980.

p. 167–68 "IT IS INCONCEIVABLE": Cited in Church Committee, *Final Report* (Book 2).

p. 168 "ALL THESE PEOPLE": Schlesinger interview.

p. 168 NIXON ATTITUDE: Morgan, *Domestic Intelligence*.

p. 169 HUSTON: Church Committee, *Final Report* (Book 2).

p. 169 HUSTON PLAN: Memorandum, Tom Charles Huston to Richard Helms DCI, Subject: Domestic Intelligence, July 23, 1970.

p. 169 HOOVER KILLS HUSTON PLAN: Church Committee, *Final Report* (Book 2).

p. 169 NIXON PRESSURE: Ibid.

p. 169 IRS: Senate Judiciary Committee, Staff Study, *Political Intelligence in the Internal Revenue Service*, December 1974.

p. 170 MITCHELL WARRANTS: Robert Rust interview (Rust was former U.S. Attorney for the Southern District of Florida).

p. 170 NIXON AND "PLUMBERS": Bob Woodward and Carl Bernstein, *All the President's Men*, New York, 1975.

p. 170 HOOVER-NIXON ESTRANGEMENT: Richard Gid Powers, *Secrecy and Power.*

p. 170 EHRLICHMAN AND HOOVER: John Ehrlichman, *Witness to Power*, New York, 1982.

p. 171 SCHLESINGER: Paul W. Blackstock, "The Intelligence Community Under the Nixon Administration," *Armed Forces and Society*, Winter 1975.

p. 171 MEDIA BREAK-IN: Nelson Blackstock, *Cointelpro*.

p. 171 "FAMILY JEWELS": Parkus, *Cointelpro*.

p. 172 ROCKEFELLER COMMISSION: Commission on C.I.A. Activities Within the United States, *Final Report*, June 1975.

p. 172 NEW CONGRESSIONAL ATTITUDE: Loch K. Johnson, *A Season of Inquiry*, Lexington, Kentucky, 1985.

p. 172 "SHUT YOUR EYES SOME": Quoted in David Wise, "Intelligence Reforms: Less Than Half a Loaf," Washington *Post*, April 23, 1978.

p. 172 CASUAL SENATE OVERSIGHT: Stansfield Turner interview.

p. 173 COLBY AND SENATE COMMITTEE: Colby interview.

p. 173 COLBY AND ANGLETON: Confidential interview.

p. 173 POISON GUN: Colby interview.

p. 174 LISTEN FOR THE SOUNDS: David Wise, "The F.B.I. Pardoned," New York *Times*, April 25, 1981. Felt and Miller were convicted, but were later granted full presidential pardons by President Reagan.

TEN: The Crown Jewel

p. 177 ODOM'S APPEARANCE: Authors' notes.

p. 178 NSA: James Bamford, *The Puzzle Palace*, New York, 1982.

p. 178–79 ODOM'S SPEECH (TO ASSOCIATION OF FORMER INTELLIGENCE OFFICERS, OCTOBER 10, 1987): "NSA Director Says Media Leaks Have Resulted in Paralysis and Misjudgment That Could Lead to War," *Periscope*, Fall 1987.

p. 179 ODOM-BAMFORD INCIDENT: as told to Mitchell Koss, present at the Association of Former Intelligence Officers meeting, by James Bamford.

p. 179–80 CHURCH COMMITTEE HEARING: Select Committee to Study Governmental Operations with Respect to Intelligence Activities [hereafter Church Committee], *The National Security Agency and Fourth Amendment Rights*, Interim Report, (Book 5), October 29 and November 6, 1975.

p. 180 JOHN TOWERS' REMARKS: Ibid.

p. 180 ROOSEVELT'S AUTHORITY: House Government Operations Committee, Subcommittee on Government Information and Individual Rights, hearings, *Interception of Nonverbal Communications by the Federal Intelligence Agencies*, 1976.

p. 181 WESTERN UNION QUOTE; FORRESTAL ARRANGEMENT WITH CABLE COMPANIES: *Supplementary Detailed Staff Reports on Intelligence Activities and the Rights of Americans* [hereafter Church Committee], *Final Report*, (Book 3,) April 23, 1976.

p. 181 OPERATION SHAMROCK: Ibid.

p. 182 MAGNETIC TAPE: Bamford, *Puzzle Palace*.

p. 182 COMPUTER MEMORY BANKS: Bamford, *Puzzle Palace*. The introduction of magnetic tape also became a source of another of the CIA's many business fronts. At the NSA's request, the CIA established Project LP/Medley, which created a New York-based television tape-processing business. Actually, it was the receiving point for the cable companies' magnetic tapes, which were being constantly shuttled back and forth for duplication. The originals were immediately returned to the companies; the duplicates went to the NSA.

p. 183 DOMESTIC SPYING: Church Committee, *Final Report*, (Book 3).

p. 183   PROJECT MINARET: Bob Woodward, "Messages of Activities Intercepted," Washington *Post*, October 13, 1975.

p. 183   "CREDIT CARD REVOLUTIONARIES": Church Committee, *Final Report*, (Book 3.) Testimony of agent C. D. Brennan.

p. 183–84   WEATHERMEN CASE: Bamford, *Puzzle Palace.*

p. 184   END OF SHAMROCK: Church Committee, *Final Report*, (Book 3).

p. 184   JUSTICE DEPARTMENT CASE AGAINST NSA: Bamford, *Puzzle Palace.*

p. 185   AIR FORCE REQUEST: Harry Rositzke, *The CIA's Secret Operations*, New York, 1977.

p. 185   PROBLEMS OF PENETRATING SOVIET UNION: Peer de Silva, *Sub Rosa—The CIA and the Uses of Intelligence*, New York, 1977.

p. 186   "GENTLEMEN, ONE OF OUR OWN RB-47s": Claud Witze, "A View From the Hill," *Air Force*, September 1970.

p. 186–87   NSA "FERRETS": Glenn Infield, *Unarmed and Unafraid*, New York, 1970.

p. 187   ARMENIA INCIDENT: Allen Dulles testimony, given in executive session and not declassified until 1982, was primarily concerned with the U-2 incident, but there was extensive questioning about pre-U-2 reconnaissance missions.

p. 187   LIMITATIONS OF FERRETS: Curtis Peebles, *Guardians*, Novato, California, 1987.

p. 187   U-2 AND JOHNSON: Clarence Johnson, *Kelly: More Than My Share of It All*, Washington, D.C., 1985; Jay Miller, *Lockheed U-2*, Austin, Texas, 1982.

p. 187   90 PERCENT: Michael Beschloss, *Mayday*, New York, 1986.

p. 188   *Discoverer*: Phillip Kass, *Sentries in Space*, New York, 1971.

p. 188   NRO REVEALED: Senate Special Committee to Study Questions Related to Secret and Confidential Documents, report #93-466, *Questions Related to Secret and Confidential Documents*, October 12, 1973.

p. 188   SCOPE OF U.S. ELECTRONICS ESPIONAGE: Anthony Kenden, "Recent Developments in U.S. Reconnaissance Satellite Programmes," *Journal of the British Interplanetary Society*, February 1982.

p. 188   *Rhyolite*: Strobe Talbot, *Endgame*, New York, 1980.

p. 188–89   RUSSIAN DISCOVERY: Ibid.

p. 189   CARTER STUDIES TECHNICAL ESPIONAGE: Stansfield Turner, *Secrecy and Democracy: The CIA in Transition*, New York, 1983.

p. 189–90   KAMPILES CASE: William E. Burrows, *Deep Black*, New York, 1986; Bob Woodward, *Veil: The Secret Wars of the CIA*, New York, 1987.

p. 190   "CHEATING" EXPERTS: Turner, *Secrecy and Democracy.*

p. 190   TRACKSMAN 2: Bamford, *Puzzle Palace.* Under a subsequent (and secret) U.S.–China agreement, Tracksman 2 was relocated to northern China near the Soviet border—with the strict understanding that the Chinese were to share in all intelligence produced by the monitoring station.

p. 191   "HERE I WAS": Turner, *Secrecy and Democracy.*

p. 191–92   "ALL ITS EGGS": Interview with Robert Seamans.

p. 192   "YOU HAVEN'T GOT": Bob Woodward, *Veil.*

ELEVEN: Desert One

p. 193–94   CIA MEETING: Confidential interview.

p. 195 CARTER VIEW OF INTELLIGENCE: John Ranelagh, *The Agency*, New York, 1986.

p. 196 1974 MEMO: Central Intelligence Agency, Untitled Memorandum, February 21, 1974 (unclassified), later given to Church Committee.

p. 196 "I FELT THAT": Remarks, President Jimmy Carter, press conference, Washington, D.C., November 30, 1978.

p. 196 DEEMPHASIS ON SOVIET UNION: CIA official Robert M. Gates, remarks, Conference on U.S. Intelligence: The Organization and the Profession, Langley, Virginia, June 11, 1984.

p. 196–97 NIT, KIQ: Loch K. Johnson, "Making the 'Intelligence Cycle' Work," *International Journal of Intelligence and Counterintelligence* (vol. 1, no. 4), 1987.

p. 197 CARTER OUTLOOK: Ranelagh, *The Agency*.

p. 197 HUGHES-RYAN AMENDMENT: Section 622, *Foreign Assistance Act of 1974*.

p. 197 SIGNIFICANCE OF ACT: Treverton, *Covert Action*.

p. 198 HEARING ON HELMS: Thomas Powers, *The Man Who Kept the Secrets*, New York, 1979.

p. 198 CIA CHILE OPERATION: Victor Marchetti and John D. Marks, *The CIA and the Cult of Intelligence*, New York, 1974.

p. 198 "I DON'T SEE WHY": *Andres v CIA* (80-0865 DDC). This court case was a successful Freedom of Information Act lawsuit restoring CIA-ordered excisions from the Marchetti and Marks book, noted above.

p. 198 "MAKE THE ECONOMY SCREAM": Select Senate Committee to Study Governmental Operations with Respect to Intelligence Activities [hereafter Church Committee], report, *Covert Action in Chile, 1963–1973*, December 18, 1975.

p. 198–99 "DID YOU TRY": Senate Foreign Relations Committee, hearings, *Nomination of Richard Helms*, 1973.

p. 199 HELMS'S CONVICTION: Treverton, *Covert Action*.

p. 199 PIKE COMMITTEE: Ibid.

p. 199–200 COLBY'S ATTITUDE: William Colby, *Honorable Men*, New York, 1978.

p. 200 CIA IN ANGOLA: John Stockwell, *In Search of Enemies*, New York, 1978.

p. 200 U.S. PERCEPTIONS IN ANGOLA: Gerald J. Bender, "Angola: A Story of Stupidity," *New York Review of Books*, December 21, 1978.

p. 201 SAVIMBI, ROBERTO: Stockwell, *In Search of Enemies*.

p. 201 FORD ADMINISTRATION ESCALATION: Seymour Hersh, *The Price of Power*, New York, 1982.

p. 201 SECRET DECISION: Stockwell, *In Search of Enemies*.

p. 201 KISSINGER'S PERCEPTIONS: Rene Lemarchand, editor, *American Policy in Southern Africa*, Frederick, Maryland, 1978.

p. 201 ANGOLA AS POKER GAME: Bender, *Angola*.

p. 201 CONGRESS ENDS OPERATION: Colin A. Legum, "The Soviet Union, China, and the West in Southern Africa," *Foreign Affairs*, July 1976.

p. 202 INTELLIGENCE COVERAGE OF CUBA: Confidential interview.

p. 202 RODRÍGUEZ-MENA: *Granma* (Havana), weekly edition, October 11, 1987.

p. 202–3 ASPILLAGA: Jack Anderson, "Defector Says Cuban Agents Duped CIA," *Newsday*, March 23, 1988. *Granma* and *Prensa Latina* in Havana have both published extensive DGI surveillance pictures of CIA agents photographed while leaving espionage equipment for their Cuban "assets."

p. 203 CARTER CANCELS SR-71 FLIGHTS: Gloria Duffy, "Crisis-Mangling and the Cuban Brigade," *International Security*, Summer 1983.

p. 203 U.S.-CUBA RELATIONS: Wayne Smith, *The Closest of Enemies*, New York, 1987. Smith was head of the U.S. Interests Section in Havana, 1977 to 1982.

p. 203 TURNER AND "COMBAT BRIGADE": Turner interview.

p. 204 BRIGADE AS POLITICAL ISSUE: Duffy, "Crisis-Mangling and the Cuban Brigade."

p. 204 TURNER FINDS SOLUTION: Turner interview. The NSA could have saved Turner and everybody else a lot of trouble by simply consulting the June 20, 1963, issue of the New York *Times*, which contained an article headlined RUSSIANS IN CUBA NOW PUT AT 12,500. That was the Soviet unit NSA claimed to have discovered sixteen years later.

p. 204 NICARAGUA INCIDENT: Confidential interview.

p. 205 SULLIVAN AND SHAH: Gary Sick, *All Fall Down*, New York, 1985.

p. 205-6 U.S. PERCEPTION OF SHAH: Ibid.

p. 206 "IRAN IS NOT": House Intelligence Committee, Subcommittee on Evaluation, staff report, *Evaluation of United States Intelligence Performance Prior to November 1978*, January 1979.

p. 206-7 KHOMEINI, END OF SHAH: Mansur Rafizadeh, *Witness*, New York, 1987.

p. 207 IRANIANS RECONSTRUCT DOCUMENTS: These documents, with Farsi translations, were later published in fifty-nine volumes by the Khomeini government under the title *Asnad Lana-i Jasusi: Volumes of U.S. Diplomatic and Intelligence Correspondence Published by the Students Following the Imam's Line in Teheran, Iran, 1980–1986*, Teheran, 1982–87.

p. 207 BANI-SADR: Ibid. (vol. 9, *A Collection of Documents Revealed in the Early Days of the Espionage Den Seizure*).

p. 208 BARZAGAN: Ibid (vol. 22).

p. 208 BANI-SADR'S LAPSE: Confidential interview.

p. 208 EVOLUTION OF U.S. INTELLIGENCE: On this point, see especially Walter Laqueur, "Spying and Democracy," *Society*, November–December 1985.

p. 209 "ROGUE ELEPHANT": Attributed variously to CIA General Counsel Stanley Sporkin, White House official Richard Allen, and Senator Frank Church.

p. 209 VIEW OF REAGAN SUPPORTERS: Much of this worldview was concentrated in the Committee for the Present Danger, a lobbying group of ex-military and intelligence officials displeased with Carter administration policies. Fifty-one of the committee's members were later appointed to high-level posts in the Pentagon, State Department, and intelligence agencies.

p. 209 REAGAN VIEWS: Lou Cannon, *Reagan*, New York, 1982.

p. 209 VIEWS ON INTELLIGENCE: Justin Gallen, "Intelligence: the Reagan Challenge," *Armed Forces Journal*, January 1981.

p. 209 CENTRAL AMERICA: The Reagan supporters were concentrated in another lobbying group called The Council for Inter-American Security, which advocated a more activist U.S. role in Latin America.

TWELVE: Ends and Means

p. 210–11 HAMILTON AND MCFARLANE: Joel Brinkley, introduction to *The New York Times Edition of the Report of the Congressional Committees Investigating the Iran-Contra Affair*, New York, 1988 [hereafter Iran-Contra Committees].

p. 212 "CONFUSION, SECRECY AND DECEPTION": Ibid.

p. 212 IRAN-CONTRA AFFAIR: Ibid.

p. 212 "TRUST AND CONFIDENCE": Senator Barry Goldwater, "Congressional and Intelligence Oversight," *The Washington Quarterly*, Summer 1983.

p. 213 CASEY ADMIRATION OF DONOVAN: Casey interview.

p. 213 CASEY IN WORLD WAR II: William Casey, *The Secret War Against Hitler*, New York, 1988.

p. 214 OSS FREEDOM: Bradley F. Smith, *The Shadow Warriors*, New York, 1983.

p. 214–15 CASEY'S OUTLOOK: Bob Woodward, *Veil: The Secret Wars of the CIA*, New York, 1987.

p. 215 CASEY AND KIRKPATRICK: Ibid.

p. 215 CASEY'S IMPATIENCE: Thomas Powers, review essay, "Casey's Case," *New York Review of Books*, January 5, 1988.

p. 215–16 ANGOLA: William Claiborne, "In Angola, It's Getting Harder to Tell the Good Guys From the Bad," Washington *Post*, October 26, 1987.

p. 216 SOMOZA AND NICARAGUA: Bernard Diedrich, *Somoza*, New York, 1981.

p. 216–17 CASEY'S NICARAGUA OBSESSION: Theodore Draper, "The Rise of the American Junta," *New York Review of Books*, October 8, 1987.

p. 217 REAGAN'S KNOWLEDGE: Treverton, *Covert Action*.

p. 217 "DIDN'T KNOW": Woodward, *Veil*.

p. 217–18 PASTORA AND CIA: Confidential interview.

p. 219 CASEY SHAPES RESISTANCE MOVEMENT: Thomas Powers, "Casey's Case."

p. 220 MINING, MANAGUA AIRPORT BOMBING: Woodward, *Veil*.

p. 220 CASEY'S EXCESSES: Robert A. Pastor, *Condemned to Repetition*, Princeton, 1987.

p. 221 FBI PARDONS: Nat Hentoff, "Our Own KGB," *Village Voice*, April 30, 1981.

p. 221 FBI INVESTIGATION OF PEACE GROUPS: Philip Shenon, "F.B.I.'s Chief Says Surveillance Was Justified," New York *Times*, February 3, 1988.

p. 221 SPECIAL OPERATIONS DIVISION: Steven Emerson, *Secret Warriors*, New York, 1988.

p. 222 CIA'S "BACK CHANNEL": Ibid.

p. 222 SPORKIN WARNING: Stanley Sporkin, testimony, hearings, Iran-Contra Committees, June 24, 1987.

p. 222 CASEY'S EVASIONS: *Final Report*, Iran-Contra Committees.

p. 222–23 OLIVER NORTH: Ibid.

p. 222 EXECUTIVE ORDER 1233: Draper, "Rise of the American Junta."

p. 223 OPERATION STAUNCH: *Report of the President's Special Review Board*, February 26, 1987.

p. 223–24 SECRET ARMS DEAL WITH IRAN: Ibid.

p. 223 CONVERGENCE WITH CONTRA OPERATION: *Final Report*, Iran-Contra Committees.

p. 223   NORTH AND PLAUSIBLE DENIABILITY: Oliver North, testimony, hearings, Iran-Contra Committees, July 10, 1987.

p. 224   HASENFUS: *Final Report,* Iran-Contra Committees.

p. 224   IRAN-CONTRA HEARINGS: Treverton, *Covert Action.*

p. 226   SPY CASES: Senate Intelligence Committee report, *Meeting the Espionage Challenge: A Review of United States Counterintelligence and Security Programs,* 1986.

p. 227   FOUNDING FATHERS' ARGUMENTS: Cecil V. Crabb and Kevin V. Mulcahy, *Presidents and Foreign Policy Making,* Baton Rouge, 1986.

Index

257

ERNEST VOLKMAN, former executive editor of *Espionage* magazine, is the author of three other books, including *Warriors of the Night: Spies, Soldiers, and American Intelligence.* He lives in New York.

BLAINE BAGGETT, executive producer for the Secret Intelligence television series, is the KCET/Los Angeles Director for National Public Affairs. His production of "Spy Machines" won the prestigious Peabody Award. He lives in Los Angeles.